A HISTORY OF
GHOSTS
SPIRITS
AND THE
SUPERNATURAL

A HISTORY OF
GHOSTS SPIRITS
AND THE
SUPERNATURAL

Senior Editor Kathryn Hennessy
Project Editor Abigail Mitchell
Editors Victoria Murrell, Fiona Plowman,
Victoria Pyke
Senior US Editor Megan Douglass
Senior Art Editor Helen Spencer
Designer Judy Caley
Managing Editor Gareth Jones
Senior Managing Art Editor Lee Griffiths
Picture Research Sarah Smithies, Jo Walton
Assistant Picture Researcher Nunhoih Guite
Senior Production Editor Robert Dunn
Production Controller Nancy-Jane Maun
Jackets Design Development Manager Sophia MTT
Senior Jacket Designer Surabhi Wadhwa-Gandhi
Senior DTP Designer Harish Aggarwal
Senior Jackets Coordinator Priyanka Sharma-Saddi
Associate Publishing Director Liz Wheeler
Art Directors Maxine Pedliham, Karen Self
Publishing Director Jonathan Metcalf
Managing Director Liz Gough

First American Edition, 2024
Published in the United States by DK Publishing,
a division of Penguin Random House LLC
1745 Broadway, 20th Floor, New York, NY 10019

Copyright © 2024 Dorling Kindersley Limited
24 25 26 27 28 10 9 8 7 6 5 4 3 2 1
001–336851–Aug/2024

A catalog record for this book
is available from the Library of Congress.
ISBN: 978-0-7440-9873-0

Printed in UAE

www.dk.com

This book was made with Forest
Stewardship Council™ certified
paper—one small step in DK's
commitment to a sustainable future.
Learn more at **www.dk.com/uk/
information/sustainability**

CONTENTS

ASKING THE ANCESTORS
Ancient world

UNDERWORLDS AND AFTERLIFE
Antiquity to medieval

MEETING THE SPIRITS
1400–1700

OCCULTISM AND THE UNDEAD
1700–1900

REVISIONISM AND REVIVALS
1900 onward

CONSULTANT

Professor Owen Davies is a historian who specializes in witchcraft, magic, ghosts, and popular medicine. He is a published author, a member of the History Department at the University of Hertfordshire, and Vice President of The Folklore Society. His research work is often interdisciplinary, applying archaeological, anthropological, and biomedical knowledge to historical topics, and reflects a particular interest in heritage, as well as landscape and public history.

CONTRIBUTORS

Ben Gazur is a freelance writer with a specialized interest in history, folklore, and popular culture. He has written articles for the BBC, the Wellcome Collection, the *Guardian*, and *All About History*.

Ted Hand is a US public school teacher and independent scholar, specializing in the history of Western esotericism—occultism, Renaissance magic, Wicca, and the occult and magical counterculture of the 20th century.

Dr. Sam Hirst is a postdoctoral research fellow at the University of Nottingham. Their research focuses on 18th-century Gothic literature and Romanticism, as well as romance, Gothic, and horror in modern genre fiction and film.

Dr. Ceri Houlbrook is a historian whose primary research interests are the heritage and material culture of ritual and folklore in the British Isles. She is a Senior Lecturer in Folklore and History at the University of Hertfordshire and has collaborated with the Ashmolean Museum, Oxford, and the Museum of London Archaeology.

Dr. Cailín Murray is an Associate Professor of Anthropology at Ball State University in Indiana. Her research focuses on both the environmental ethnohistory of settler colonialism in North America and the anthropology of the supernatural, and how the two are interlinked.

Helen Nde is a Cameroonian-born, Atlanta-based writer and artist. Helen curates the online community Mythological Africans, which explores mythology, folklore, spirituality, and culture from the African continent. She has also published *The Runaway Princess and Other Stories*.

Andrew Hock Soon Ng is an Associate Professor at Monash University, Malaysia, where he teaches literature and creative writing. His primary research is in Gothic studies and horror narratives, including the literary tradition of Asian monstrosities.

Philip Parker is a historian and former British diplomat, who studied history at Trinity College, Cambridge, and international relations at the Johns Hopkins School of Advanced International Studies. He was a contributor to DK's *A History of Magic, Witchcraft & the Occult* and is the author of many critically acclaimed books.

Dr. Francis Young is a historian and folklorist, specializing in the history of religion and belief. He is an award-winning author and regularly appears on BBC radio, as well as writing for *History Today*, *BBC History Magazine*, *The Catholic Herald*, and other publications.

PREFACE

Throughout recorded time and around the world, the living have been haunted by ghosts and other supernatural beings. The spirit world has teemed with a diverse and enduring array of benevolent and malevolent beings, whose characteristics have been shaped by different human cultures—from the jinn of Arabic belief to the fairies of Ireland, and from the demonic yōkai of Japan to the divine òrìṣà spirits of the Yoruba of West Africa.

Religion and myth have played a huge part in shaping the nature of supernatural beings. But while some spirits were and, in some cases, still are considered divine beings, related to gods and goddesses, many cultures also developed notions of ghosts and spirits that had no link to organized religion. Societies create spirits to reflect different aspects of the human condition, and to explain the seemingly inexplicable workings of the natural world.

In the beliefs of many cultures through history (though by no means all), humans, through death, also end up as spirits or ghosts. Anthropologists have shown that, although there are similar core notions around the world about the spirits of the dead (such as their ability to leave the physical body), there is also a range of different interpretations and beliefs: whether or not they are sentient (capable of feeling or perceiving things), what they do, and their relationship to the living and to other categories of supernatural being. Across the spectrum, it is no surprise that in the spirit realm, just as in the human world, we find the good, the bad, and the ugly. The spirits we create mirror human qualities and weaknesses.

Ghosts and spirits have been venerated, appeased, conjured, and exorcised, depending on different cultural contexts. They have variously been thought to be frightening, comforting, aggressive, peaceful, or enigmatic. While some spirits reveal themselves visually, others can be detected by the noises they make, by certain odors, or through touch. Spirits rarely speak aloud or engage in lengthy conversations with humans, but they can communicate in various ways. Restless ghosts, for instance, were sometimes believed to be on a mission to rectify some injustice or to warn the living of some impending doom by gesture or groans. Others had no such purpose, but appeared to the living as silent memorials of the past.

Both people and places can be haunted by spirits. As well as myths and legends, personal experiences were (and still are) fundamental to the upholding of belief. The supernatural world has remained relevant across time because people continually claimed to have close encounters with ghosts and spirits. These often occurred at night, when the boundary between the human and other worlds was thought to be most porous. It was also a time when the imagination was excited by the darkness and dreams merged with reality. In many traditions, however, people did not seek out spirits, nor did spirits necessarily desire to seek out humans. The two lived parallel lives with only occasional interaction. Yet there were places in the landscape—liminal or boundary spaces—where humans and spirits were more likely to encounter one another for good or ill.

The amazing array of ghosts and spirits presented in this book, which covers cultures around the world, showcases how the supernatural can both entertain and educate. The topic is sometimes dismissed as a rather frivolous subject for scholars, but these spirits reflect the cultures that produced them, and represent universal notions and emotions, including the meaning of life and life after death, and the clear human need to believe that we are not alone. What this book also illuminates is the extraordinary hold that spirits and the supernatural have had on artistic creativity over the centuries, from medieval grimoires illustrated with drawings of demons and planetary spirits to modern artwork inspired by spirit communication, and from William Shakespeare's purgatorial ghosts to spooks in the television series *Scooby-Doo*. The world of the supernatural continues to play on our imaginations, and its long history provides plenty of inspiration. New spirits are also being created in cyberspace, confirming that they are eminently adaptable to the ever-changing landscapes of the human world.

OWEN DAVIES

◀ **Frolicking ghosts**
Robert Blair's *The Grave* (1743) was an early example of graveyard poetry, which used macabre imagery to reflect on life, death, and immortality. *The Gambols of Ghosts* was drawn by William Blake for the poem's 1808 edition.

ASKING THE
ANCESTORS
ANCIENT WORLD

Introduction

For millennia, humans have looked to the spirits of their ancestors and other supernatural beings for protection both in life and death. Although what is known about the spiritual beliefs of prehistoric peoples rests solely on the archaeological remains of past cultures—the images they left on cave walls and rocks; how they buried their dead; and how they constructed their ritual monuments in the landscape— Stone Age burial practices provide the earliest and most intimate sense of the idea of an afterlife. The laying out of bodies and inclusion of grave goods, such as drink and food, suggest that the dead were equipped for a journey to another place—but the archaeology reveals little about the nature of this other place. Ritual deposits in the ground, including sacrifices, hint at attempts to placate unknown gods or spirits.

The first writing, from more than 5,000 years ago, sheds light on how spirit worlds were believed to work and the role of the ancestors within them. Ancient

Mesopotamian cuneiform clay tablets reveal a world teeming with gods, demons, and the spirits of the dead. The living guarded themselves and their homes against such supernatural threats, and the *ašipu* (professional priest-exorcists) were important figures in society.

In the royal tombs of ancient Egypt, hieroglyphic texts and colored wall paintings divulge a highly sophisticated relationship between the living and the dead, and the judgment of the soul by Osiris, god of the afterlife and Underworld. The aristocracy and priesthood commissioned elaborate papyrus scrolls called the "Book of Coming Forth by Day" (known today as the "Book of the Dead"), which contained a series of spells to protect the dead on their journey to the afterlife. Ancient Egyptian texts also include the first recorded ideas about the concept of the human soul. The ancient Egyptians believed that the soul had several constituent parts, one of which—the *ib* – was situated in the heart. Two millennia later, ancient

First Australian rock art *see p.21*

Circling the Zoroastrian dead *see p.27*

Old Testament necromancy *see p.41*

Greek philosopher-physicians such as Plato and Aristotle wrote at length about the nature of the soul and its location in the body.

Writing developed in ancient Asian civilizations around 1200 BCE. Records from several centuries later show a preoccupation with ancestral spirits, while incantations written on bamboo slips suggest that, as in early Mesopotamia, ghosts and night demons were an everyday concern. Religious texts, such as the *Rigveda* and *Upanishads* of Hinduism, include the first references to the concept of reincarnation. Instead of entering an afterlife, the immortal soul is believed to transmigrate to another body—human or animal—upon biological death. This idea of rebirth can be found in Eastern religions such as Buddhism and Hinduism, in classical Greek philosophy, and in ancient nonliterary religious traditions around the world.

By the time of the Western Han dynasty (206 BCE–9 CE) in China and the Roman Empire (27 BCE–476 CE) in the West, the range of human ideas about death, the soul, and the afterlife that shaped the world's major religions had already been recorded. These early sources also provide clues to the beliefs that led prehistoric human ancestors to create their enigmatic monuments.

"I am noble, I am a spirit, I am equipped;
O all you gods and all you spirits, prepare a path for me."

ANCIENT EGYPTIAN BOOK OF THE DEAD, SPELL 9

Chinese oracle bones *see p.50*

Anglo-Saxon grave goods *see p.52*

The good people *see p.58*

THE BIRTH OF THE AFTERLIFE
early human beliefs

Humans are unique as a species in their reverence for the physical remains of the dead and in the belief that some of a person's essence survives after death. Spiritual beliefs and burial practices emerged very early in human evolution, perhaps with the awareness that life must end and that—if only for reasons of hygiene—the dead must be kept separate from the living.

Burying the dead

Deliberate burials predate even the appearance of modern humans (*Homo sapiens*). Around 430,000 years ago, at Sima de los Huesos cave in Atapuerca, Spain, 28 members of the *Homo heidelbergensis* species were interred in shallow pits. Some 70,000 years ago, Neanderthals (*Homo neanderthalensis*) buried several corpses at Shanidar cave in Iraq's Zagros mountains. Traces of pollen were found on one of the Neanderthal bodies, suggesting that flowers were laid over the corpse in its grave.

Archaeological evidence of the first grave goods (objects buried alongside the dead) dates back to the Middle Paleolithic period (about 28,000 years ago), hinting at the emergence of a belief in an afterlife. At Sungir, in Russia, a young boy and girl from this time period were found buried together with more than 10,000 ivory beads, a mammoth figurine, and a belt of fox teeth.

Neolithic practices

The development of agriculture in the Neolithic period, from around 10,000 BCE, created more settled societies, and with them the first formal cemeteries and more complex religious beliefs. The increasing evidence of grave goods such as pottery, beads, agricultural implements, and flint arrowheads buried in Neolithic graves suggests that in these societies, the deceased were believed to have needs beyond death that must be met.

▼ **Spirit mask**
Found in a cave in Nahal Hemar, Israel, this and similar spirit masks from c. 7000 BCE are decorated with strips of asphalt on the back. Depicting a range of ages, the masks have cavities for eyes and mouth, suggesting that they may have been worn in shamanic ceremonies.

▲ **Passage to the Underworld**
The 130-ft- (40-m-) long eastern passageway that leads into the interior of the tomb at Knowth, Ireland, is the longest of its kind in Western Europe. Passage tombs reflect the sense of the Underworld as a real place the dead must travel to.

Similar evidence of a cult of the dead comes from Çatalhöyük in central Türkiye, between 6000 and 5000 BCE. There, skeletons and skulls were interred beneath mud-brick houses, some of which were decorated with paintings of bulls, felines, and vultures. At about the same time, in China's Yangshao culture, Neolithic agriculturalists buried their dead in pit graves, and later exhumed and

"… the importance of the dead was that they move through the cosmos. Like the Sun, they were a dynamic element …"

DAVID LEWIS-WILLIAMS AND DAVID PIERCE, *INSIDE THE NEOLITHIC MIND* (2018)

reburied them. This practice may indicate that death and the passage into an afterlife was a process that was not considered to be completed with the first "physical" death.

By the Late Neolithic period, monumental architecture had appeared in Europe. Large megalithic structures such as Stonehenge in the UK and the stone alignments at Carnac in Brittany, France, appear to line up with cosmic bodies, suggesting a belief in the connection between cosmic bodies, the living bodies of worshippers, and the dead bodies of ancestors. Passage tombs such as Newgrange and Knowth in Ireland (dating from c. 3200 BCE), in which access to the burial chamber is gained through a narrow connecting passageway, provide a sense of transition into the afterlife, while the frequently found decoration of spirals, lozenges, and concentric circles may have been a way of altering consciousness to enter the domain of the dead.

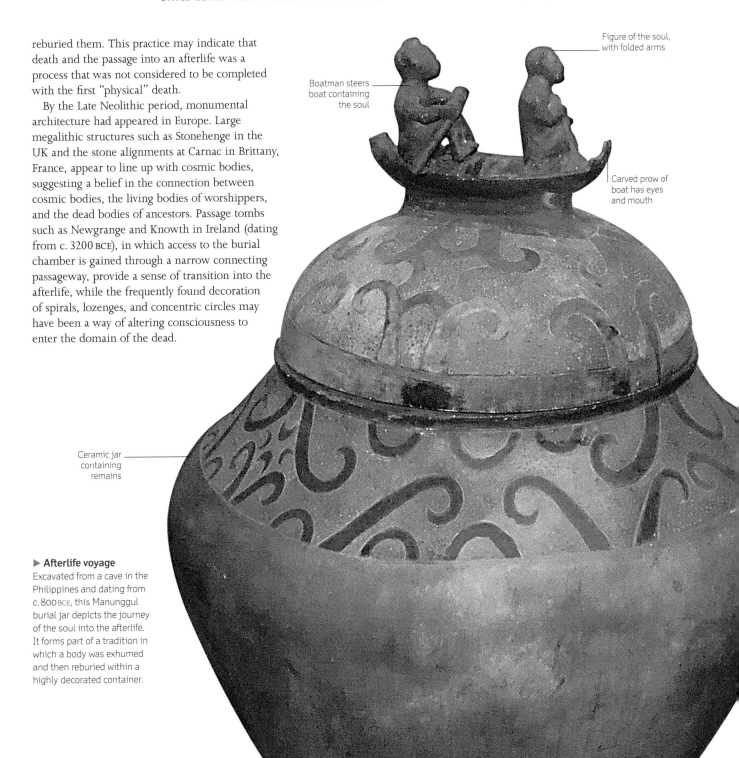

Figure of the soul, with folded arms

Boatman steers boat containing the soul

Carved prow of boat has eyes and mouth

Ceramic jar containing remains

▶ **Afterlife voyage**
Excavated from a cave in the Philippines and dating from c. 800 BCE, this Manunggul burial jar depicts the journey of the soul into the afterlife. It forms part of a tradition in which a body was exhumed and then reburied within a highly decorated container.

▲ **Dressed in her finery**
This reconstruction of the regalia of the Bad Dürrenberg shaman shows the special status deer-antler headdress and pendant of boars' teeth and tusks in which she was buried. It is possible that the abnormality of vertebrae in her neck and at the base of her skull led her to experience hallucinations.

Artificial underworlds

Some megalithic tombs have roofless semicircular courts, which may have been the site of rituals held in honor of the dead. Caves—the sites of the earliest Paleolithic burials—continued to be revered as places where the Underworld met the upper world. The Underworld may have been seen as a physical place to which the dead went. At Alepotrypa, Greece, people made pilgrimages to leave offerings at the mouth of the cave there, while at Carn Euny in Cornwall, UK, inhabitants of the Iron-Age village created a *fogou* (underground chamber) in the 1st century BCE—a possible symbolic passageway into the afterlife. The sense of a journey into the land of the dead is an often-repeated theme in early art, from the burial urns of the Philippines (see p.15), to the memorial picture stones of pre-Viking Scandinavia (around 500 CE), which frequently depict ships.

Ancestor spirits

The inhabitants of the earliest agricultural villages seem to have venerated ancestral spirits. At Ein Mahal in Israel, dozens of bodies were buried close to the hearths of houses, perhaps signifying the need to keep the dead close to the living. At Ain Ghazal, a farming village of the Natufian culture (in present-day Jordan), the heads of corpses were separated from the rest of the skeleton and covered in white plaster; the eyes were then inset with shells (see p.18). Children's bodies were not treated in this way, suggesting that only adults could become ancestral spirits. In other places, the dead were commemorated with images, as seen in the plank figurines of Cyprus,

◀ **Plank figure**
Flat, rectangular clay figurines like this one, adorned with geometric patterns indicating jewelery and clothing, are unique to the Middle Bronze Age (2000–1600 BCE) in Cyprus. Each figure may have been created to represent the spirit of a single dead person.

or the decorative cremation urns produced by the Iron Age Pomeranian culture of northern Poland and Germany.

The birth of shamanism

Little evidence has been found of the prehistoric practitioners of cults of the dead. Nevertheless, the common presence of animal imagery in burials and the interment of some corpses with special offerings of animal remains suggest a belief in shamanism, which may date back to pre-Neolithic times. The term "shaman" comes from the Evenki people of Siberia but is used by scholars more generally to describe a broad set of beliefs and practices that center around spirit communication.

At Bad Dürrenberg in Germany, the grave of a 30–40-year-old woman from around 7000 BCE was found buried with an array of grave goods, such as the bones and antlers of a deer. Analysis of her skeleton revealed a spinal malformation, and it is possible that this gave her a special status in the community—perhaps that of a shaman. Similarly, excavations in various Neolithic cemeteries across Europe have revealed a handful of bodies buried in seated positions—as opposed to the usual flat or flexed (with bent knees) position. These individuals' roles in life seem to have demanded special treatment in death. By accessing the spirit world while alive, such shamans—the first priests—must have given people reason to hope for an afterlife. Without written records, however, their specific beliefs regarding the supernatural remain a mystery.

▲ **Spirit face**
Dating from c. 600–200 BCE, the burial urns of the Pomeranian culture are topped with hat-like lids and decorated with faces. Each urn has a unique face, which possibly represents the deceased within.

"You travel in other worlds on behalf of your people with the help of your spirit animal."

HARALD MELLER, DIRECTOR OF THE STATE MUSEUM OF PREHISTORY, HALLE, GERMANY, ON THE ROLE OF THE BAD DÜRRENBERG SHAMAN, 2023

◄ **This ivory statuette** from Brno, Czech Republic, dates from 29,000–25,000 years ago. Such figures were believed to capture the spirit of a person, animal, or disease.

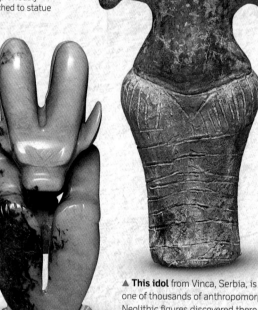

Red paint decoration typical of Vinca idols

Arm previously attached to statue

▲ **Sandstone heads** such as this one were excavated by the river at Lepenski Vir, Serbia. Dating from 5000 BCE, they are thought to depict either river spirits or the dead.

▶ **A cowlike figure** from China's Neolithic Hongshan culture, this dates from 4700–2920 BCE. It was probably worn as a pendant around a shaman's neck, with the jade believed to provide protection.

▲ **This idol** from Vinca, Serbia, is one of thousands of anthropomorphic Neolithic figures discovered there. Dating from around 4000 BCE, it is thought to have had a ritual purpose.

▲ **A skull** (C. 7000 BCE) from Ain Ghazal, Jordan, has been covered with plaster and had its eye sockets filled with shells—an early example of ancestor skull veneration.

▼ **This necklace** of wolves' teeth was buried with a man 4,000 years ago in Upton Lovell, UK. The grave also contained a ceremonial cloak, animal bones, and tools, suggesting the man was both a metalworker and a shaman.

Prehistoric rituals

In the absence of written records, it is difficult for archaeologists to ascertain the exact purpose and meaning of many of the finds from early human societies. Without evidence to the contrary, objects are often assumed to have been used in rituals. Yet some clearly indicate their role in early human spiritual beliefs. As well as afterlife beliefs and the practice of ancestor veneration, shamanistic elements emerged in the prehistoric period as an early aspect of religion, and saw people attempting to engage with spirits in the natural world. These objects, dating from the Neolithic period to the Iron Age, are believed to have served a shamanic, talismanic, or otherwise spirit-related function.

◀ **This human figure** was found with eight others on an altar at a stone circle in Xaghra, Malta. Dating from 3000–2400 BCE, the figures are thought to have belonged to a shaman.

▶ **The Knowth macehead** is a piece of carved flint discovered in an Irish passage tomb (see pp.14–15), and dates from 3300–2800 BCE. It may have been used in a funerary ritual.

◀ **This female *dogū*** (figure) dates from Japan's final Jomon period (1000–300 BCE). Many similar examples have been found with deliberate breaks, leading experts to suggest they may have been used in healing rituals.

The corners are masks with rectangular mouths

Markings could indicate shaman's face paint

Decorated with a snake pattern

◀ **A shaman's face** is thought to be depicted on this urn lid from China's Yangshao culture (2600–2300 BCE). The lid's red decorations suggest that shamans (see p.17) might have tattooed or painted their bodies with animal and geometric symbols.

▲ **Jade congs** such as this one were ritual objects in Neolithic China. This one from 2400 BCE was found in a circle of congs surrounding the deceased in a tomb at Sidun, in Jiangsu Province.

SPIRITS OF THE DREAMTIME
First Australian beliefs

▼ Art of the Dream
This 1971 work by Pintupi artist Johnny Warangkula Tjupurrula is called *Old Man's Fighting Dreaming* and shows three ancestor figures. Dreamtime art often depicts ancestral spirits and their stories.

The belief systems of First Australian peoples are incredibly diverse, and more than 250 languages are spoken by Indigenous peoples across the vast continent. However, they share in common the concept of the Dreamtime. This term, coined by European anthropologists, describes a world inhabited by creation spirits and ancestral beings, who descended to the Earth to create its landscape of rivers, trees, waterways, and deserts, and to give life to animals, plants, and humans. Within this world view, all things—landscapes, peoples, and spirits—are interlinked, and the Dreamtime remains present always. A person's spirit exists before birth and is reborn after death, and each person has a life spirit, one of the Dreamtime spirits, which helps and guides them.

Wandjina and Mimi spirits

Among the Ngarinyin, Worrorra, and Wunambal peoples of the Western Kimberley, Dreamtime spirits include the Wandjina. According to legend, these "sky-beings" came down from the Milky Way and created all life. They are particularly associated with clouds, rivers, and other water features, and produce rain and "child seeds," the source of human life.

Among the peoples of Arnhem Land (sacred land in Australia's Northern Territory), Mimi spirits, with their spindly bodies, are said to be shy creatures who live in caves and rock crevices during the day. In the Dreamtime, they taught useful skills to the Indigenous peoples, such as hunting, cooking kangaroo meat on the fire, fishing, weaving, and the performance of ceremonial songs and dances. The Mimis also created rock art, which became the primary medium through which First Australians depicted images of the Dreamtime spirits and their stories. Mimis are generally believed to be benevolent, only creating mischief if their pets—animals such as echidna, goanna, and rock-wallabies—are harmed.

Warning of danger

Just as the desert and the tropical regions contain natural perils, so they are home to less benevolent beings. In the salt lakes of the Pilbara region of the Western Desert lurk the legendary Ngayurnangalku—monstrous beings with sharp teeth and talon-like fingernails—who prey on unwary Martu people. Farther north, the Anangu people fear the Mamu, with their large protruding eyes and fangs that could rip a person to shreds. In Warlpiri country, the hairy Pangkarlangu allegedly use their claws to kill babies. All these legends about dangerous spirits are associated with the features of particular landscapes and the stories therefore serve as a reminder to Indigenous peoples, and in particular their children, that the environment in which they live, if not respected, could prove to be perilous.

▲ **Teacher spirits**
Painted by the Indigenous artist Jimmy Midjawmidjaw, who came from Crocker Island, northeast of Darwin, this work uses ocher on bark to show three Mimi spirits, with their spindly torsos and flowing limbs.

"Those who lose dreaming are lost."

FIRST AUSTRALIAN PROVERB

▲ **Spirits in the caves**
This ancient First Australian rock art from the Kimberley Desert shows Wandjinas with white faces, large black eyes, and a type of halo. The faces are depicted without mouths, and this is said to stop them from producing too much rain.

THE LAND OF NO RETURN
Mesopotamian spirits and demons

Over a time period of more than 3,000 years, from c. 4000 BCE, many cultures inhabited ancient Mesopotamia, part of the modern Middle East. Despite their differences, these cultures—among them the Sumerians, Akkadians, Babylonians, and Assyrians—shared a set of beliefs about the Underworld and the spirits that lived there.

According to these beliefs, the essential spirit of a person—called the *gidim* in Sumerian and the *etemmu* in Akkadian—survived death. It then embarked on a perilous journey through demon-infested lands to the seven gates of the Underworld. There, the spirit was admitted by the gatekeeper Bidu to be judged by the 600 Anunnaki ("those who see"), before being assigned a place among the dead.

Place of darkness

Ancient Mesopotamians believed the Underworld was a real location, a subterranean place of darkness and pale shadows. It had a definite hierarchy, and the place assigned to the dead was determined not by whether they had been virtuous or wicked when alive, but according to their previous social position. The judgment of the deceased, marked in a book by Belit-Tseri, the infernal scribe, could consign the *gidim* or *etemmu* to an eternity of misery, drinking stagnant water and eating dust, or for

◄ **Power to protect**
The most feared of demons, Lamashtu was blamed for blighting crops, polluting rivers, causing miscarriages, and feeding off babies' blood. Amulets like this, showing her standing on a donkey and suckling a jackal and wild pig, were seen as a way of binding her power.

dead rulers such as Ur-nammu, king of Ur, to one of comparative ease. It was deemed vital that the dead be given offerings of food and wine. This task was usually performed by the eldest son of the deceased or, for the rulers of Mesopotamian cities such as Ur or Nippur, by priests in the temples they had endowed. Without offerings, it was believed, the dead would starve in the afterlife and be reduced—be they former kings, priests, or merchants—to the condition of beggars.

No way out

Presiding over the host of spirits was Ereshkigal, goddess of death. From her palace of Ganzir she made sure that no dead person crossed back to the upper world. For this reason, her realm was known as *erset la tari* ("the land of no return"). None but a handful of heroes visited the Underworld and came back: there was said to be a ladder in the city of Uruk that led there, but to venture safely into Ereshkigal's domain, a person must not wear clean clothes, carry a weapon, or make any kind of noise. Even Inanna, sister of Ereshkigal and the goddess of love, who came to Ganzir to

◄ **Naked and powerless**
Also known as Ishtar, Ereshkigal's sister Inanna (depicted on this Babylonian relief from c. 1750 BCE) was one of the few to visit the Underworld and return. At each gate she had to take off one piece of magical clothing, so she entered powerless.

▲ **Lord of the wind**
Depicted here with a doglike face and wings, Pazuzu brought winds of famine and pestilence. But his power also protected against other demons, so statues like this and amulets were common.

> "Who has ever ascended ... unscathed from the Underworld?"

INANNA'S DESCENT TO THE NETHERWORLD, SUMERIAN POEM, c. 1750 BCE

▶ **Driving out Lamashtu**
Pazuzu, the wind lord, holds this bronze plaque (934–612 BCE), which shows an exorcism. The second row from the top depicts the seven *galla* demons, while the third shows the sick person in bed as priests of the water god Ea drive out the demon. Lamashtu is at the bottom, clutching two snakes.

witness the funeral of her brother-in-law, barely escaped. According to legend, Inanna was stripped of her magical powers in the Underworld, and died after sitting on her sister's throne. She was rescued by her servants, but was only allowed to leave the Underworld to rejoin the living if she promised to send others in her place. These substitutes were Geshtinanna, the fertility goddess, and Dumuzid, the shepherd god. Their absence from the world of the living, each for half the year, was thought to explain the progression of the seasons.

Demonic neighbors

As well as housing the spirits of dead people, the land of no return was the haunt of demonic beings. Most terrifying among these were the *galla*, the messengers of Ereshkigal, whose duty it was to drag the souls of the unwilling dead down into the Underworld. There was also Lamashtu, a demon goddess with the head of a lion, donkey's teeth, and bloodstained hands, who was said to prey on pregnant women, babies, and infants. Pazuzu, the bird-winged lord of the wind demons, was both a destructive and a protective force, as he had the power to level houses and expel other demons.

Warding off evil

While the ancient Mesopotamians sometimes blamed ailments such as headaches or seizures (epilepsy) on demonic possession, these afflictions were also seen as the work of *gidim* or *etemmu* whom Ereshkigal had allowed to return to their former homes in the land of the living. They came as ghosts to right some wrong done to them in life, or because their burial rites had been faulty or the proper offerings had not been made.

To guard against spirit hauntings and the malevolent influence of demons, Mesopotamians carried amulets engraved either with dogs, of which demons and ghosts were believed to be afraid, or with images of Pazuzu. They also employed magical ointments and special knots, which were believed to bind the haunting spirit and render it powerless.

Exorcising spirits

If amulets and other measures failed to prevent ailments caused by malicious beings, those affected might consult an *ašipu*. This specialized exorcist would come armed with spells, such as an incantation to Gula, goddess of health, to drive out the bad spirit. More extreme measures included making an image of a sick person, sprinkling it with incense, and feeding it with a cake baked in ashes—intended symbolically to "resurrect" and cure the patient. Finally, if the *ašipu* knew the identity of the ghost, they might make an image of this spirit, write the name on it, and then break the statue's feet and place a dog's tooth in its mouth. Now unable to wander or to speak, the ghost would be forced back to the land of no return.

▶ **Bound for the afterlife**
This Babylonian clay tablet from around 1500 BCE depicts a figure leading a bound spirit back to the Underworld. British Assyriologist Irving Finkel has called this the first-ever image of a ghost.

Cuneiform text on back of tablet explains how to deal with ghosts

Young woman may be ghost's lover

Ghost is a bearded male figure

▲ **Demonic attack**
In a scene from an illustrated manuscript of the Persian epic poem *Shahnameh*, the *daeva* Akvan/Akoman, who can transform

DESTRUCTIVE DEMONS
the Zoroastrian *daevas*

Zoroastrianism—the dominant religion of ancient Persia (now Iran) from the mid-6th century BCE to the Islamic conquest in the 7th century CE—is one of the world's oldest living faiths. Founded by the prophet Zoroaster some time between 1500 and 600 BCE, its dualist worldview sees the universe as the backdrop to a cosmic struggle between Ahura Mazda, the divine force of light and truth, and his evil counterpart Angra Mainyu, the embodiment of falsehood and chaos. Today, small Zoroastrian communities still exist, mainly in Iran and India.

Servants of falsehood

Zoroastrians believe that *daevas* (or *devas*) are the servants of Angra Mainyu. Their name means "shining one" in Old Persian and in the *Gathas*, the oldest Zoroastrian scriptures, they are referred to as "deities to be rejected," possibly remnants of an earlier Persian pantheon. From being indistinct ambiguous entities, they evolved in later Zoroastrian belief into spirit-demons that corrupt and tempt humans into evil.

The *daevas* acquired individual names and characteristics, such as Dehaka, a fearsome *azi* (dragon or serpent) with three heads, able to swallow men and horses whole. Each is associated with a particular sin or blight, such as Apaosha, the demon of drought and thirst, or Bushanta, the *daeva*

of idleness. They are ruled over by six chief *daevas*: Akoman, Andar, Savar, Naikiyas, Taprev, and Zairich.

Raising the dead

Associated with death, *daevas* are said to cluster around *dakhmas*, or Towers of Silence, circular raised structures where Zoroastrians expose the corpses of their dead to be picked clean by birds of prey, as dead bodies are believed to be unclean and likely to be contaminated by demons. *Daevas* are also thought to inflict agonizing tortures in the *druj-demana* ("House of Lies") to which sinners are condemned pending final judgment at the end of time.

Daevas present a constant source of temptation and avoiding their attention is vital. Lapses such as cutting fingernails and leaving the clippings unburied could attract them, as could immoral acts. Particularly evil behavior, such as sexual crimes or worshipping demons, could result in becoming a *daeva* after death. Only virtuous acts—a commitment to Ahura Mazda's way of light, or the recitation during the hours of darkness of the *Vendidad*, a book of rituals and prayers about the *daevas*—will keep them at bay.

▲ **Sky burial**
Daevas are thought to gather at *dakhmas*, such as this 17th-century Tower of Silence in Mumbai, India. This tower is still used by the Parsees, a community descended from ancient Persian Zoroastrians.

IN CONTEXT

Angra Mainyu

Angra Mainyu ("Evil Thought"), also known as Ahriman, is the dark counterpart in Zoroastrian belief to Ahura Mazda ("Wise Thought"). Both spirits came into being at the same time, and Angra Mainyu tried to destroy everything good his opposite created. A shape-shifting demon and lord of an army of *daevas*, Angra Mainyu whispered sin into the ears of Mashya and Mashyanag, the first man and woman. Neither spirit can overcome the other before the end of time, when Ahura Mazda will finally triumph.

This c. 4th-century CE bronze winged dragon is thought to represent the destructive, shape-shifting spirit Angra Mainyu.

RAISING THE DEAD
ancient necromancy

Necromancy—the summoning of the spirits of the dead to seek their advice—is a feature of many ancient societies. It may have originated through the practices of shamans, who achieved an altered state of consciousness to commune with ancestors in a spirit world. Later customs—such as the plastering of skulls (see p.17) around 7000 BCE to depict the faces of the dead—are indicative of ancestor worship, suggesting a belief that communication with their spirits was possible.

Diviners of the dead

Clearer evidence of necromancy rituals to bring the dead back, consult with them, and learn about the future comes later. The word derives from the ancient Greek νεκρομαντεία—nekrós or νεκρός ("corpse") and manteía or μαντεία ("divination")—and Greek historians provide much of the known information about its prevalence. According to Strabo in his *Geographica* (written in the 1st century CE), diviners of the dead were to be found among communities in Etruria (Italy), Babylonia,

◀ **Protector of souls**
This Egyptian amulet shows Nephthys, the protector of the dead and goddess of mourning. Amulets featuring her are a component of several necromantic spells in *The Demotic Papyrus of London and Leiden*.

and Egypt. Greek accounts suggest these necromancers were respected and often consulted by rulers. Other necromantic practitioners were recorded in Persia (where they were known as magi, or wise men, and indulged in fire magic), and among various other peoples of the Middle East, including the Chaldeans and the Sabaeans.

The netherworld

Among the Sumerians, necromancers were referred to as *manzuzuu* or *shae'etemmu* (from *etemmu*, the word for "spirit"), and included a class of female necromancers known as *mušelitum*. The oldest account comes from the poem "Enkidu and the Netherworld," an early form of the *Epic of Gilgamesh* written around 2000 BCE. In it, the hero Gilgamesh accidentally drops

IN CONTEXT

Aeschylus's *The Persians*

The Western world's oldest surviving play features necromancy. *The Persians*, written in 472 BCE by Greek playwright Aeschylus, relates the defeat of Xerxes' Persian forces at the battle of Salamis (480 BCE). In it, Atossa—the mother of Xerxes, who has not yet returned from the war—summons the ghost of her son's father, King Darius I, by offering libations of honey, milk, wine, and flowers. When he appears, Atossa tells Darius's specter of their son's defeat and Darius laments Xerxes' folly: in deciding to invade Greece and build a bridge over the Hellespont, Xerxes defied the gods, causing his own downfall. Darius's ghost then prophesizes a further Persian defeat at Plataea in 479 BCE.

Darius I of Persia was one of the greatest rulers of the Achaemenid dynasty. In Aeschylus's play, his ghost speaks with awe and reverence of the Underworld.

◀ **How to raise a ghost**
This 7th-century BCE Babylonian cuneiform tablet contains incantations on how to raise a ghost and how to prevent it from causing harm. It describes a necromancer's eye ointment containing lion fat, frog intestines, and grasshopper wings.

two magical objects into the underworld, which his friend Enkidu tries to retrieve, but becomes trapped. Gilgamesh appeals to the god Enlil to summon Enkidu back, and Enkidu fleetingly appears, like a rushing wind, to give Gilgamesh an account of the (largely miserable) life of the dead. Later Sumerian and Babylonian necromancers performed rituals that included applying magical eye ointments in order to see spirits and using skulls to contain the conjured ghosts and allow them to communicate.

Practical magic

In ancient Egypt, the Book of the Dead's spells to help souls on their journey into the afterlife were mirrored by a darker form of necromantic magic. *The Demotic Magical Papyrus of London and Leiden*, an Egyptian magical text, or grimoire (see pp.156–159), from the 3rd century CE, is filled with practical magic, including spells to conjure up a damned spirit or kill an enemy. It also instructs how to summon the dead by putting stones in a burning brazier for the spirits to enter. Directions include the addition of ass dung for invoking a murdered man's ghost. Extreme care had to be taken, because evil spirits could enter a corpse and reanimate it, and defying the god Osiris, who oversaw the normally one-way passage to the land of the dead, was highly dangerous.

Such Egyptian magic was transmitted to the Greeks and Romans, and is reflected in ancient Jewish texts (see pp.40–41), which condemn those "who consult a skull." The Bible repeatedly forbids necromancy. Clearly hard to eradicate, the (by then) more than 2,000-year-old practice survived well into the Middle Ages and beyond.

> ## "Å a Å À gul-gul-la-ta li-pu-la-an-ni.
> ## ("May he who is in the skull answer [me!]")

AKKADIAN NECROMANCY TABLET, 1ST MILLENNIUM BCE (TRANSLATION BY DR. IRVING FINKEL)

LEGIONS OF HELL
demons

▲ **Demonic guardians**
Six pairs of colorful *yaksha* demons flank all entrances to the Temple of the Emerald Buddha in Bangkok, Thailand, to ward off evil spirits. As demonic nature spirits, they protect sacred places, but can also be malevolent, vindictive, and murderous.

The earliest peoples recorded in history blamed powerful entities, such as devils and demons, for the fearsome forces of nature—storms, famines, disease, and so on. Over time, these demons acquired names and characteristics. Their appearance was often hideous, or part-human and part-animal, perhaps influenced by historical worship of animal spirits.

Between good and evil
Demons were not generally seen as fundamentally evil, or morally corrupt. In Mesopotamia, the *galla* (see p.24) who dragged souls to the Underworld were terrifying, but were considered part of the natural arrangement of things, and could be warded off with the right incantations or amulets. Similarly,

in Ancient Egypt, Ammut—the female demon who devoured the souls of the dead whose sins outweighed a feather—was simply a part of the cosmic order. In the ancient Hindu epic *Ramayana*, Ravana, king of the demons, is the personification of brute force and ill-controlled passions. However, neither he nor his *rakshasas*, demons who haunted graveyards, were considered to be essentially evil.

As polytheistic religions developed, they included beliefs in demons with both good and bad attributes. In ancient Greece, the Agathos Daimon was literally a "spirit of good nature," who could act as a personal companion and ensure health and good fortune. Japanese lore includes a panoply of demons, such as the *oni*, who lurk in forests and

classification systems were devised to account for the many ways in which demonic forces were believed to manifest themselves in the world.

A demonic revival

The Romantic movement of the 18th and 19th centuries led to a renewed fascination with demons. Henry Fuseli painted an incubus in *The Nightmare* (see pp.218–219) and an interest in the dark side of unseen powers spawned a genre of Gothic novels, such as Mary Shelley's *Frankenstein* (see pp.196–197). This fascination continues to this day and the paranormal romance novels of the 21st century (see pp.278–279) have returned demons to the morally ambiguous, or even alluring, figures that they were in ancient times.

▲ A catalog of infernal types
This illustration from Collin de Plancy's 1863 *Dictionnaire Infernal* shows a birdlike demon. In previous editions, the author had satirized belief in demonic powers, but his growing Catholic faith led him to believe in their existence.

eat the flesh of unwary passers-by, or the skeletal *gashadokuro*, who crush humans to death. While they must be avoided, they often have contradictory impulses and are not entirely repugnant.

Judeo-Christian demons

In the Jewish Tanakh (Hebrew Bible), the word for demons appears a few times in reference to the worship of false gods, who are described as *shedim*. In early Christianity, demons were often connected with pagan deities and the occult. However, over time, they became associated with the fallen angels who had rebelled against God. Led by Satan, these entities embodied evil and a temptation toward sin.

In 1215, the Fourth Lateran Council of the Christian Church ruled that demons had once been good, but had chosen evil. This sinister characterization preoccupied the medieval mindset and elaborate

▼ The Great Duke of Hell
This illustration from the 1775 German *Compendium of Demonology and Magic* follows the medieval tradition of classifying demons into hierarchies, and shows Astaroth, who makes up the highest-ranking evil trinity with Beelzebub and Lucifer.

Serpent alluding to the temptation of Eve

"Everything daemonic is between god and mortal."

PLATO, *SYMPOSIUM*, C. 385 BCE

JOURNEYS FOR SPLIT SOULS
ancient Egyptian *ka*, *ba*, and *akh*

▲ **Weighing the heart**
This modern copy of ancient papyrus art depicts a common scene in Books of the Dead—the crucial heart-weighing ceremony. The heart had to be judged "as light as a feather" for the *akh* to be granted eternal life.

The ancient Egyptians believed in several different types of "soul," which outlived the physical body and depended on proper funerary rites being observed. After burial, the vital life force (an animating spark known as the *ka*) remained in the tomb, separate from the mummified corpse. The *ka* required sustenance from the living—this could be food as well as symbolic offerings, which were represented by paintings on the tomb walls.

The *ba* or "traveling spirit," depicted in Egyptian paintings and sculpture as a large bird with a human head, was the part of the soul that could fly between the worlds of the living and the dead. Even when a person was still alive, the *ba* was believed to travel during sleep and dreams.

Becoming immortal

The *akh* (or "effective spirit") was the transfigured aspect of the soul, which could only be fully achieved after a perilous journey through the netherworld, ending in a final judgment. The *akh* was therefore not present during the deceased's lifetime. The final verdict on the life of the dead person was decided by the Forty-Two Judges, alongside Osiris, god of the underworld, who weighed the deceased's heart against an ostrich feather representing Truth, Justice, and Balance. If the heart was light enough, the *akh* was granted eternal life in the Field of Rushes—a paradise.

Calling on ghosts

The *akh* was believed to be able to return to earth as a ghost in order to help or inflict harm upon the living. Around a dozen letters from the time have survived that address the *akh* of a departed family member and appeal for its help with (or cast blame on it for) various problems.

The letters were often written on dishes that held food offerings in burial chambers, for the *ka* to read when it came for sustenance. Many contain requests for the *akh* to appear to the writer in a dream. Such interactions between the living and the dead were seen as a means to maintain order and balance in society, which was highly prized. Some historians have compared rituals to honor the *akh* to the Catholic veneration of holy saints.

IN CONTEXT

Khonsemhab and the ghost

One of the oldest ghost stories in written form was discovered in fragments, inscribed on shards of pottery (or *ostraka*) dating from the Ramesside Period (1295–1069 BCE). They tell the story of Khonsemhab, the High Priest of Amun, who confronts a desperate spirit: the *akh* of Nebusemekh, a Middle Kingdom official, whose grand tomb has been left to deteriorate over the centuries. The ghost fears that, without a burial chamber to house his soul, he may soon cease to exist. Khonsemhab weeps for the spirit. He sends servants to make offerings and pledges to rebuild the tomb, which will allow the departed soul (*ba*) to continue to live in the afterlife.

This pottery fragment (dating from 1186–1077 BCE) contains part of the story of Khonsemhab.

▲ **Protecting the heart**
In ancient Egyptian religion, the sun was thought to die each night and be reborn each morning as a scarab beetle. This scarab amulet, placed by the heart (the seat of the "soul"), symbolized eternal renewal and ensured the spirit's safe passage through the netherworld.

THE WHEEL OF REBIRTH
reincarnation

Belief in reincarnation—the idea that the soul outlives the body and returns in a new physical form—was held by many ancient cultures. It may have arisen from a sense that dead ancestors returned to the living world to help their kin once more. Many cultures around the world today retain this idea. Among the Arrernte people of Central Australia, newborn babies are believed to be the reincarnations of totem spirits who have returned to Earth from the Dreamtime realm (see pp.20–21). In southern Africa, the Zulu people believe that the soul progresses gradually, life-by-life, being born first as lower animals, such as insects, and moving on to be reborn as humans and, ultimately, ancestors.

◀ Eternal knot
The endless knot is one of the Eight Auspicious Symbols of Tibetan Buddhism. It represents *samsara*, the endless cycle of rebirth, from which only the following of Buddhist teachings will allow escape.

Life cycles

The idea of a progressive reincarnation is also central to Hinduism. The earliest Vedas (Hindu scriptures) spoke of the soul going to Devlok, the realm of the gods, after death—a journey eased by veneration by the deceased's descendants. By the time of the Upanishads (texts from c. 1100–500 BCE), this idea had evolved into a doctrine of reincarnation, in which the *atman* (the immortal soul) undergoes *samsara*, a potentially endless succession of cycles of rebirth. A person with bad *karma* (the balance of good and evil acts performed in their life) might be reincarnated as an unclean animal, such as a dog, while one who has fulfilled their *dharma* (duties in life) could be reborn as a Brahmin priest. For Hindus, the ultimate aim is to achieve *moksha* (final release), when the cycle of reincarnation will end and the *atman* will be reabsorbed back into Brahman, the universal spirit.

Path to Nirvana

Established in the 6th century BCE by Siddhartha Gautama (Buddha), Buddhism teaches that the soul is chained by worldly desires to the cycle of *samsara*. A person's actions in a previous life are said to condition their rebirth into one of six realms— that of gods, angry gods, hungry ghosts, Hell, animals, and humans (see right). Only reaching a state of enlightenment through following the Buddhist Eightfold Path will release the soul from attachment to earthly things, so ending the *samsara* cycle and leading it to Nirvana, the state of final release. Other ancient cultures also believed in forms of reincarnation. The Greek mathematician and philosopher Pythagoras (c. 570–490 BCE) held

▼ Avatars of Vishnu
In Hindu belief, even deities such as Vishnu, the preserver god, undergo rebirth. His 10 incarnations, or avatars (shown here), include a fish, a boar, the hero Rama, the Buddha, and Kalki, the final avatar, who is yet to come.

KEY

1 The first section of the wheel shows the Realm of the Gods, a place of perfect happiness and no suffering.

2 The second realm is inhabited by the *asuras* (angry gods), who are known for their paranoia.

3 *Pretas* (hungry ghosts, see pp.46–49) belong in the third realm.

4 Hell, made of fire and ice, is the fourth realm.

5 The fifth realm is that of animals (*tiryakas*).

6 Human existence is the sixth realm—the only one from which beings can leave the wheel to reach Nirvana.

◀ **Wheel of life**
A *bhavacakra* is a Tibetan depiction of the Buddhist wheel of life. It symbolizes the Buddhist view of an eternal succession of lives, with each section of the wheel depicting one of the six realms of existence. Yami, lord of death, threatens to devour the wheel.

► **Soul food**

In this illustration from the
16th century, Pythagoras is
shown avoiding a fava bean
plant. Beans were one of the
foodstuffs he ordered his
followers not to eat, because
he believed they contained
the souls of the dead.

that souls were immortal and entered new bodies after death. By living pure lives and abstaining from eating meat, fish, and beans, humans might, he suggested, escape this cycle of rebirth and gain immediate access to the land of the gods. Otherwise, their souls were doomed to be reborn, with virtuous acts in one life counting for nothing in determining the next. This Greek idea of "metempsychosis" (the transmigration of souls to another body) taken up by the Greek philosopher Plato, who, in his *Phaedrus* (c. 370 BCE), argued that the soul is destined to be reincarnated for a cycle of 10,000 years.

Secret knowledge

Greek mystery religions, such as Orphism (said to have been founded by the legendary hero Orpheus; see pp.82–83), are believed to have taken much of their secret knowledge from Egypt, where the Greek historian Herodotus claimed the origins of the reincarnation doctrine lay. The Orphics believed that souls, originally pure, were polluted by contact with the material world. According to Orphic principles, living through three life cycles allowed the soul to be purged, so it could enter the company of the gods. Similarly, the Manichaeist religion, founded in Mesopotamia in the 3rd century CE by the prophet Mani, taught that special knowledge, or *gnosis*, allowed an escape from reincarnation. Only by spurning things of the flesh—such as meat-eating, material possessions, and procreation—could a believer finally enter paradise.

◀ **Spirit writings**
Charles d'Orino's illustration of a reincarnated spirit appears in *Nos Invisibles* (1907) by Clotilde Briatte, who produced books she claimed were channeled to her by the spirit of the deceased French author Honoré de Balzac.

Reincarnation reborn

Early Germanic religions may have contained some element of reincarnation; for example, the Norse Vikings believed that the *hugr* (personality) of the dead could survive and pass into the body of a newly born relative. While Christians rejected the idea of reincarnation, the study of Eastern religions and medieval Jewish kabbalah (see pp.122–123), which included the cycle of *gilgul*, or rebirth, led to a revival of interest in the 19th century. In 1857, French author Hippolyte Rivail, writing as Allan Kardec, founded Spiritism (see pp.228–229), with reincarnation as a central belief. This was followed in the US by the formation of the New York Theosophical Church in 1875, which mirrored Hindu and Buddhist beliefs by teaching that souls, after a time on the astral plane (see pp.262–263), are reborn into human bodies. With this, and similar modern borrowings, the ancient notion of reincarnation itself had, in a sense, been reborn.

▼ **Back from the dead?**
This photograph from 1930 shows a British woman, Miss E. C. Butt, alongside a bust of the Egyptian queen Nefertiti. Butt claimed to be Nefertiti reincarnated.

RESTLESS SPIRITS
South and Southeast Asian *bhutas*

The *bhuta* (or *bhoota*), a spirit of the dead, is feared and venerated across large areas of South and Southeast Asia. Originally a generic term for a spirit, the *bhuta* came to be identified with those who had failed to pass through to the otherworld after death, or to be reborn. They might linger on earth for a number of reasons: misdeeds in life; lack of proper burial rites; or some unfinished business, such as the need to punish their killer.

Hindu religious texts feature stories about *bhutas* and instructions for dealing with them. The *Sushruta Samhita*, for example, covers *Bhutavidya*, the science of *bhutas*, and how people who are possessed by the ghosts of such ancestor-demons may be cured.

The ghosts cannot be exorcised directly, but only by performing a ritual from another text, the *Atharva Veda*. This is done by finding out what is preventing the *preta* (the disembodied spirit released from a corpse after death) from moving on, and promising to remove this obstacle. In Indonesian *wayang* puppet theater, which features stories drawn from Hindu culture, *bhutas* appear as evil giants.

Temptresses and flesh-eaters
There are different kinds of *bhuta*. Some are the ghosts of people who were not buried with the proper rites, or not buried at all. These restless spirits can be appeased by performing funerary

rituals. More troublesome are the *bhutas* of those who have died by suicide; *bhavanis*, the ghosts of unmarried women; and *churails*, those of childless women, who entice young men to their doom. But the most dangerous *bhutas* are the *brahma rakshasas*, said to be the spirits of members of the Brahman priestly caste who have committed grave misdeeds in life, such as accepting gifts from evil people. Supernaturally strong, they inflict curses on those who anger them and even consume human flesh.

Keeping *bhutas* at bay

Remote places such as crossroads, fields, or the places where they died are thought to be popular haunting spots for *bhutas*, although *brahma rakshasas* are apparently fond of the sacred bodhi tree. Expert in deceiving the people they prey on, these ghosts usually appear in human form, and accounts in South and Southeast Asian folklore often describe a figure dressed in white, with feet that point backward, and, in some cases, inverted palms or no nose. *Bhutas* also manifest as fierce creatures such as tigers, a remnant of their possible origin in shamanistic beliefs about animal spirits.

Having identified a *bhuta*, there are various ways to deal with it. Lying on the ground is said to confuse *bhutas*, as they fear touching the earth, and refusing to show fear may lead them to find another victim. Water, iron, and burning turmeric are also used to drive them off. Alternatively, their attacks can be halted by welcoming and celebrating them, or by making them offerings of meat, blood, or milk, in which case they may turn into guardian spirits.

▲ **Rabble-rousers**
This carved panel from the 8th-century Kailasanatha temple in Kanchi, Tamil Nadu, India, shows a row of *bhuta-ganas*, fearsome spirits who inhabit cremation grounds and act as attendants of the Hindu god Shiva.

> "… the two evil spirits, of the form of brahma-ghosts, with their bodies oppressed by hunger and thirst, roamed over this earth."

SHIVA SPEAKING, FROM BHĀVASARMAN'S STORY, *PADMA PURANA*

IN CONTEXT

Bhuta Kola

In some regions of India, including Tulu Nadu in the southwest, communities enact a shamanic ritual designed to invoke their guardian spirits. Performing to special music, dancers and priests wear masks representing *bhutas* such as Panjurli, said to ward wild boars off crops, or Bobbarya, a spirit that protects fishermen. As well as appeasing *bhutas* by giving them offerings and allowing them to take a physical form, the Bhuta Kola ritual also plays a role in maintaining social harmony, as the spirits can pronounce judgment on difficult local disputes.

This dancer's mask takes the form of Panjurli, the boar spirit.

THOU SHALT NOT CONJURE SPIRITS
Old Testament condemnations

In the 2nd millennium BCE, the Jewish Israelites of the Middle East were surrounded by peoples steeped in magical traditions. Canaanites, Philistines, and Israelites, who all inhabited Canaan (present-day Southern Levant), held rituals centered on "ghost pits" (see pp.42–43) in an effort to raise the dead. The Jewish faith differentiated itself from these pagan practices. Communing with the spirits of the dead was condemned as an attempt to manipulate God's will.

Later, Christians also adhered to the Old Testament's prohibition of spirit conjuring. The Book of Deuteronomy includes dealing with spirits in its list of forbidden magic, warning that "one who consults ghosts or familiar spirits, or one who inquires of the dead" is "abhorrent to the Lord."

Waking the dead

Necromancy (the raising of the dead) challenged the divine order of things, in which the deceased went to Sheol, a place of silence and darkness; to heaven; or—according to later rabbinic literature—to Gehenna (the land of the damned). The spirits of the dead were distinct from evil spirits and demons in Jewish belief. Nonetheless, many Jewish people believed God had ordained the final abodes of the dead, and summoning spirits back among the living was considered unnatural. The Book of Job states: "As the cloud is consumed and vanishes away, so he who goes down to the grave shall come up no more." Manasseh, the king of Israel, is condemned (but ultimately forgiven by God) in the Old Testament Book of II Chronicles because "he practiced divination, and sorcery, and witchcraft, and dealt with mediums." Only where God permitted a vision of the dead, as he did to the

Prophet Ezekiel in the "valley of dry bones," was such communication sanctioned. Similarly, there are many examples in the Old Testament of oneiromancy (divination through dreams).

Laws against magic

The penalties for necromancy could be severe, as the Book of Leviticus commands: "A man or woman, impersonating a necromancer or a medium, shall be put to death." The Sanhedrin, the Jewish council, warned against those who fast and then sleep in graveyards in order to be possessed by the spirits of the dead. Conjuring spirits might be forbidden, but nonetheless, necromancy was clearly practiced in the Holy Land—even by kings and prophets—and it remained a preoccupation for the guardians of the Jewish religious laws.

▲ **Protective spell**
This Jewish Aramaic incantation bowl, which dates to late antiquity, features an incantation for protection against the demonic spirit of Lilith, who in Jewish lore was sometimes considered to be Adam's first wife.

▶ **Jaws of Hell**
In the Middle Ages, Christians imagined the entrance to Hell as like the jaws of a fierce beast. Here, an angel locks the gate, preventing the spirits of the damned from returning to Earth.

"There must not be found among you anyone that ... uses divination, a soothsayer ... or a medium, or a wizard, or a necromancer."

BOOK OF DEUTERONOMY 18:10–11

▲ **Valley of dry bones**
The prophet Ezekiel is shown commanding the skeletons of the dead to reconstitute themselves so he can consult them. God himself had commanded Ezekiel to perform necromancy.

▲ **This 1753 painting by Januarius Zick** portrays the woman of Endor in the image of a hag/witch, with the robed spirit of Samuel behind her.

The Endor ghost pit

The biblical Book of Samuel relates how Saul, the first king of Israel, sought the services of a necromancer to raise the spirit of the prophet Samuel. Saul wanted to know how to defeat the Philistines—a people from the southern coasts of Canaan who often warred with the Israelites—in battle the following day. The woman Saul sought out is described in the Hebrew text as *eset balat ov*, or "female master of the *ov*," which refers to a "ghost pit," a hole dug into the ground as part of ceremonies for raising the dead.

Saul must have been desperate, as such rituals, common in the pre-Israelite Canaanite culture, were now strictly forbidden. Reluctantly, the woman performed the ritual and *elohim*, or spirits, arose from the pit in the village of Endor. Among the spirits was the prophet Samuel (as "an old man wearing a robe"), who warned Saul that he had lost God's trust and that he and his sons would die at the hands of the Philistines. As prophesied, Saul's sons perished in battle, and he chose to die by suicide rather than be captured.

Over the centuries, this brief story has inspired much theological debate. At first, this centered on whether the apparition really was Samuel's spirit, and why he would rise up through the ground, which for Christians had a strong association with Hell. However, by the time of the European witch trials (see pp.146–149), attention had turned to the woman, who was widely cited as providing biblical evidence for the existence of witches. In later translations of the Bible she became known as the Witch of Endor.

"I see a ghostly figure coming up out of the earth."

1 SAMUEL 28:13

▶ **More fool you**
In this illustration from Joel Chandler Harris's 1892 version of the folktale, Brer Rabbit has fooled Brer Bear into tying himself up, in a typical trickster role-reversal.

FRIEND OR FOE?
trickster spirits

Almost every region of the world has its trickster spirits. These figures play an ambiguous role; they are able to break the rules, but their deceit often protects the common people against higher powers. In children's stories, they help teach young people about social norms and, even when their tricks fall flat and they themselves are tricked, their experiences can create a feeling of communal solidarity by showing that a certain amount of misfortune is an inevitable part of life.

A state of "in between"

Many tricksters are beings who live between realms, or have dual natures. Loki, the Norse god, was the son of a giantess and so only half-divine; his tricks included causing the death of the god Baldur with an arrow made of mistletoe. Positioned "in between," tricksters are often associated with thresholds. For example, the West African Yoruba figure Èṣù, usually presented as a trickster òrìṣà, or spirit, is associated with many transitional symbols, including crossroads, gates, keys, and doors.

Èṣù uses the power of divination as a means of answering difficult questions, just as many tricksters use pranks to resolve apparently impossible situations. These situations may include oppression by outsiders—as dealt with by Brer Rabbit in the stories that were told among enslaved people in the US American South, which show how wit and humor can help overcome adversity.

Shape-shifting teachers

Tricksters often have the ability to change shape or are themselves part animal. Sun Wukong, the Chinese Monkey King, made himself immortal by erasing his name from the Book of Life and, with typical trickster mischief, is not above turning up drunk to the gods' banquets and stealing their food.

In North American tales, tricksters can take the shape of a bird, such as Wisakedjak, the crane spirit of the Algonquin people, or a land animal, such as Coyote of the Indigenous peoples of the Great Plains and US American Southwest. Coyote's useful exploits include leading people from the underworld to Earth, and creating the first horse, but always with the initial intention to deceive.

Some tricksters take human forms, such as the Polynesian hero Maui, who is revered for pulling the Hawaiian Islands up from the ocean floor by his fishing hook. Whatever form they take, tricksters illustrate how the way of the world does not always play by the rules, and that sometimes it can be necessary to break them.

▲ Shifting trickster
Èṣù takes many forms, from old man to young child, and in this late-19th-century wooden carving is depicted as female. Èṣù's exploits illustrate that there are always two sides to every situation.

IN CONTEXT

Japanese *kitsune*

Kitsune are Japanese fox spirits, endowed with supernatural trickster abilities. They are the messengers of Inari (the rice goddess of worldly success), and their powers, and the number of tails they have, grow with age: a nine-tailed *kitsune* is said to be almost invincible, and able to see and hear all things in the world. These untrustworthy spirits often create illusions, such as a second moon to lead travelers astray. It is said that a *kitsune* can be controlled by seizing the magical pearl in which it hides its soul.

Kitsune **masks** are commonly worn during rice harvest festivals in Japan.

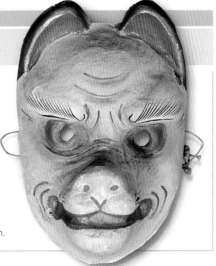

FAMILY MATTERS
ancestor veneration in Asia

Originating in Neolithic times, the veneration of ancestors plays a vital role in religious belief across much of East and Southeast Asia. The practice combines a generalized respect for the elders in society with a sense that this must be carried on into the afterlife, where ancestral spirits require regular offerings to sustain and appease them.

Divining ancestor needs

Respect for the ancestors appears in varying forms across all the region's main religious traditions, including Taoism, Confucianism, Buddhism, Shinto, and animist and Indigenous belief systems. In China, ancestor veneration dates back to at least 5000 BCE and the Yangshao culture (see pp.14–15) of the middle Yellow River valley. By the Shang dynasty

◀ **Ritual vessel**
Bulbous-based bronze *hu* wine vessels were placed in Chinese tombs as offerings, or used in ceremonies to honor the dead. This Western Zhou example, with a bird-shaped lid and stylized *taotie* demon head decoration, is from the 8th century BCE.

(c. 1600–1049 BCE), divination using oracle bones—tortoise shells or ox bones that were heated to produce cracks that could be interpreted—prescribed regular sacrifices to appease the spirits of ancestors. By the time of the Zhou dynasty (1046–256 BCE), ancestor worship had become more elaborate, with temples dedicated to the spirits of former emperors.

Split souls

As well as the cults of imperial ancestors, the ancient Chinese revered members of their own families, worshipping them at home and in frequent rituals at their tombs. They believed that a person has two soul elements: the *hun* and the *p'o*. The *hun* was destined for the afterlife. It was first assessed by the City God, and then judged by the Ten Magistrates of Hell. If virtuous, it could choose either to cross a Golden Bridge to Nirvana and eternal bliss or a Silver Bridge to the land of the gods. Those who had transgressed in life, such as by disrespecting their parents, were thought to suffer a period of punishment before being permitted to cross one of the bridges. The *p'o* stayed with the physical body, and required regular nourishment in the form of offerings of food and "spirit money." In some traditions, a third spiritual element was said to reside in or near the wooden ancestral tablets that formed a key part of ancestor veneration.

Hungry ghosts

Making regular offerings was especially important during the lunar month of July, when ghosts were believed to return to the land of the living. Festivals

---

IN CONTEXT

Ancestors in the *Analects*

Although his writings ushered in a new code of ethics and morality in China, the 5th-century-BCE Chinese philosopher Confucius did not reject traditional ancestor worship. In the writings collected after his death as the *Analects*, he

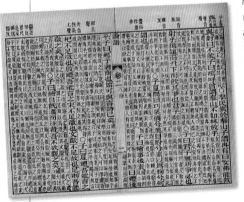

recommended the detailed rituals necessary for the veneration of ancestors, such as fasting, the wearing of ceremonial dress, and the offering of food. Confucius regarded these practices as a form of filial piety, which continued the respect due to elders in life after death.

The *Analects* is a collection of sayings attributed to Confucius and his followers.

◄ **Ancestral lineup**
This Chinese portrait from the early 19th century shows six generations of ancestors, with the most recently dead occupying the front row. The altar at the back of the room contains offerings and an ancestral tablet.

▲ Paying respects
This 19th-century Japanese woodblock depicts men dressed in traditional kimonos making offerings of food and flowers to the *kami* and the spirits of their dead ancestors.

such as the Buddhist Ullambana and the Taoist Zhongyuan (see p.102) are still held in China to remember and appease these spirits. People who committed evil acts in life, died by suicide, died violently, or whose families did not make offerings might be punished by becoming "hungry ghosts." These restless spirits wandered the Earth, inflicting vengeance on those who had wronged them. They could only be put to rest by rituals and sacrifices.

Spirit protection

In Korea, ancestor veneration may have originally occurred at prehistoric megalithic dolmens. It was formalized around the imperial family during the Joseon dynasty (1392–1897 CE), when shrines were constructed for the worship of the ancestral ruler, Jongmyo, with sacrifices made at elaborate altars

such as Sajikdan, in Seoul. Many Koreans believed that a dead person's soul had three spirits. The *hon* was said to rise to heaven, while the *baek* was buried in the tomb. There it remained for four generations before ascending to heaven to become a spiritual protector to the person's descendants. The *baek* and a third spirit, which resided in the ancestral tablets on the family altar, needed to be honored with regular offerings. This third spirit had a special box constructed for it to prevent it from wandering, and was also given spirit money, which it could ultimately use to pay for passage at the 12 gates of the Underworld. For those who had died through violence or accidents, the services of shamans were called upon to cleanse the spirit of its anger and allow it to pass through to the next world.

> ## "To forget one's ancestors is to be a brook without a source, a tree without a root."
>
> CHINESE PROVERB

▲ **Home burial**
This set of "grandfather bones" was buried under a house in the Philippines. In many Filipino traditions, bodies may be exhumed and reburied several times, often to appease or quieten the ancestor's spirit.

Nature spirits and restless souls

In Japan's Shinto religion, there is a distinction between the human dead and the *kami*, spirits that inhabit natural features such as rocks, trees, and streams. The *kami* are venerated mainly at Shinto shrines, while the human ancestors are revered at domestic altars; in visits to family graves; and at festivals such as Bon, in July and August. People make offerings of food, drink, and symbolic money to nourish and appease the dead—both the peaceful dead, who are thought to protect the living, and the restless dead (those who lived an unhappy life or experienced an unnatural death). These tragic spirits wander the world, struggling to enter the afterlife. Only veneration by the living can help them escape this fate. In one version of Shinto, the *sangaku* (mountain cult), human spirits are believed to live among the *kami*. After 13 years, they too become *kami*, further blurring the distinction between the two types of spirit.

The sleeping dead

In Southeast Asia, customs are similarly focused on venerating the ancestors. In the Philippines, feasts were traditionally held for departed ancestors. The ancestors were believed to share the afterlife with nonhuman spirits, so might, if properly honored, be able to intervene and prevent these beings from harming their descendants.

In Tana Toraja, on the Indonesian island of Sulawesi, people have long had an intimate relationship with their ancestors, keeping their departed loved ones in their home for years before the funeral. Until they are buried, the deceased are referred to as simply "sleeping." The funerals are hugely elaborate, 11-day events, which end with the final interment of the body in a cliff-face tomb. Even then, the dead return—each August, in the Man'ene ceremony, the corpses are exhumed and paraded through their former home villages. This practice is yet another form of honoring the dead and stressing the links between the elders who have gone before and the living, whose duty it is to revere the ancestors and perpetuate tradition.

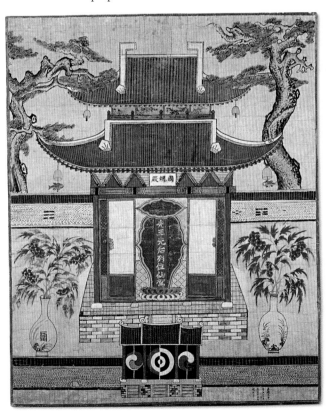

▶ **Painted shrine**
In Korea's later Joseon dynasty, paintings sometimes replaced ancestor shrines as a focus of devotion. This 1811 example commemorates a former king and queen and may have been hung where government workers could pay homage.

▶ **Chinese oracle bones** (see p.48) were inscribed with questions to the ancestors, then heated to produce cracks, or "answers."

Ornately decorated headdress

▲ **This *tavu*** (ancestral altar) is from the Indonesian Tanimbar Islands. Often adorned with heirlooms and bones, the *tavu* is a point of contact between the living and the dead.

▲ **Ancestor skulls**, such as this one, are preserved and decorated by the Asmat people of Papua New Guinea to channel their spirit to their clan.

▲ **This Māori *amo*** ("house-post figure") dates from c. 1800. It once adorned a meeting house, where it represented the spirit of an ancestor.

A headdress of textiles, feathers, and plant seeds.

Venerating the dead

One of human history's oldest beliefs is that when family members die, they enter a spirit world that is closer to the gods than to the living. Ancestor spirits are, therefore, believed to be able to offer protection and assistance to their descendants, so long as they are venerated with dutiful offerings and prayers. Many cultures have also produced fetishistic objects to affirm this connection between the ancestors and the living, and these are believed to be imbued with supernatural power.

▲ ***Mbulu-ngulu*** ("images of the dead"), such as this 19th-century one, were placed on reliquaries housing ancestors' bones by the Kota of Gabon.

▼ **Zapotec funerary urns**, such as this 6th-century CE example from Monte Alban, Mexico, were visited by descendants, who brought offerings of incense, chocolate, and blood.

▲ **This jade funerary mask and collar**, from the Maya site of Calakmul, date to 600–900 CE. Masks such as this one depicted the dead and established a link with the spirit world.

▲ **Medieval bust reliquaries** held the skulls of Christian saints (in this case, Saint Balbina), and were placed on or near altars, or carried in processions on feast days.

Naturalistic and "portrait-like" in style

Figures are almost always shown seated

▲ *Aloalo* **sculptures** marked the tombs of the Antandroy, Mahafaly, and Sakalava people of Madagascar. The word *alo* means "intermediary": between the living and the dead.

▲ **This house model** comes from the Mesoamerican Nayarit culture (300 BCE–300 CE). Placed in a tomb, it depicted the thin divide between the living (above) and the dead (below).

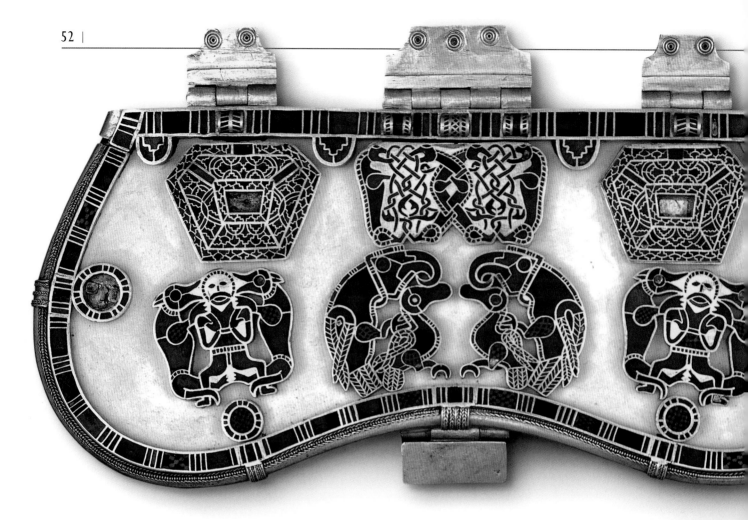

▲ **Gifts for the afterlife**
Inlaid with gold and garnets, this purse lid was just one of the precious grave goods buried with a high-status male (possibly a king) in a 7th-century CE Anglo-Saxon burial mound at Sutton Hoo, Suffolk, England.

EYES EVERYWHERE
spirits in Northern European folklore

Relatively little is understood about the ancient religions of Northern Europe, because accounts of pagan beliefs by later Christian writers often distorted or misunderstood what they heard. Much of what is known survived in the form of folk customs and stories, passed down orally from one generation to the next across a vast landscape that once stretched from the steppes of Asia to the Atlantic.

"The Smith and the Devil" is one such story, taking much the same form throughout the Indo-European-speaking world. It describes how a metalworker makes a bargain with the Devil (or other demonic being) that allows the man to weld any materials together. When the Devil comes to collect the man's soul a decade later, the man welds him to a tree, and the Devil is forced to release the metalworker from his side of the bargain.

Worship of the gods in forest groves and clearings was a common feature of pre-Christian European religions, especially in Scandinavia and northern Germany, where the Saxons venerated the Irminsul. This sacred pole was destroyed when the Frankish ruler Charlemagne massacred Saxon pagans in the late 8th century CE.

Lost souls and demonic dogs

In Scandinavia and elsewhere in the Germanic and Celtic world, the dead were buried in mounds. The rich were laid to rest with sumptuous grave goods, but even the poor were buried with a pot or two to serve them in the afterlife. Beliefs about where the deceased ended up varied, however. The Norse dead (see pp.104–107) were believed to go to the various halls of the gods, some of which were forbidding places—for example, Náströnd, the corpse-shore in Hel's domain, where murderers were sent. But there was also a belief that the dead person's spirit—their *sawul* or soul—remained close to the place of burial for a while, particularly if the deceased still had business (such as righting a wrong) in the land of the living.

Ghosts and other apparitions stalked the landscape in many guises. In the folklore of Brittany, France, the Iannic-an-ôd ("little John of the shore") were the lost souls of those drowned at sea. They swam close to the shore, crying out pitifully, but only attacked those who addressed them directly. More frightening was the Wild Hunt (see pp.118–121), which flew across the night sky with its pack of demonic dogs. Other ghostly hounds—black dogs, known in England as barghests, or shugs (from their shaggy appearance)—howled near houses where someone was doomed to die.

Living landscape

Some supernatural beings were closely associated with features of the landscape. Forests and hills were thought to be the domain of goblins (see

▲ **Burial ritual**
Germanic burial rites were designed to help the soul leave the body. In this scene, the deceased has been given offerings, including a pot and a sword—weapons are often found in male graves—for use in the afterlife.

pp.198–199), elves, and sprites—small, shy, and mischievous creatures similar to fairies (see pp.62–63) that largely avoided human company. Remote wastelands were said to be populated by trolls, depicted as large, ungainly, and ugly, with greenish-blue skin, dressed in skins and wielding clubs. Although violent to intruders, trolls were considered easy to trick.

◀ **Demon dog?**
This woodcut of the English Civil War Battle of Marston Moor (1644) shows the killing of Boye, Prince Rupert's dog, which was said to have magical powers such as shape-shifting. Boye was actually a white dog; this depiction plays on the European folkloric tradition of huge, demonic black dogs, such as barghests, associated with death and ill omens.

▲ Marsh lights
German artist Hermann Hendrich's 1823 painting *Will-o'-the-wisp and Snake* forms part of his body of works that concentrate on themes from Northern European mythology and folklore.

Watery places teemed with spirits in Germanic folklore. In marshlands, the will-o'-the-wisp or jack-o'-lantern (see p.99), which appeared as a dancing string of lights, led travelers deep into bogs, where they drowned and were devoured. In Scandinavia, the *fossegrim* was a type of aquatic troll whose skill at playing the fiddle belied its hideous appearance. Although it could be appeased with offerings of meat—and might even teach fortunate humans to play its instruments—this troll's haunting airs were also said to lead its victims to a watery doom.

Selkies, kelpies, and kobolds
In Scottish folklore, the selkies (see p.90) were seal folk who frolicked in the water but sometimes shed their skins to take human form. The selkies' archrivals were the Finn Folk of Orkney, sea-dwelling sorcerers who kidnapped humans to live with them in their underwater homes. More dangerous still were the kelpies, water-horses made of foam that could also shape-shift into the form of beautiful women. Kelpies lured children into riding

them, but would not allow their victims to dismount; instead, they galloped into the water, drowning their helpless riders.

Even the home was not immune from spirits. The *nisse* or *tomte* in Scandinavia and the *kobold* (see p.198) in Germany were considered to be guardians of the farm or homestead, and were often associated with its first inhabitant. They supposedly carried out domestic chores, but were likely to play tricks on the homeowner if neglected. One type of *nisse*, the *tomtenisse*, is particularly associated with the winter solstice, and today Scandinavians still decorate their homes at Christmas with its likeness.

Folklore rediscovered
From household spirits to hellhounds, trolls, and yet more ferocious beasts like dragons—such as Nighogg, who gnaws at the roots of the world tree (see p.104) in Norse mythology—supernatural beings formed the bedrock of the folktales that authors such as German brothers Jacob and Wilhelm Grimm and Danish writer Hans Christian Andersen rediscovered in the 19th century. By recording versions of these tales, many of which have ancient origins, these writers ensured that the spirits that inhabited the landscape of pre-Christian Europe are still part of the region's heritage today.

▶ Surprised by a kelpie
The 1821 print "Sees a Water Kelpy," by the London cartoonist Thomas McLean, is a humorous depiction of a man being attacked by a kelpie. This one has shape-shifted into the form of a monstrous fish with a lionlike face.

◀ **Forest troll**
Norwegian artist Theodor
Kittelsen's 1899 *Skovtrold*
("forest troll") was one of
a series of troll paintings
he produced, capturing
the menace of these dark
creatures and their intimate
connection to the ancient
northern landscape.

DRUIDS, DISGUISES, AND BONE FIRES
the Celtic festival of Samhain

After the harvest, when summer turned to winter, the ancient Celts celebrated Samhain. A festival that lasted for three days and nights, it marked the end of the harvest and the approach of the hungry winter months, a time when death and the dead could visit the living.

Danger in the dark

The Celts were a cultural grouping of distinct tribes who originated in Iron Age Europe and shared a culture and similar languages. What is known about Samhain comes from the traditions of the Insular Celts of the British Isles and Brittany.

At Samhain, communities celebrated the harvest with feasting and drinking in honor of the gods, whose blessing was sought to ensure good fortune prevailed. Failure to attend was believed to invite divine curses. Towering communal bonfires were lit from discarded crops, animals were slaughtered, and Druid priests offered sacrifices to the gods (hence the original term "bone fires"). The embers of these fires were then used to light the hearth of every home, to bind the community together. The ashes of the fire were spread on the fields to bless the earth, and people also smeared ash over their faces to create a disguise that would protect them from evil spirits. At this time of year, roaming spirits and supernatural creatures were said to escape the Otherworld (see pp.58–61)—such as the shape-shifting púca, which blighted unharvested crops and kidnapped children, or Lady Gwyn, a headless woman with a black pig.

Feeding the spirits

Using a disguise meant that people only had to reveal themselves to good spirits, who were believed to help divine the future. Fire rituals were popular, such as roasting hazelnuts in a hearth fire, asking questions, and interpreting how the nuts behaved for answers (exploding nuts did not bode well). Marriage divination was also performed by bobbing for apples. Families left food and drink outside their homes for ancestor spirits and laid places for them at their tables—known as a "dumb supper." Paying respect was believed to appease the spirits and ensure survival through the hard winter.

◀ **Spiritual leader**
Samhain was a religious event guided by Druids (Celtic priests, as depicted here), and was believed to protect the community from spiritual dangers and the oncoming winter.

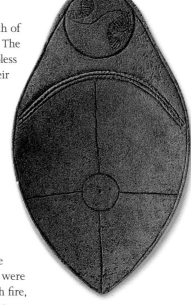

▲ **Divination spoon**
Decorated with symbolic motifs, this copper Iron Age spoon (50 BCE–100 CE) was possibly used by Druids for divination. Many similar spoons have been excavated, suggesting they were ritualistically significant.

IN CONTEXT

Modern Samhain

The British Isles experienced a Celtic revival in the 19th century, and renewed interest in the Druid faith led some people to convert to Neopaganism (see pp.264–265). The often-cited concept of the "veil" between life and death being thinner at Samhain probably originated in this period. Today, many pagans honor Samhain with rituals, feasts, and fires. Some celebrations are private, but others have become public spectacles, such as the annual Samhuinn Fire Festival in Holyrood Park, Scotland.

A celebrant dressed as the Winter King carries a flaming sword at a 2017 Samhain celebration in Glastonbury, England.

THE PEOPLE OF THE MOUNDS
the Aos Sí

▲ **Eternal youth**
The Irish Celtic Otherworld was known as *Tir na nÓg*, or "Land of the Ever Young"—as seen here in a 1920s depiction of Aos Sí in a thriving landscape by English illustrator Arthur Rackham.

By around 500 BCE, Celtic peoples inhabited a swathe of land across northwestern Europe that encompassed Spain, France, Britain, and Ireland. The Celts brought a rich system of beliefs and deities from their original homeland (possibly in Central Europe). While these beliefs varied from region to region, the Celts were united by a deep reverence for the land. They believed that the natural landscape was suffused with the divine, with particular places acting as gateways to the land of the gods.

The Otherworld of the gods and other supernatural beings came closest to the mortal realm in watery places, such as springs, rivers, lakes, and bogs; in caves and hills; and in groves of sacred trees—especially hawthorn—where druids, the Celtic priests, carried out ceremonies. In Ireland, the Shannon River is named for the goddess Sionna, but for the Irish Celts the most common gateways to the Otherworld were the burial mounds and Iron Age forts—which later Celts called "fairy forts"—that dotted the country. Fairy forts, the Celts believed, were home to the

Aos Sí, or "people of the mounds." Also called the Aes Sidhe (and in Scotland the Aes Sith), they were considered to be the descendants of the Tuatha Dé Danaan, an ancient race of supernatural beings who had lived in Ireland before the Milesians (the ancestors of the Celts) forced them underground. Some Christian writers believed that the Aos Sí were fallen angels who had rebelled against God, while others believed them to be the souls of unbaptized dead humans.

Dealing with the good people

Later writers used the generic term "fairies" (see pp. 62–63) to refer to the Aos Sí, but the Irish Celts gave them a variety of names, such as *na daoine maithe* ("the good people") or *na deone beaga* ("the little people"), designed to flatter the Aos Sí and avoid angering them. Although they were generally regarded as neither good nor evil, they could, if provoked, punish humans by spoiling their butter, making cows' milk dry up, or causing sickness. Those who caught sight of these (normally invisible) beings without permission might even be blinded.

The Irish Celts sought to appease the Aos Sí, leaving gifts and aligning the front and back doors of cottages perfectly so the "good people" could walk along their unseen fairy paths unhindered. Often depicted as tall, human-like beings with pointed ears, dressed in forest hues of red and green, the Aos Sí lived much like humans in their parallel world, drinking whiskey, dancing, and keeping cows. They had some peculiarities, though, such as their hatred of iron, fire, and salt—which the human Celts sometimes used as charms to keep the Aos Sí at bay—and a particular love of white quartz.

◀ *Riders of the Sidhe*
John Duncan's 1911 painting shows the Aos Sí out hunting. They carry symbols of their power, such as the Tree of Life and the Stone of Quietness, believed to reveal the past and future.

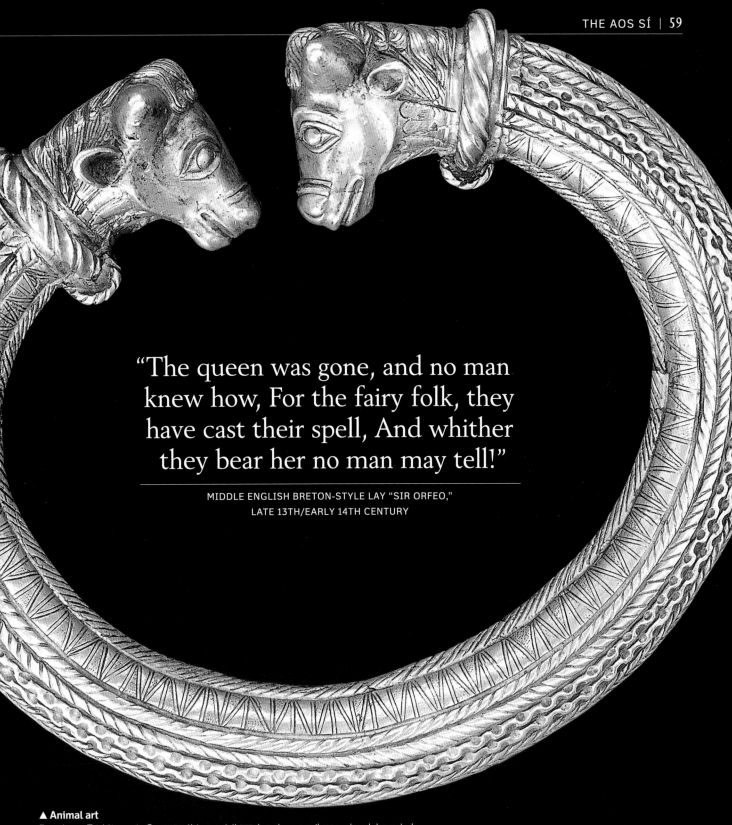

"The queen was gone, and no man knew how, For the fairy folk, they have cast their spell, And whither they bear her no man may tell!"

MIDDLE ENGLISH BRETON-STYLE LAY "SIR ORFEO,"
LATE 13TH/EARLY 14TH CENTURY

▲ Animal art
Found near Trichtingen in Germany, this exquisite 2nd-century BCE silver armband decorated with bull-head endings is typical of Celtic craftsmanship—and of a people who believed that the divine resided in everything, including animals, plants, hills, and rivers.

In Celtic folklore, dealing with the Aos Sí was fraught with peril. They might help with the harvest or ruin it, depending on their mood. Humans invited to enter a fairy mound might leave it to find years gone by and their loved ones dead. For others, such as the shepherd boy asked to join the Welsh equivalent of the Aos Sí, the Tylwyth Teg ("fair family"), after meeting them in the woods, no time passes at all: one moment, he is in a luxurious palace, wanting for nothing; the next, after drinking from a forbidden fountain in the Otherworld, he finds himself back on the hillside with his sheep.

Changelings

Another trick the Celts believed they had to guard against was the abduction of their children. The Aos Sí would switch a healthy human baby for a sickly child of their own. This replacement child, or changeling, would feed voraciously, but would nonetheless gradually fade away and die. When this happened, the abducted human child would be trapped in the Otherworld, doomed forever to be a servant to the fairy folk, alongside human midwives—who alone could assist at the birth of Aos Sí babies—and any others they deemed useful, or simply wanted to ensnare. The Celts placed iron scissors in their cradles, hoping that the good folk's hatred of that metal would protect their babies from substitution by changelings.

Malevolent beings

Other inhabitants of the Celtic Otherworld were far more dangerous than the Aos Sí. The Dearg Due was the ghost of a woman forced by her father into a loveless marriage that ended in her suicide. In revenge, her spirit sucked her husband's and father's blood dry, and her vampire-like phantasm was thought to stalk remote areas, feeding on the blood of unsuspecting young men. Only rocks piled on her grave could keep her quiet for a year.

The Bean Sí, or banshee, the apparition of a woman with long, streaming hair, was said to travel the countryside in a cart drawn by six coal-black horses. Anyone who heard her unearthly scream three times was doomed to die soon after. Though the tradition might be an echo of keening, the practice where professional mourning women were paid to wail at funerals, fear of the banshee's cry terrified generations of Celts. It was better, they believed, to stay away from bogs and remote moors, and not to stray too close to the fairy mounds. The good folk might be feasting there, and might offer a passing human their hospitality—but only the foolhardy would accept.

▲ **Child swap**
Joseph Bouvier's 19th-century painting depicts a group of Aos Sí carrying away a human baby, having left a mischievous-looking changeling nestled in the vegetation on the ground.

IN CONTEXT

Fairy darts and thunderbolts

Celtic peoples found prehistoric artifacts scattered around the ancient mounds in which they believed the Aos Sí lived. They concluded that these artifacts must have magical properties. Flint arrowheads, for example, were thought to be "fairy darts" shot by the Aos Sí, while polished stone axes were thunderbolts that had fallen to earth. Fairy darts were blamed for ailments such as paralysis, blindness, or sickness in cattle, but placed in water that was then drunk by the patient, the darts (or thunderbolts) could also be used as a cure.

This thunderbolt-like Neolithic polished stone ax with flattened sides and a sharpened blade was excavated in Pendle, Lancashire, UK.

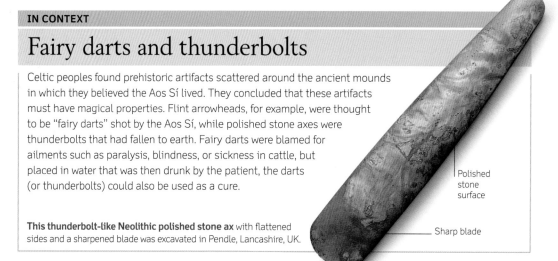

Polished stone surface

Sharp blade

▲ Deliverer of death
In this 19th-century illustration, the spectral image of a banshee hovers over an Irish village, her hair streaming as she emits the scream believed to foretell the imminent death of a villager.

▶ Fairy or angel?
In Persian and later Islamic sources, such as this 16th-century miniature, the *peri* is usually depicted as a beautiful, winged woman whose goodness contrasts with the mischievous jinn (genies) and evil demons.

THE WEE FOLK
fairies

In European folklore, a fairy is a mythical, often small being that is usually hidden from humans, despite living among them. The term "fairy" may come from the Latin word *fata*, meaning "fate." Modern depictions of fairies stem from the 19th century, but these magical beings, in their many guises, have been talked about for much longer.

Different but equally dangerous

Fairies exist in traditions all over the world, so descriptions of them vary widely. They are often associated with natural sites, such as rivers, hills, or forests, but they can also be attached to human-built places—for example, English brownies were believed to integrate themselves into households. Some fairies are described as beautiful, such as the *peri*, a benevolent fairy race from Persian—and later Islamic—folklore. Others are said to be grotesque, among them the Scottish *fachan*, which had one leg, one eye, one arm sprouting from its chest, and a single tuft of hair on its head. Fairies might be child-size, such as the Irish leprechaun, or minuscule, like the *aziza* of Dahomey (now Benin), West Africa, which were so small they lived in anthills.

There are many more differences: some fairies are winged, others not; some dwell together, others are solitary creatures. The one thing fairies have in common is that, while some are believed to be generally good and some generally bad, they are all dangerous. This is because they have their own set of rules, and if an unwitting person breaks those rules, even the kindest of fairies will punish them, perhaps with a curse (see p. 58). People developed different ways to protect themselves against this perceived threat. In Britain, for example, fairies were thought to be repelled by iron, which perhaps explains why people nailed horseshoes to their doors, deterring fairies—and other unwanted supernatural beings—from paying them a visit.

Friendly fairies

Over time, stories of fairies have cast them as more benevolent creatures. Seventeenth-century versions of Cinderella (the Italian *Cenerentola* and French *Cendrillon*) feature kind-hearted fairies who provide gifts. For the puppet Pinocchio in the 19th century, it was a blue-haired fairy who helped. By the early 20th century, *Peter Pan* author J. M. Barrie had created Tinker Bell, originally portrayed on stage as a darting light, while the enduring Flower Fairies drawn by British illustrator Cicely Mary Barker in the same period are sweet and childlike.

▲ **Fairy ring**
This classic 19th-century European depiction of fairies by Nils Blommér shows them dancing in the moonlight—a favorite pastime. It was said to be risky for a human to enter the ring, evidence of which would linger in a circle of mushrooms or flowers.

IN CONTEXT

The Cottingley fairies

Between 1917 and 1920, British cousins Frances Griffiths and Elsie Wright produced five photographs of alleged fairies. The girls, aged 9 and 16 at the time, claimed to have been playing with the fairies at the stream behind Elsie's house in Cottingley, Yorkshire. The pictures were considered genuine by some English spiritualists (see pp. 222–225), including Sir Arthur Conan Doyle, but in the 1980s Elsie and Frances admitted to having faked them.

Elsie Wright is offered a flower by a fairy hovering beside her in the fourth Cottingley photograph, taken by Frances Griffiths in August 1920.

UNDERWORLDS AND AFTERLIFE

ANTIQUITY TO MEDIEVAL

Introduction

In every recorded culture since antiquity, humans have lived with a range of spirit beings, supplicating or warding them off as necessary. Some were celestial beings, such as the angelic messengers of Christianity and Islam or the guardian angels of Zoroastrianism. Others dwelt below ground, in underworlds such as Hell—home to the Devil and tortured souls—or the Greco-Roman realm of Hades, occupied by the souls of the dead and their divine masters. Similarly, in Norse mythology, Niflheim was a cold, dark place, situated beneath the roots of the world tree Yggdrasil. Various African religious traditions also feature underworlds populated by spirits.

In animistic religions, all natural things on Earth are believed to be imbued with a spiritual essence that determines the way humans live or lived. While early anthropologists condescendingly dubbed animism the most "primitive" form of religion, their 20th-century counterparts focused instead on the personification of animistic spirits and their organic interactions with humans. For instance, the Ojibwe communities of Canada were much concerned with "rock people" and "bear people," and, similarly, relations with "jaguar people" were and still are central to the beliefs of some Amazonian peoples.

As well as the concept of celestial spirits and subterranean worlds, and that of animism, the idea that humans shared their everyday lives on Earth with other beings was widespread. The Roman pantheon included the *lares*, minor deities who presided over homes, farms, roads, and fields, and it was common practice for homes to have a little domestic shrine, or *lararium*, to ensure the well-being of the resident family.

Other members of the spirit world were believed to live in humanlike family and community groups. In the pre-Islamic and Islamic Arab world, there were the jinn, spirit beings who were thought to have their own tribes. Jinn often minded their own business, but could

Dealing with the dead *see p.69*

Laboring jinn *see p.72*

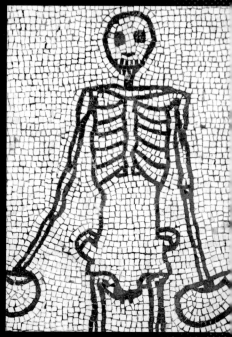

Ancient Roman reminder *see p.87*

cause illnesses in people who offended them. Like humans, they could have good and bad characters, but unlike humans, they were said to have the power to shape-shift into animal forms. According to legend, the trolls of Scandinavia and the fairies of Ireland lived similar parallel earthly lives, sharing the landscape and its resources with people, and occasionally coming into conflict over those resources or territories.

Whether spirit beings occupied other realms or lived alongside humans, communication and interaction with them was more likely to occur in particular places in the landscape or at certain times of year—known as "liminal" or threshold points. In Africa and Europe, for example, waterfalls, pools, caves, and mountain tops—places that reached into the sky or went deep into the Earth—were all places where the boundary between human and spirit worlds was believed to be permeable. In the Christian calendar, All Hallows' Eve (Halloween) and All Saints' Day were moments in the sacred year dedicated to the dead, and a time when dead ancestors were said to be able to visit the living. But each culture also had its powerful people, conjurers, shamans, or diviners, who could communicate with the spirits at will, through birthright, training, or secret knowledge.

"No one can hurry me down to Hades before my time, but if a man's hour is come … there is no escape for him …"

HOMER, *THE ILIAD*, 8TH CENTURY BCE

Saving souls *see p.96*

Magic circle *see p.112*

Protection against spirits *see p.122*

CITIES OF THE DEAD
ancient necropoleis

The deliberate burial of the dead is a very ancient practice, and recent evidence suggests it may date back at least 300,000 years to when *Homo naledi*, a now-extinct species of hominin, deposited the remains of 15 individuals deep inside the Rising Star Cave in South Africa. The places of burial, the way in which corpses were buried, and the grave goods that early cultures left in tombs tell us much about their beliefs regarding the afterlife.

The lands of the living and those of the dead were almost always seen as realms that should be kept apart, so graves were situated outside the area of settlement, in cemeteries or larger necropoleis ("cities of the dead", from the Greek words *nekros*, meaning "dead," and *poleis*, meaning "cities").

In cultures such as those of the early Christians, where it was believed that the dead body would be physically resurrected in the afterlife, the dead were buried, but in those where the corpse was believed impure or served no purpose—as in Hinduism—they might be cremated.

◀ **Protective talisman**
This gilt figurine of Horus the sky god as a falcon represented the divinity of the pharaohs and offered protection. Mummified falcons were also placed in ancient Egyptian tombs as funerary offerings.

▼ **Opening the tomb**
This engraving shows a scene from 1923, when British archaeologist Howard Carter; his sponsor, Lord Carnarvon; and his assistants lifted the pharaoh Tutankhamen's coffin from one of the massive stone sarcophagi, amid piles of precious grave goods.

▲ Marble monument
This 4th-century CE Roman funeral stele, from the vicinity of the Vatican necropolis, combines Christian imagery—the two fish—with traditional pagan elements, such as the invocation to "D. M." (or *dis manibus*; the "spirits of the dead").

In the Neolithic necropolis Hal Saflieni Hypogeum, in Malta, the burials seem to have been conducted in stages. First the flesh was left to decompose, then the skeletons were moved to the burial chamber and covered in red ocher, and then finally buried in a communal grave. Red ocher, a pigment made from ground-up iron ore, was symbolically important because—associated with the color of blood—it signified regeneration.

Many cultures believed that the dead required grave goods—physical objects they could somehow use in the afterlife. Such grave goods can be spectacular, such as the golden objects found in the Varna necropolis in Bulgaria. Dating to around 4300 BCE, and one of the oldest such sites, the rich burials, including those of chieftains who had made their wealth in the salt trade, included many items (such as jewelery and weapons) made of gold.

Egyptian elites
The tombs of ancient Egypt provide an unparalleled account of Egyptian beliefs about life after death. The elite and, above all, the ruling pharaohs, were mummified by treating the body with preserving salt and wrapping it in bandages, as it was believed the deceased would need their body again after death. The walls of tombs were richly decorated with scenes from their Book of the Dead, sets of spells to help souls navigate the trials they would face after death (see pp.32–33). The tombs—considered to be new palaces for the dead rulers—were spectacular, from the 482-ft- (147-m-) high Great Pyramid at Giza to the royal necropolis in the Valley of the Kings, near Luxor. This necropolis contains the famous burial chamber of the pharaoh Tutankhamen, who died around 1323 BCE. His tomb housed elaborate interlocked sarcophagi and grave goods that included a golden funerary mask.

▲ Ancient burial
This grave was excavated at the Varna necropolis in Bulgaria. It held the skeleton of a prosperous male who died in his 40s, possibly a chieftain, with rich grave goods, including a gold-handled ax and gold bangles and necklaces.

▶ **Afterlife textile**
Dating from around 600 BCE, this embroidered poncho was used as a wrapping for a mummy of the Paracas culture in Peru. It is decorated with iconographic motifs depicting a variety of otherworldly animal beings.

Many pharaohs' tombs notably contained *shabtis*, miniature statues that were expected to be the dead ruler's servants in the next world.

Underground cities

Roman tombs were often on the outskirts of cities due to a religious prohibition on burying bodies inside the city boundaries, but the streets leading to cities were lined with a ribbon of tombs and monuments inscribed with the names, and often the professions, of the dead. From around the 1st century CE, the Romans built catacombs, or underground necropoleis, within larger Roman cities, including Rome. Families went

◀ **Buzzing with life**
This famous gold pendant was excavated from the Chrysolakkos necropolis near Malia, in Crete, established by the Minoan people around 1800–1700 BCE. In their religious ideology, bees were an important symbol of fertility and rebirth.

there to honor their dead with funerary feasts in chambers that contained stone couches in imitation of *triclinia* (Roman dining rooms). As well as serving as memorials, catacombs acquired a religious purpose when used by early Christians to bury their dead (and to hide from religious persecution in the tunnels). The belief that burial close to a prestigious or holy person could help the deceased enter heaven led Christians to house their dead in tombs near those of saints such as St. Peter, beneath the Vatican in Rome, where there are five stories of catacombs.

Painted chambers

Dating from the 9th–1st centuries BCE, the Etruscan necropoleis at Cerveteri and Tarquinia (city-states of this Mediterranean civilization) are made up of tombs cut into rock, and covered inside with exquisite frescoes. These paintings, showing scenes of Etruscan mythology and daily life, and often depicting the grave's occupant, were intended for the benefit of the deceased in the afterlife, glimpsed only briefly by the living.

Notable sites

Necropoleis are a feature of cultures worldwide. In South America, the Paracas culture of Peru wrapped the dead in cloaks (or "mummy bundles") and placed them in shaft graves at the site of Cerro Colorado. The largest of the necropoleis, containing more than 400 burials, was in use for 1,000 years from around 800 BCE. In China, at the 4,000-year-old Ordek's Necropolis at Xiaohe (on the edge of the Taklamakan desert), the arid climate preserved the remains of 300 mummies buried upside down.

Among the grave goods were the oldest remains of cheese ever found. In both of these examples, the grave goods and the efforts taken to preserve the corpse suggest a belief in an afterlife where both the body and the goods would be needed.

Necropoleis did not die out once these ancient cultures collapsed, and monumental burial sites continue to be used. The largest necropolis of all, the Paris catacombs, was built only in the late 18th century, when city graveyards became too full. The bones of 6–7 million people remain there.

▼ **Game for the dead**
In this painting from the necropolis at Tarquinia (c. 530 BCE), two wrestlers are shown grasping each other's hands as part of funerary games held in honor of the deceased.

KEY

1 The legendary king Dhu al-Qarnayn is identified with figures including Alexander the Great and Persian king Darius II. In the Qur'an, he is instructed by Allah to build a wall to hold off evil forces.

2 In Islamic depictions, jinn usually have horns. Coincidentally, the name Dhu al-Qarnayn means "the two-horned one."

3 The wall represents a division between oppression and civilization.

4 Crafted from blocks of iron and coated in brass or copper, the wall built by the jinn was said to be so strong that the enemy could not even make a hole in it.

▶ **Helpful jinn**
Jinn in the service of Dhu al-Qarnayn are shown building a wall to keep the two evil forces, Yājūj and Mājūj (Gog and Magog), away from the ruler's lands in this 16th-century Persian miniature.

FORGED IN SMOKELESS FIRE
Arabic jinn and ghouls

In pre-Islamic Arabia, belief in jinn—unseen supernatural beings of great power—was widespread, and this belief was carried forward into the Islamic faith from the 7th century CE. Their name derives from an Arabic word meaning "hidden," and these invisible beings have parallels with the winged creatures depicted in Assyrian reliefs (see pp.22–25) and with the *mal'akh* (angels) of Jewish literature, who act as messengers between God and humans.

◀ **Protective magic**
This 19th-century Islamic talisman was believed to offer protection against malicious jinn. It is decorated with a figure of a horned jinni (singular) astride a beast with the head of a lion and tail of a snake, surrounded by cloven-hoofed attendants.

Before the advent of Islam, the veneration of spirits associated with particular locations or natural elements was common practice. Jinn were believed to inhabit desolate places, shape-shifting between human form and that of animals such as cats or snakes. They were considered by some to be the earliest inhabitants of the world, with ancient ruins such as those of Mada'in Saleh (in northern Saudi Arabia) seen as their original homes. Often ascribed superhuman characteristics such as great strength or exquisite beauty, jinn were also reported to be skilled artists and healers, able to inspire poets by whispering into their ears.

Flesh-eaters and demons

Other spirits appeared in Islamic folklore, such as the shape-shifting *ghul* ("ghoul"), which lurked in graveyards and devoured human flesh, and the ifrit, a demonic being similar to a jinni, but usually regarded as malevolent. Tales of such beings were popularized in collections like *The Thousand and One Nights*, which ultimately shaped modern portrayals of jinn and other spirits.

Life in the shadows

As the religion of Islam spread across the Arab world, beliefs about jinn shifted. They were regarded as one of Allah's creations, but unlike humans, who—according to the Qur'an—were made from clay, jinn were fashioned from smokeless flame. They dwelt in a shadow world known as al-Ghaib, but lived much like people, in tribal units and nations, some nomadic and others sedentary. When jinn interacted with humans, it was said that they could help them, grant wishes, or even marry them and have half-human children. But like humans, jinn had free will, and could accept Islam or, like Iblis (the Devil and, in some accounts, leader of the malicious jinn), reject it and torment and corrupt people. Malicious jinn were believed to cause sickness or even possess their human victims.

◀ **Death or glory**
In this illustration from a manuscript of the Persian epic poem the *Shahnameh* (977–1010), the hero Rostem is depicted killing Div-e Sepid (the "white demon"), the lord of the *divs*, or demons, as one of his seven labors to free his own king.

Driving out a jinni

The belief that unseen spiritual beings, such as jinn, lived alongside humans and were able to possess them was widespread during the early Islamic period. Possession could be positive, such as when the spirits were believed to inspire a poet or musician to create beautiful work. However, more often than not, it was interpreted as malicious, or a consequence of the victim offending the jinn or committing a sinful act. The symptoms of jinn possession often included amnesia, seizures, or speaking incoherently, and it was believed to prevent the person from thinking or speaking according to their own free will.

To ward off the attentions of jinn, people carried protective talismans. However, if this failed, the family of the afflicted person might call on a specialized exorcist. This was often a Sufi, a practitioner of a mystical form of Islam, who would perform a ritual to expel the bad spirit.

First the exorcist would recite prayers and scriptural verses. He might then ask the jinni why it had possessed the victim and try to persuade it to leave. If this did not work, he would blow in the ear of the patient, curse the jinni, and demand in the name of Allah that it leave the body it had possessed. Exorcists also employed the power of music—such as haunting melodies played on the oud (a type of lute)—because this was considered to help release the spirit's grip on its victim.

"We have created for Hell many of the jinn."

THE QUR'AN, SURAH AL-A'RAF: 179

▲ **A group of Arab musicians** perform to drive a jinni from the body of a young child in this 1884 painting by Pierre-Andre Brouillet.

Spiritual protection

The belief that a material object can be imbued with magical powers, capable of conveying spiritual protection to its owner, is common to almost every culture throughout human history. These amulets, or lucky charms, were made from a diverse array of materials, including precious metals and stones, and were often inscribed with symbols and religious texts. Most were designed to be worn close to the body, as rings or pendants, or to be placed in the home or the grave. Whether protecting, healing, or attracting good luck, each talisman was considered an essential part of survival in a world inhabited by both malevolent and benevolent spirits.

▲ **The Eye of Horus** (or wedjat eye), a popular amulet in ancient Egypt, represents the healed eye of the god Horus and harnesses the power of regeneration and health.

▲ **Objects depicting the evil eye** guard against the real evil eye, which allegedly kills or injures with a glance. A crescent moon secures help from the Roman goddess Diana.

▲ **A hagstone**, worn around the neck or hung in windows or doorways, saw off witches, nightmares, and illness. Looking through the hole supposedly revealed other realms.

▲ **This jade burial suit** belonged to Dou Wan, a princess of China's Western Han dynasty (206 BCE–9 CE). Such suits served as immortal armor for the elites, preserving the body and soul after death and protecting against evil spirits.

Sewn together with gold wire

Jade plaques with pierced corners

▶ **Witch bottles** were used in early modern England as a cure against bewitchment. This one contains iron nails and a piece of an iron blade—to inflict pain and end the spell.

A protective
item was often
inserted inside

Blood-colored
rubies symbolize
the power of life

▲ **This Tibetan *ga'u* or amulet box** harnesses powerful
Buddhist symbols: the geometry of squares and stones
creates a mandala, symbolizing the universe in its ideal
form and protecting the wearer.

▲ **Japanese *omamori*** are amulets
that derive their power from Buddhist
or Shinto blessings. They traditionally
protected against evil spirits but now
often represent good luck.

▲ **This seated antelope figure** comes from
ancient Egypt. The antelope was considered
a creature of chaos and an enemy of the gods,
yet its depiction on amulets transformed this
threat into a protective power.

▶ **Incantation bowls** from the Persian
Sasanian Empire (400–700 CE) were
inscribed with spells to protect
against the curses of demons
or humans. They invoked the
power of spirits.

The bowl must
be ritually turned
to read the text

▲ **This Kuna *nuchu*** (medicine doll)
comes from Panama. Carved from the
wood of a sacred tree and imbued
with protective spirits, it would either
assist healing or repel evil.

▲ ***Lakakare*** **or coconut charms** from
Papua New Guinea, carved to look
like a sea creature, ward off evil. The
coconut shell is filled with substances
with magical properties.

The spiraling
design ensnares
a demon

THE REALMS OF HADES
spirits and the Underworld in ancient Greece

For the ancient Greeks, death was marked by the final exhalation of breath, when the spirit, or *psyche*, would travel to the Underworld, accompanied by the messenger god Hermes. There, it was judged by Hades, god of the dead—along with the demigods Minos, Aiakos, and Rhadamanthys—and then assigned to one of the realms of Hades: the Elysian Fields for the elite; the infernal depths of Tartarus for the damned; or the Asphodel Meadows for the majority, where the spirit would live as a "shade" of its former self.

◀ **Funerary plaque**
This plaque from a tomb in Attica (c. 520–510 BCE) depicts the elaborate rites of *prothesis*, or laying out of the dead.

in Tartarus, were often bound as part of their punishment—the Lapith king Ixion, for example, was tied to a flaming wheel for eternity for his crime of attempting to seduce Hera, wife of the great god Zeus.

The land of the dead

Hades had many precautions in place to ensure the dead did not stray back to the world of the living. Five rivers encircled the Underworld, including the great river Styx—only crossable by paying an *obol* (the coin used in burial rites to close the eyes of the dead) to the ferryman Charon—and the Lethe, whose waters caused any drinker to forget their own earthly existence. The entrance was guarded by the ferocious three-headed dog Cerberus, who would savage anyone who tried to get past. The damned,

Restless spirits

The Greeks went to great lengths to ensure that the dead were properly buried. Otherwise, they feared their spirits might become trapped between life and death. Their elaborate funerary rituals included the *prothesis*, or laying out of the body; the *ekphora*, the predawn procession to the cemetery; the interment of the body in a grave or burial mound; and the *perideipnon*, or funeral feast, with libations of wine and offerings of milk and honey to the deceased. The name for the dead who had not been given a proper burial was *ataphoi*, meaning "unburied." In Homer's epic poem *The Odyssey*, the hero is so desperate to flee the island of the sorceress Circe that he delays burying the body of Elpenor, his companion who died falling from a roof. Elpenor's *ataphoi* returns to threaten the wrath of the gods if Odysseus neglects the proper rituals.

The restless dead also included the *biaiothanatoi*: the spirits of those who had suffered a violent death, like the more than 6,000 Persians who had fallen at the Battle of Marathon against the Athenians and whose ghosts were said to haunt the battlefield. The *aoroi* were the untimely dead—such as

Inscription hammered into gold foil

Text instructs the deceased to drink from the Lake of Memory

◀ **Underworld instructions**
This gold funerary tablet from the 3rd–2nd centuries BCE was created for a devotee of an Orphic mystery cult. Orpheus, a mythical Greek hero (see pp. 82–83), was believed to possess special knowledge that could result in a better afterlife.

The king of Tiryns, on whose orders Hercules captures Cerberus, hides from the beast inside a jar

Hercules wields a club to subdue Cerberus

▲ Hound of Hades

This black-figure vase, dating from c.525 BCE, depicts the three-headed beast Cerberus, who guarded the entrance to the Underworld, being caught by the hero Hercules. The Greek writer Hesiod described Cerberus as "the dreaded hound on watch."

▲ Vengeful ghost
In *The Eumenides*, the third play in Aeschylus's *Oresteia* trilogy, the ghost of Clytemnestra summons the *Erinyes*, or Furies—vengeful Underworld spirits—to pursue and punish her son Orestes, who murdered her.

"Arouse them for me, the spirits, the dead; rouse their souls and forms at the mouths of my vessel."

SPELL FROM THE GREEK MAGICAL PAPYRI, 3RD CENTURY CE

unmarried youths, or anyone who had died before their telos (life goals) had been fulfilled. These spirits were believed to roam the earth, haunting the living.

Repelling and inviting spirits

In early spring, the Athenians celebrated *Anthesteria*, a festival of wine that was also a festival of the dead. The ghosts of the deceased were believed to wander freely through the city during the festival, and so temples and businesses were closed. The Athenians made offerings to appease the restless spirits and protect themselves and their homes; chewed hawthorn leaves; and covered their doorways with tar to repel any who tried to enter.

There were times when, instead of warding off spirits, the Greeks actively sought them out. The term *nekya*, meaning necromancy (magic invoking or communing with the dead), was first used by Homer as a title for Book 11 of *The Odyssey*.

▶ **Deathly deity**
This marble relief fragment shows Hecate, a goddess who became particularly associated with ghosts and necromancy. Athenians offered a feast each new moon to appease her and the spirits she controlled.

Odysseus, longing to return home, is desperate for advice and so he descends to Hades and summons the shade of the prophet Tiresias using spells from the sorceress Circe. Tiresias appears and tells him how to get home safely. In a similar vein, the Greek playwright Aeschylus included a scene of necromancy in his play *The Libation Bearers*, in which Orestes and his sister, Electra, summon the ghost of their father, Agamemnon, to seek advice on how to punish his murderer (and wife), Clytemnestra. In both works, *nekya* rites are described. Odysseus pours votive offerings of milk, honey, barley, and sheep's blood into a trough, while Electra pours libations on her father's tomb and calls on the gods of the Underworld.

Link to the Underworld

Many who sought to speak to the dead did so at oracular shrines, called *necromanteion*. These were often caves or gorges that were believed to connect directly to the Underworld. Plutarch, for example, describes how the Spartan king Pausanias traveled to the *necromanteion* of Heraclea Pontica, on the Black Sea. There, he raised the spirit of Cleonice, whom he had accidentally stabbed to death and who had been haunting him.

Such stories show that necromancy was not regarded by the Greeks as a form of evil magic, but more as a means of negotiating with the dead. Restless or vengeful ghosts could perhaps be appeased, enabling them to enter properly into the Underworld and remain there for good. The dead might have valuable knowledge to impart, but it was nonetheless essential that they remain dead after sharing it.

IN CONTEXT

Asclepius

The son of Zeus and a mortal woman, the mythical Asclepius was taught medicine by the centaur Chiron and went on to become a great healer. According to the legend, he was so skilled that he had the power to bring the dead back to life; for example, using an herb to resurrect the Cretan prince Glaucus. Zeus saw such work as a breach of the natural order and, fearing men would use the technique to abolish death altogether, he killed Asclepius with a thunderbolt. However, Asclepius himself achieved immortality of a kind, as Zeus brought him back as the Greek god of medicine.

A marble statue from c. 160 CE shows Asclepius holding a staff intertwined with a serpent—a symbol of his healing powers.

Orpheus and Eurydice

The Greek heroine Eurydice was a young bride, newly married to the musician Orpheus, when she died of a venomous snake bite. Orpheus followed Eurydice to the Underworld, also known as Erebus, determined to bring her back. The myth of this ill-fated couple has inspired many classic works of art and literature, plenty of which describe the ghostly inhabitants of the Greek Underworld.

Plato wrote of Orpheus's quest in his 4th-century BCE *Symposium*, and the story was expanded upon three centuries later by the Latin poets Virgil and Ovid. Their poems describe how, when Orpheus played his lyre for Hades and Persephone—god and goddess of the Underworld—the ghosts of that realm were drawn in by his song of love and loss. Virgil wrote of how "the insubstantial shadows, and the phantoms of those without light, came from the lowest depths of Erebus, startled by his song ...."

Touched by Orpheus's song, Hades allowed Orpheus and Eurydice to return to the land of the living, on the condition that Orpheus was not to look back at his wife until they reached the surface. Either not heeding or forgetting their warning, Orpheus turned to glimpse her, and Eurydice was condemned to remain among the ghosts below.

> "The bloodless spirits wept as he spoke, accompanying his words with the music ..."

OVID, *METAMORPHOSES*, 8 CE

▲ This painting by Jan Brueghel the Elder (c. 1594) shows Orpheus in the Underworld amid the souls of the dead—and their tormentors.

PARALLEL EXISTENCE
African spirit realms

Traditional African religions have a long history of beliefs in both spirits and the existence of a sacred spiritual realm. While their conceptions of the universe vary, most African peoples share a belief in the interconnectedness and interdependence of all of its parts. In these traditional religions, the physical realm—inhabited by humans, animals, plants, and other forms of life—exists alongside both otherworlds and underworlds, which are inhabited by supernatural beings, such as the spirits of the unborn, deities, nature spirits, and the spirits of ancestors (see pp.130–131).

Living with spirits

No rigid boundaries exist between worlds, but certain people, animals, plants, places, activities, and times are believed to have easier access to the spirit realm. Among Cameroon's Oku people, designated sacred places—usually lakes, mountains, and waterfalls—as well as the plants and animals in the countryside, are inhabited by spirits called *emyin*. Through dreams and other encounters with these spirits, Oku healers and diviners gain the knowledge they need to support their communities. Ritual dance ceremonies (see pp. 170–171), especially at funerals, also grant participants access to the spirit realm.

Some otherworlds and underworlds are believed to exist apart from the physical world, rather than alongside it. These include hospitable places like Samanadzie—a dark, fertile realm said to be inhabited by the spirits of those found worthy to be resurrected by Onyankopon, the Supreme Being of the Akan (Ghana)—and inhospitable places like Magombe, the underworld of the Baganda of Uganda, which is sometimes described as cold, fetid, and haunted.

Circle of life

Life is cyclical in the traditional African worldview. People live, die, and are reborn, or their spirits linger in the spirit realm (for better or worse) or are retained by the community through induction into ancestorhood. Death is therefore seen as a journey to the next stage of life. Requirements for ancestorhood (a desirable status) are often met by the person's standing as a beloved elder in the family while alive. Over time, the departed blend into the community of those who have died. The Swahili call this community of souls the *mizimu*, and their domain is called Kuzimu.

▲ **Protective shell**
This turtle-shaped Senufo amulet is worn to appease and gain the protection of the turtle spirit. The Senufo believe that turtles, snakes, crocodiles, and chameleons were created before humans, and therefore represent every form of life.

IN CONTEXT

Twin spirits

The birth of twins, for many African peoples, is a noteworthy occasion. The Senufo of Cote d'Ivoire, and many other African peoples, believe that twins are linked to the spirit realm. Twins were feared in some past societies, but were and are generally perceived as a demonstration of fertility, abundance, and divine favor, and/or as a powerful embodiment of the mystical equilibrium necessary for life. Because twins are believed to have perfect knowledge of each other, diviners often seek to establish twin-like relationships with clients to facilitate their divinations.

Yoruba *ibeji* twin figures memorialize deceased twins. The Yoruba of Nigeria have the highest recorded rate of twin births in the world.

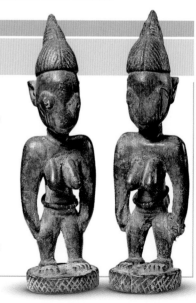

Top half features carvings of spirit realm

Bottom half depicts cosmic ocean

▲ **Calabash of creation**
"Two halves of a gourd create one universe" is the Yoruba saying illustrated by this carved calabash (a hollowed-out gourd shell). The top half represents *isálòrun*, the spirit realm. The bottom half represents the primeval waters from which *ayé*, the physical world, was created.

"The world is a marketplace we visit; the other world is home."

YORUBA SAYING

THE RESTLESS SHADES OF ROME
Roman *lares*, *manes*, and *lemures*

While the great heroes and statesmen of ancient Rome were believed to go to the Elysian Fields after they died (like the ancient Greeks; see pp.78–79), the remaining deceased were thought to become *umbrae*—shades of the dead condemned to perpetual gloom. These insubstantial ghosts needed to be appeased, and so, each new moon, women would garland the *lararium* with rosemary and garlic and give offerings of corn and wine. The heart of every Roman household, the *lararium* was a miniature shrine that honored the family's ancestor spirits (*lares*). The *manes*, on the other hand, were the spirits of particular individuals, who were honored every February at the *Parentalia*—part of a nine-day festival when Romans would privately honor their ancestral dead.

Sinister beings
The Roman spirit world also included *lemures* and *larvae*: grotesque, malevolent, and restless ghosts who preyed on the living. Their festival, the *Lemuralia* or *Lemuria*, was celebrated on May 9, 11, and 13, marking a period so ill-omened that even the temples were closed. It was a time when the spirits of the dead were believed to roam and so the head of each household would perform rites

◄ **Shadow selves**
This obsidian mirror from Pompeii's House of the Gilded Cupids reflected shadows, giving viewers a sense of how they would appear after death.

to banish them. This included spitting out nine black beans for the *lemures* to swallow, beating together copper objects, and reciting spells.

Ghostly apparitions
To avoid a corpse becoming a *lemur*, it had to be properly anointed and buried. Even if only part of a body could be found, that, too, required the proper rites. These rites were essential, or else a *lemur* might haunt the place of death. Roman literature is rich with such stories: the letters of Pliny the Younger include the tale of a house haunted by a spirit wrapped in chains. Pliny recounts that the philosopher Athenodorus saw the apparition in the house and followed it to the courtyard. The ghost pointed to a particular spot, which, when dug up, revealed the remains of a murdered man. The bones were buried with the proper rites, and the haunting ceased. Ghosts, too, had needs, and for the Romans, righting a wrong that a spirit had suffered in life was just as vital as the offerings made during festivals.

► **The cheerful dead**
This mosaic from Pompeii (3rd century BCE) depicts an ominous grinning *larva* holding two jugs. It was intended to remind feasting guests that earthly fortunes are fleeting.

▼ **Family spirits**
This fresco from a *lararium* in the House of the Vettii, Pompeii, shows the *lares* as young men bearing drinking horns, on either side of the *genius loci*, another protective household spirit.

"It will be the ancient sacred rites of the Lemuria, When we make offerings to the voiceless spirits."

OVID, *FASTI*, BOOK V, 8 CE

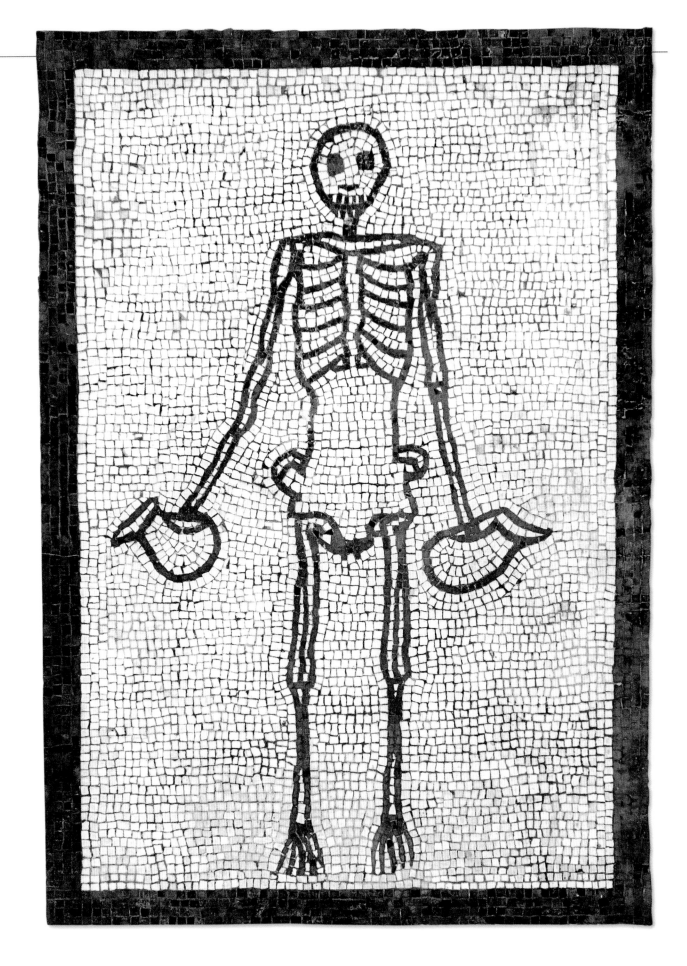

▶ **Underworld mirror**
This mosaic-decorated skull represents
Tezcatlipoca, a Mexica god whose name
means "smoking mirror" in Nahuatl.
He was believed to be the prince
of Mictlan, and could take many
forms, such as a moaning
bundle of ashes or a
shrouded corpse.

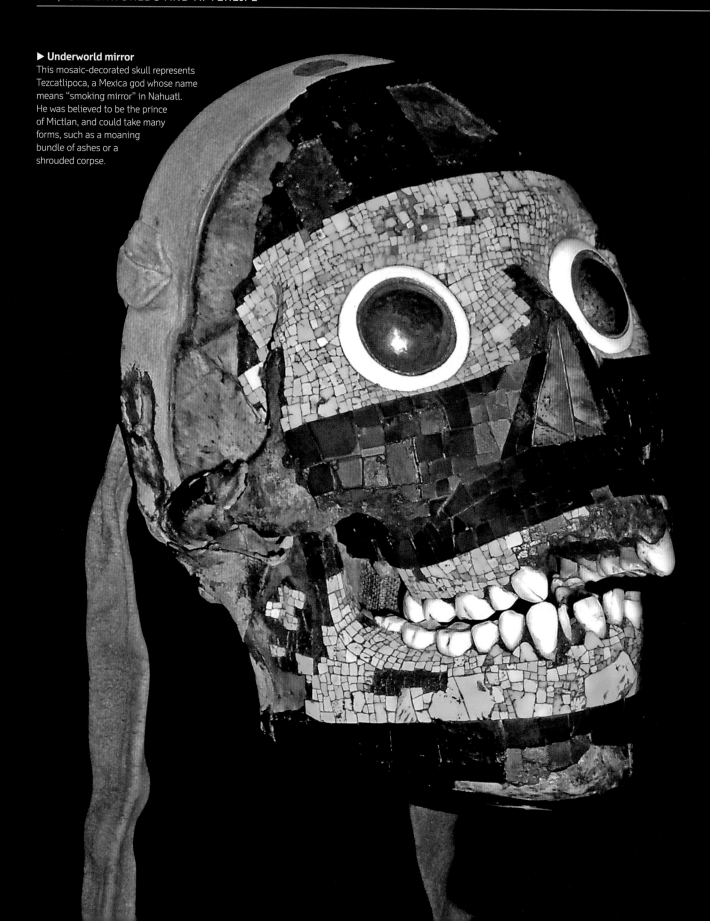

COSMIC DISORDER
Mesoamerican spirits

Ghosts and deadly spirits stalked the landscapes of Mesoamerica. The diverse cultures of this region in the era before 1493—among them the Olmec, Zapotec, Maya, Toltec, and Mexica (Aztec or Nahua)—had many differences, but their religious beliefs and ideas about the cosmos were closely related. Mesoamerican peoples treated death with respect rather than fear, and saw it as a key regenerative moment in the cosmic process. Each culture believed that human spirits could return to the world of the living if conditions were right.

Deadly cosmology

Death was central to Mesoamerican concepts of creation. According to the Nahua creation myth, the gods had to kill themselves in order to make the sun move, and only human sacrifice would keep it in motion. In the Maya religion, the sun and moon were formed from the souls of two heroes who had been defeated in a ball game by the lords of Xibalba ("place of fright"), the underworld where souls went after death.

According to the Mexica, where a spirit ended up depended on how they died. For example, those who died of illness or old age went to a different afterlife from those who died in battle or at birth—the latter went directly to paradise. For others, nine levels had to be crossed, passing through many obstacles to reach the place of the dead known as Mictlan. Many individuals were cremated with a dog or buried with a dog figurine, because

◀ **Earth monster**
Olmec art often features an open-mouthed monster figure, as seen in this statue from Chalcatzingo in south-central Mexico. The open jaws are said to represent the entrance to the Underworld, which was thought to be located within a cave.

▲ **Divine mothers**
This 16th-century Mexica image from the *Codex Borgia* shows Cihuateteo, the ghosts of women who died in childbirth. Normally they helped guide the sun's motion, but on five days of the year they were thought to haunt crossroads and attempt to steal children.

dogs were thought to be able to protect and guide the dead on their difficult journey to the afterlife. Those who drowned were buried with seeds, often corn, in their mouths as a symbol of rebirth.

Lost souls

Once a soul had gone to the afterlife, it was never supposed to return. Those who came back as ghosts represented a failing in the cosmic order and served as omens of doom. The Maya used amulets and shamans to send them back to rest. They believed that restless souls might be reborn as plants, which might be medicinal or toxic, depending on the intention of the ghost.

There are many examples of vicious ghosts in Mesoamerican cultures—many of them female (see pp.132–133). One such example is Xtabay, from Yucatec Maya folklore: the ghost of a spurned woman who lures men into woods to devour them.

SOULS OF THE DEEP
mermaids and sirens

The dual nature of the sea, as both a giver of life and a potentially destructive force, has given rise to stories of part-human aquatic creatures who haunt its depths, and who can either help sailors and travelers, or lead them to their doom. Often depicted as beautiful women, these mermaids (from *mere*, an Old English word for the sea) are a symbol of the ocean's mysteries, and they appear in the mythologies of many cultures.

The first fish-woman

Merfolk first appear as mythical monsters in ancient Mesopotamia (c. 4000 BCE). The *kullulu* ("fish-man"), said to be a child of the primordial sea goddess Tiamat and described as having a fish tail and a human upper body, was sometimes paired with a *kuliltu* ("fish-woman").

The first mermaid tale can be traced to Assyrian legend (c. 1000 BCE), in stories about the goddess Atargatis. While different versions give different reasons for her transformation, most include a heartbroken Atargatis diving into a lake and the gods turning her into a mermaid to save her.

The mermaids of Greek mythology were called sirens, and were originally imagined to be part bird, rather than part fish. The name *seirén* ("entangler") referred to their seductive song, used to lure men to their deaths. In Homer's *Odyssey* (725–675 BCE), the hero Odysseus has his men strap him to the mast of his ship and plug their ears with wax so they cannot hear it. The Roman writer Pliny the Elder described many mermaid sightings in his *Natural History* (77 CE), claiming that their bodies were covered with fish scales.

▲ Mer-monster
Finding a Japanese *ningyo*, or "human fish"—represented here by Baien Mouri in his *Baien Book of Fish* (1835)—was said to be a bad omen. Yet the flesh of a *ningyo* was also believed to confer eternal life and youth on any human who ate it.

▶ Shape-shifting spirits
This woven pandanus-leaf sculpture by Samantha Malkudja depicts a Yawkyawk, a shape-shifting ancestor spirit from Western and Central Arnhem Land, Australia, who inhabits pools and streams.

▶ Famed musicians
This late-15th-century illustration by French illuminator Robinet Testard shows mermaids helping the god Neptune in a contest against the goddess Athena. Playing trumpets and stringed instruments, they assist him with their musical powers.

Sea wives

By the medieval period, mermaids were generally depicted with fish tails. In Ireland, merrows were seen as beautiful women with long, green hair. Merrows might fall in love with and marry human men, who would hide the merrow's *cohuleen druith* (the magical cap that allowed them to live underwater) because the merrow would be tempted to return to the sea. This motif recurs in tales of Scottish selkies: in the water, they are seals, but on land, they shed their skin to take on human form and marry human men. The husband would similarly conceal his wife's sealskin, to prevent her from transforming back into a seal. However, mermaids were not always loving. In South American legend, the *lara* ("lady of the lake") is a siren-like enchanter of men.

Modern merfolk

By the 19th century, belief in mermaids had diminished in Europe to become folk stories, retold by writers such as Hans Christian Andersen, whose *Little Mermaid* is perhaps the most famous of all. Yet beliefs in mermaid-like deities live on: Mami Wata (see p.172) is often portrayed as a mermaid, and the Inuit of Canada and Greenland venerate Sedna, a powerful half-human, half-fish goddess. If enraged, she may send storms but, if placated, can ensure the fishermen enjoy a bountiful catch; she is also known as "mother of the sea."

"O, train me not, sweet mermaid, with thy note,
To drown me in thy sister's flood of tears."

WILLIAM SHAKESPEARE, *COMEDY OF ERRORS, 1594*

▲ **The living and the dead**
This manuscript illustration depicts the popular medieval ghost story or morality tale of the three living and three dead. While out hunting, three young noblemen are suddenly confronted by the animated corpses of their ancestors, who reveal that their mortal sins have led to an eternity of torment.

SPIRITS, SOULS, AND THE HOLY GHOST
Christianity and the supernatural

Belief in the resurrection of souls was central to early Christianity and the most popular funerary inscription of the time—*Vivas*; "May you live"—expressed the hope of each believer that God would grant them eternal life. According to Matthew's Gospel, many holy people were raised from the dead at the moment of Jesus' death (Matthew 27: 52–53), and the Bible also left open the possibility of a return of the dead before the final resurrection.

Necromancy—the idea that a person's body could be reanimated by magic or their soul brought back to be consulted for divination purposes—was considered a form of sorcery and expressly forbidden. However, contrary to this, the Bible includes the story of a woman who seems to raise the spirit of Samuel at the request of King Saul (see pp.46–47); this suggests that necromancy might work, even if it was outlawed.

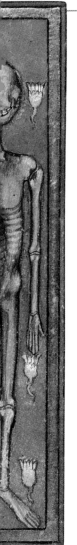

Fasching

Customs intended to "scare away" evil spirits can be found throughout the Christian world. In the liturgical calendar, the precedent for the 40-day fasting season of Lent was the temptation of Christ by the Devil, and so this period always represented a battle with evil spirits who worked hard to tempt people into sin. *Fasching* is the German name for pre-Lent festivities and is related to *Fastenschrank*, meaning the last alcoholic drink before Lent. In different parts of Germany, *Fasching* is called *Karneval* and participants frequently don masks— originally intended to confuse and repel evil spirits.

This *Fasching* or *Karneval* mask is exquisitely carved from wood; many such masks have been handed down through the generations.

Theological debates about the returning dead have featured prominently in the history of Christianity. The Church refers to the relationship between the living and the dead (excluding the damned) as the "communion of saints," but Catholics and Protestants hold different beliefs about the closeness of this relationship.

The spiritual world

In medieval English, the word *ghoste* simply meant "spirit," so the Holy Spirit (in the divine trinity of Father, Son, and Holy Spirit) came to be known as the Holy Ghost, representing the spiritual presence of God in the world. From Judaism, Christianity took the idea of angels (disembodied spirits who serve God), and borrowed *daimons* (intermediary beings) from the ancient Greeks, reimagining them as demons: fallen angels who serve Satan. Christian saints (recognized after death for their holiness in life) provided another level in the spiritual hierarchy, with powers to intervene in the world on behalf of those who sought their help.

Escaping souls

The Catholic doctrine of Purgatory, defined at the Council of Lyon in 1274, states that the souls of Christians who die in a state of repenting sin undergo purification in the afterlife before their admission to heaven. Therefore, for an undefined period, these souls are caught between Heaven and Hell. It was believed that the living could perform rituals—masses, candle lighting, prayers for the dead—to advance the atonement of their sin. The idea that souls might return from Purgatory to right the wrongs they had committed in life was widely believed in folk Christianity. However, people also feared more sinister revenants (the returning, reanimated dead).

Belief in Purgatory underpinned belief in ghosts and so, when the Protestant Reformation of 1517 abolished the former—Protestantism claims the dead go straight to either Heaven or Hell—reformers hoped also to eliminate beliefs and practices surrounding the latter. According to the new religion, "faith alone" could save a soul from eternal damnation, and this meant an end to the rituals that the living performed for the dead. Requests for prayer were even erased from tombs, and ghosts came to be considered demons in disguise, or priestly hoaxes to fool the people.

▶ **Ghost in the glass**
A fragment in the window of Chester Cathedral depicts a skeletal revenant, still wearing a burial shroud. Fear of reanimated corpses was a concern in medieval England.

"His ghost would not rest, and he would get in the buildings in the shape of a bull, and roar till ... the tiles would fly off the building."

EDWIN SIDNEY HARTLAND, *THE ROARING BULL OF BAGBURY*, 1890

However, without Purgatory, the living were deprived of a close relationship with the dead, and interpreting ghosts of departed loved ones as demons offered very little comfort to the grieving. Perhaps unsurprisingly, reports of ghosts only increased in the 16th century. Popular beliefs proved more wide-ranging than church dogma and, in Protestant nations, often resembled a patchwork of Catholic ideology, reformist ideas, and old folkloric superstitions.

Anti-Sadducists

The fate of the dead was contested again in England during the 1650s, when the country was made a republic and religious liberty briefly prevailed. Some sects ("mortalists") claimed that the soul was mortal and also expired at death. After the Restoration of the monarchy, many theologians became concerned by the spread of such ideas, accusing mortalists of following the Sadducees of the New Testament—who had denied Christ's resurrection and also the existence of spirits.

"Anti-Sadducists" such as Joseph Glanvill argued that ghosts provided evidence of the reality of the spiritual world, and thereby the existence of God. In his book *Saducismus Triumphatus* ("Sadducism Overthrown," 1681), Glanvill collected ghost reports, such as the "Drummer of Tedworth," a poltergeist-like manifestation in Wiltshire.

◀ Unfinished business
The "Guildford Ghost," a murdered man, appears "crying Vengeance" in this image from an English ghost pamphlet of 1709. Early modern ghosts often seemed to appear for judicial purposes, such as to avenge a crime or extract a confession.

In the 18th century, the Methodists, led by John Wesley, also embraced the notion of ghosts as evidence of a spiritual reality and justification for religious belief. Wesley even recorded the tale of "Old Jeffrey," the ghost of a long-departed relative who was believed to haunt the rectory where he grew up. Such reports were countered by rational, skeptical thinkers, and yet, even after the Enlightenment, these represented a minority.

"Laying the ghost"

In 18th- and 19th-century England, there were many stories of "ghost-laying" clergy, who claimed special powers: the ability to banish troublesome spirits. Tales describe parsons conducting exorcism ceremonies in Latin and "reading down" a spirit—making it small enough to be trapped in a small container, such as a bottle or box. This might then be thrown into a body of water, where it was confined. In *English Fairy and Other Folk Tales* (1890), Edwin Sidney Hartland relates the story of an evil squire who haunted his village as a monstrous bull. After much fervent preaching and praying, the spirit was shrunk inside a boot and buried beneath the doorstep of the local church.

Spirits were often banished to a strange place, transformed into an animal or inanimate object, or cursed to toil at an eternal task. There were a few ghosts who could not be laid, and these returned to their place of haunting for a single "cock-stride" (a short period of time) each year.

▼ Sized up
Drawn in 1792, Richard Newton's satirical cartoon shows a member of the clergy attempting to "read down" a ghost. This was supposed to shrink the spirit, but here seems to have had the opposite effect.

KEY

1 A preacher holds up two puppets depicting a witch and the devil, terrifying his congregation. The paper beside him reads "I speak as a fool."

2 Another preacher pushes a religious icon into the breasts of a young woman, as Hogarth compares religious "enthusiasm" to sexual excitement.

3 A thermometer shows the various stages of madness brought on by religion, all stemming from a diseased brain at the bottom.

4 This paper references George Whitefield, a founder of the Methodist movement satirized by Hogarth.

◄ *Credulity, Superstition, and Fanaticism*
This 1762 engraving by English satirist William Hogarth mocked people who believed in a poltergeist known as the "Cock Lane Ghost" (see p.282).

THE NIGHT OF THE DEAD
All Hallows' Eve and Halloween

The modern festival of Halloween, with its costumes, pumpkin lanterns, and expenditure (more than $9 billion annually in the US), can be traced back to the medieval Christian church. According to some, it was an attempt to co-opt older pagan traditions, though this is debated. Many pagan practices are still discernible in today's Halloween celebrations.

From old to new

The ancient Romans celebrated two festivals in May: *Lemuralia* or *Lemuria*, when they exorcised spirits from the home (see pp. 86–87), and *Feralia*, when they laid tributes on the graves of the departed. In 609 CE, keen to harness the power of the ancient festivals, Pope Boniface IV reestablished May 13 (previously *Lemuralia*) as the Christian All Saints' Day—dedicated to saints without a specific date of celebration. In the 8th century, Pope Gregory III moved this date to November 1, and in the 11th century, St. Odilo of Cluny, a Benedictine monk, made October 31 All Souls' Day, a time when families could pray for the release of their loved ones' souls from Purgatory (where sinners were punished or purified to prepare to enter Heaven).

Another word for All Saints was All Hallows (meaning "all holy") and so the period from October 31 to November 2 became known as Allhallowtide—a time dedicated to prayers for the souls of the dead. The night before All Saints' Day was referred to as All Hallows' Eve, or Halloween.

It has been suggested that, in the Celtic lands, the absorption of pagan practices into church festivals meant Halloween was greatly influenced by Samhain (see pp. 56–57), the ancient festival of the dead, when bonfires were lit to ward off malevolent spirits and a portion of the feast was set aside for the returning dead.

Praying for souls

Accounts from the 16th century detail the practice of "souling," when groups of people would go from door to door asking for "soul-cakes"—small round loaves or cakes—believing that for each one they ate (alongside a prayer said for the dead), a soul would be released from Purgatory. Young people took part, dressed in disguise ("guising"), and singing or telling jokes. In time, this tradition became more elaborate, with traveling, costumed troupes putting on shows ("mumming") in

▼ **Medieval masquerade**
This 14th-century manuscript of *Le Roman d'Alexandre* ("The Romance of Alexander") shows amateur actors, or "mummers," whose grotesque animal masks form part of the entertainment.

▶ **Hallowed days**
A 17th-century Greek icon shows a seated Christ surrounded by a host of saints commemorated on All Saints' Day, which was preceded by All Souls' Day, a time for remembering the dead.

▶ **Halloween superstition**
This greetings card illustrates the 19th-century craze for divination games at Halloween—a candle-bearing woman stares into a mirror, which apparently shows the face of the man she is destined to marry.

ON HALLOWEE'N LOOK IN THE GLASS, YOUR FUTURE HUSBAND'S FACE WILL PASS.

"Little Jack, Jack sat on his gate
Crying for butter to butter his cake."

TWO LINES FROM A TRADITIONAL BRITISH "SOULING" SONG

exchange for food, wine, or money. Soon, however, these practices were endangered; the Reformation, started by Martin Luther in 1517, led to the establishment of the Protestant Church, which did not teach the doctrine of Purgatory. Prayers were no longer thought to be needed for the safe passage of the dead and Allhallowtide was not recognized in the Protestant calendar. Nonetheless, the secular term "Halloween" appeared for the first time in Scotland in 1556, and in Shakespeare's *Two Gentlemen of Verona* (1598), one character accuses his master of "puling like a beggar at Hallowmas."

Halloween revived

While Halloween had lost its significance in the Protestant faith, the 18th-century revival of interest in folk traditions helped resurrect it in the popular imagination. Robert Burns's 1785 poem *Halloween* is full of references to pranks, mischief-making, and fairies, which are all staples of later Halloween celebrations. By the mid-19th century, the festival was widely celebrated in Britain, with torch-lit Samhain processions taking place in Ireland in the 1850s. Even Queen Victoria helped popularize Halloween, celebrating it with great pageantry at Balmoral Castle in 1876, where she led a procession of estate workers that ended with the tossing of a witch's effigy onto a bonfire.

Many Halloween traditions were transported to America by Irish immigrants escaping the potato famines of 1845–1852. Their traditions merged with more sedate harvest festivals to produce riotous celebrations, which included divination games, such as apple bobbing, and general mischief-making, which one ladies' magazine in 1872 termed "vandalism." Organized Halloween parties began to be held to keep children from wreaking too much havoc.

◀ **Ghost turnip**
This plaster cast from Donegal, Ireland (taken from a turnip carved to look like a ghost), is a reminder of the legend of Stingy Jack, which gave rise to Halloween jack-o'-lanterns.

Modern Halloween

Today, many Halloween traditions still retain echoes of the past. Candy has replaced "soul-cakes" and carved pumpkins allude to the legend of Stingy Jack, who tricked the Devil into banning him from Hell and was condemned to wander eternally in the dark with only a lantern to guide his way. The practice of leaving out food to appease wandering spirits has its echo in trick-or-treating, a form of which arose with the "guisers" of the Middle Ages who would sing songs or tell jokes for soul-cakes. The masks once worn to conceal people's identity from vengeful ghosts have today become mere caricatures of vampires and ghouls.

◀ **Dressing up**
These two girls (c. 1898) show the enduring popularity of wearing Halloween masks— originally intended to conceal people's identities from marauding, malevolent spirits.

WILD AND WANDERING SPIRITS
early Slavic mythology

The beliefs of the pre-Christian Slavic peoples of Eastern Europe were intimately linked to the landscape. Forests, swamps, lakes, and rivers were thought to be inhabited by a host of spirits, many highly dangerous to those who angered them. Much knowledge of traditional beliefs was lost when Slavic rulers converted to Christianity, culminating in the baptism of Vladimir the Great of Kiev in 988 CE. The pagan temples of great gods such as Perun, the lightning god, were dismantled, despite fierce resistance by the *volkhv*, the pagan priests.

Water and woodland

Their leaders may have embraced Christianity, but most ordinary Slavic people continued to revere their local gods, among them the *Rozhanitsy*, female deities who decided a child's fate, and lesser spirits of nature, such as the *rusalka* or *mavka* water nymphs, the ghosts of girls who had drowned in lakes or rivers. Their hair green and silky, their robes of shimmering silver, the *rusalki* apparently enticed men to dance with them until they died of exhaustion or drowned in the nymphs' watery home.

Water was not the only danger; it was also risky to venture into the woods. People feared the Baba Yaga, a deformed witch who lived in a house built on stilts made from chicken bones. In some tales, she was said to eat any children who strayed into the forest. Other nature spirits, such as the *polyovyk*, or field spirit, and the *leshy*, the guardian of the forest, tolerated human hunting or harvesting in their domain—to an extent. These spirits were often blamed for leading people astray from the path, never to be seen again.

▼ **Hen keeper**
Not all *kikimori* were malevolent. Some more benign forms, such as this *kikimora* with the features of a chicken, might marry the *domovoy* of a house and then perform useful household chores, such as caring for the hens.

◄ **Watery temptress**
This illustration of Russian author Alexander Pushkin's poem *Ruslan and Lyudmila* (1820) depicts a *rusalka* that Ruslan meets on his quest to find Lyudmila, who has been kidnapped by monsters at their wedding feast.

Household spirits

The home was not a safe haven from troublesome spirits. Each building was thought to have its own guardian or guardians, such as the *domovoy*, a male spirit who protected the main house, or the *gumenik*, who looked after the storehouse—but people had to be careful not to annoy these helpful spirits.

If a keyhole was left exposed, a *kikimora* might sneak through and enter the house. Deformed female spirits with animal parts such as dog snouts, *kikimori* were rumored to lurk in dark places like attics, and could crush people to death in their sleep. They might also kidnap a human child and leave a changeling in its place, which would then grow up to become a new *kikimora*. According to Slavic folklore, the only way to rid a home of this tricky spirit was to keep the house so clean that the *kikimora*, who loved chaos and mess, became bored and left.

Unpredictable visitors

At certain times of year, such as Velja Noc (New Year's Eve), the spirits of the dead were believed to wander abroad, knocking on the doors of their living relatives. In early summer, too, the spirits became dangerous: *rusalki* were able to leave their waterways and climb into birch trees, descending at night to lure men to dance with them until they died. The best approach at such times was to keep close to home, or consult the witches and shamans, who could offer amulets and advice to fend off the wandering spirits.

KEY

1 There are many variations of the firebird story, but this glowing bird is a valuable yet troublesome prize.

2 The golden apples come from a magical tree in the king's garden, and are said to bring strength and youth to those who eat them.

3 As the bird flies off, the prince succeeds only in catching a tail feather, which emits a fiery glow.

4 Prince Ivan is the king's youngest son, who, after seeing the thieving firebird, sets out on a dangerous quest to bring it home.

◀ **Fiery plumage**
An eastern Slavic folktale recounts Prince Ivan's discovery of the firebird—a mythical spirit with magical and ever-glowing feathers—stealing apples from his father's tree.

TALES OF THE UNEXPECTED
ghosts in Chinese literature

The supernatural heritage of Chinese literature dates back to ancient times, with tales about ghosts and ancestor spirits being passed down orally before the advent of writing during the Shang dynasty (1600–1046 BCE). While earlier records are rare, archival evidence from the Tang dynasty (618–907 CE) suggests that these story collections were a regular feature of the Chinese literary tradition.

Religious origins

Before the Tang era, Chinese ghost stories were uncommon and often overlooked, but some of the earliest examples were brought together in Gan Bao's collection *In Search of the Supernatural* and Liu Yiqing's *A New Account of Tales of the World*, both from the Six Dynasties period (220–589 CE). Belief in the otherworldly in China stems from two of its main religious practices: ancestor veneration (see pp.46–49)—originating in both animist religion and Taoism—and the concept of filial piety (reverence for forebears), which stems from Confucianism. The idea that the observance of these practices, or lack of it, may lead to reward or retribution (such as being haunted) relates to the Buddhist concept of karma.

Collected tales

Gods, ghosts, and demons came to prominence in literature during the Tang period, when a genre of supernatural tales known as *zhiguai xiaoshuo* ("records of anomalies") increased in popularity. *Miscellaneous Morsels of Youyang*, a compilation of anecdotes by the poet Duan Chengshi, featured ghosts, as did stories from various Tang texts collated as *Records from the Taiping Reign* during the Song dynasty (960–1279). The large size of the latter tome, which included works such as Zhang Jian's *Collection of the Numinous and Weird* and Chen Han's *Collection of Strange Reports* underscores the wealth of spectral tales being (re)produced in the Tang era. Notably excluded were stories from Li Fuyan's *Strange Records Continued*, seemingly due to their reactionary political themes. The story of Zhong Kui—queller of evil spirits and demons, but himself a ghost—is also thought to date from the Tang period.

While Chinese ghost-story collections came to prominence under the Tang, the most iconic example was not published until 1740. Containing 491 macabre tales, Pu Songling's *Strange Tales from a Chinese Studio* used ghosts both for entertainment and for political and social criticism, disguised as allegory.

▲ **Guardian beast**
Ming chi, or spirit objects, were part of Tang ancestor worship, providing the dead with whatever they might need in the afterlife. This ferocious example is a tomb guardian, believed to offer protection to the ancestor.

IN CONTEXT

Festival of the hungry ghost

The Ghost (or Hungry Ghost) Festival (known as Zhongyuan festival in Taoism and Yulanpen festival in Buddhism) is an annual tradition observed throughout the Chinese diaspora. It begins on the 15th night of the 7th Chinese month, when ghosts and spirits of the dead are allowed to return to the world of the living for a month to visit family and friends. The term "hungry ghost" signifies the person's reduction to animalistic cravings and existence upon death.

Hungry ghosts need to be treated with respect and appeased with offerings, as depicted in this 13th-century silk fan painting by Li Song.

◄ **Demon queller**
Zhong Kui is pictured with his demon attendants in this Ming dynasty (1368–1644) scroll painting. Zhong Kui had the power to command demons and was variously called a Demon Hunter or King of Ghosts.

SEERS, SPIRITS, AND THE NINE REALMS
afterlives in Norse mythology

The cosmology of the Old Norse world, which stretched from their Scandinavian homeland as far west as Greenland, and as far east as Novgorod in Russia and Kyiv in Ukraine, was a complex one. The gods, such as Odin, his wife Frigg, Thor, and Freyja lived in palaces in Asgard, the highest of the nine realms that made up the Norse universe. Midgard, the land of the mortals, was in the middle, and the gloomy halls of Hel, the goddess of death, were at the bottom. All were linked by Yggdrasil, the vast world tree.

Fate and death

The realm a person was destined to end up in after death lay in the hands of the Norns, three mystical female figures who sat at the base of Yggdrasil,

▼ Seer's tools
Found in what is thought to be the grave of a *völva* at Fyrkat, in Denmark, this gold box brooch contained white lead (lead carbonate), which may have been used as face paint for divination rituals. Other unusual grave goods included a metal wand and poisonous henbane seeds.

◄ World tree
Midgard, the world of humans, is the focus of this 19th-century depiction of Yggdrasil. The world tree linked all nine Norse realms, home to elves, dwarves, giants, gods, and the dead, as well as people.

weaving the threads that made up an individual's fate and cutting them when they died. Only a *völva*, or seeress, had the power to see a person's fate, using *seidr*, spirit magic that was highly perilous to employ. Much of what is known of the Norse view of the afterlife comes from the *Völuspá* ("Prophecy of the Seeress")—an 11th-century Icelandic poem in which Odin himself comes to a *völva* seeking knowledge of the future—and from the Sagas, a large collection of epic tales set down in written form around 1200.

Afterlife voyages

The highest ambition of a Viking (a seafaring Norse warrior) was to die in battle and be taken by the Valkyries, female war-spirits who served Odin, to feast eternally in one of the gods' homes in Asgard. However, some went to the underworld of Helheim, which, according to the Prose Edda, was located in Niflheim, a cold, dark realm of mists; other sources tell of the dragon Nighogg sucking the blood from the dead at Náströnd, the "corpse-shores."

Burial mounds were portals to the afterlife. Some elite mounds contained ships packed with treasure, such as the ship buried at Oseberg in Norway around 820 CE, which contained the remains of two women, one possibly a queen, along with ornate carvings, textiles, and jewelery. In such vessels, the dead were believed to voyage to the next world.

Not everyone gained entry to another realm. Some Norse dead were said to remain tied to the mortal world, because they were cursed or too evil of temperament to enter the afterlife, or simply because they wished to stay close to those they had known in life, or to guard the treasures interred with them in their burial mounds.

Locked between the worlds of the living and the dead, these beings became *haugbui*—reanimated corpses, generally of men, which were endowed with superhuman strength. They were normally not dangerous unless intruders broke into their burial place, as Grettir, the hero of *Grettir's Saga*, did when he investigated a supernatural fire burning

▲ Crossing over
This 19th-century German painting shows the gods using Bifrost, the Rainbow Bridge, to enter their new home, Valhalla, for the first time. Odin stands in the center with his spear.

Hermöd til Heliar reyd. Kana þan æ
Na strondu. Hvörgi slybur hesti æ Isbeyd
hleipti ad Vytz Kiaptinum.

Þo Helia þarfa hefdi þan, hiulin svör
tum Daudanz Inock, Hermödr ey hræda³
van, Kälz blaalita þenan Skrock.

Les XLIII. Eddu, Dæmisögu

Balldur hin Bödi

Hüngurdißr

Sulltur Anyfur

> "… difficult as [Hrapp] had been to deal with during his life, he was now very much worse after death, for his corpse would not rest in its grave …"

LAXDAELA SAGA, TRANSLATED BY MAGNUSSON AND PALSSON

around a mound. Inside, Grettir found Karr the Old, the former lord of the area, sitting on a chair. A titanic tussle ensued, ending with the hero decapitating the *haugbui*.

The walking dead

Believed to be more dangerous still were the *draugr*, who could wander abroad from their mounds. Bloated, foul-smelling beings, their skins were green, blue, or *ná-fold* ("corpse pale"), and they were vengeful. In *Grettir's Saga*, a *draugr* crushes a shepherd to death before Grettir beheads him, too. In a sign of the magic the most powerful ghosts were thought to wield, the dying *draugr* curses Grettir to live forever as an outlaw.

The *draugr* could shape-shift into seals, cats, or wolves and create supernatural clouds or areas of darkness to mask their movements. They were said to crave their former lives, and often came back to their old homes in search of the life they had lost, such as the crew of Thorodd's ship in the *Eyrbryggja Saga*, who return to their lord's hall dripping with seaweed and saltwater. If denied entry, the *draugr* would "house-ride," by mounting the roof of the building and breaking in through the rafters.

Safer spirits

Some spirits were less ferocious than the *draugr*. These included the *fyribudr*, who had no physical form but appeared in dreams or visions; and the *mylingar*, the ghosts of children murdered by their parents, who occasionally manifested as *nattramnar*,

◀ **Instructions for the dead**
Found on the Danish island of Fyn, this 9th-century Viking rune stone tells Thormundr, the grave's occupant, to "enjoy the monument"—in other words, not to wander from it as a ghost.

ghosts in the form of ravens. Yet it was still necessary to guard against them, especially at Yuletide, the winter festival, or when the weather was unusually foul. At these times, ghosts were particularly likely to break free from their graves.

Halting hauntings

Unwelcome spirits could be deterred by simple measures, such as only answering the door to someone who knocked three times (ghosts were thought to announce their presence by striking the door only once), or by leaving a pair of iron scissors open on a corpse—a custom said to immobilize it. More dramatic measures included inscribing runes inside the burial chamber to trap the corpse inside, binding the dead person's head so the spirit could not see, or sewing its toes together so it could not walk. Sometimes, the families of the dead made "corpse doors," knocking a hole into the wall of the house and then passing the dead body through it. The hole was sealed afterward, since the Vikings believed that a ghost could only enter its former dwelling by the opening through which its body had left. Beheading the corpse, as in Grettir's story, was a sure way to stop it wandering—and cremation even more so, as it deprived the spirit of a physical body in which it could return to wreak havoc.

▼ **Buried bounty**
The ornate stern of the 9th-century Oseberg burial ship, carved with intricate interlocking patterns of mythical animals, is typical of the riches interred in the burials of elite members of Norse society.

Calling up the seeress

The Old Norse poem *Grógaldr* ("The Spell of Gróa") is known for being one of a handful of such poems to reference necromancy. The poem's hero, Svipdagr, is cursed by his cruel stepmother: he must undertake a perilous quest and "journey where one cannot" to find the healing goddess Mengloth, whom he is destined to marry. Faced with this almost impossible task, Svipdagr visits the burial mound of his deceased mother, the *völva* (seeress) Gróa, and burns some of her hair in a spell of *valgaldr* ("magic of the fallen," or necromancy). He braves the anger of Hel, goddess of the underworld (Helheim), by raising the spirit of Gróa to seek her counsel. Before she died, Gróa had advised her son to do this when he needed her, as her spirit would retain her prophetic powers even in death.

Hel breaks her normal rule against anyone leaving Helheim and grants Gróa's spirit nine days' freedom, during which time the seeress teaches Svipdagr nine spells. These include charms to fend off the cold, cross impassable rivers, protect his boat at sea, prevent him from being bound, and enable him to defeat his enemies. Armed with Gróa's spells, Svipdagr journeys to Mengloth's castle, where he finds the goddess has been waiting for him for 20 years. Gróa appears to her son one last time on his wedding night, and then her specter disappears forever, back to Helheim.

> "Wake thee, Gróa! wake, mother good! At the doors of the dead I call thee …"

GRÓGALDR, c. 12TH CENTURY

KEY

1 Father Jean Tinel, Curé of Cideville, was the parish priest in 1849, when the haunting happened.

2 The tongs from the hearth were said to "give themselves up to wild dances."

3 Tinel reported the chairs and tables stamping, spinning, and moving around as if playing hide-and-seek.

4 Knives were described as being "hurled by some occult and irresistible force," embedding themselves into the presbytery walls.

5 Window panes were broken by flying penknives and inkstands.

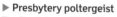

▶ **Presbytery poltergeist**
The Presbytery of Cideville in France is haunted by a poltergeist in this 1850 illustration. The priest blamed a local shepherd for the disturbances, leading the shepherd to sue him for libel and the case to be recorded.

NOISY GHOSTS

poltergeists

Strange phenomena, such as inexplicable noises, levitating objects, and items thrown across the room, are often attributed to spirits known as poltergeists. The name, deriving from German, translates as "noisy spirit," and many accounts throughout history report the activity of such ghosts, who seem to have malevolent intent.

Ghostly commotions

In 94 CE, Roman historian Flavius Josephus described the first recorded poltergeist attack in his account of an exorcism: the spirit, once exorcised, seemed to turn over a bowl of water on the far side of the room. Centuries later, in 856, a poltergeist allegedly haunted a German farmhouse, making banging noises, throwing stones, and starting fires. Gerald of Wales, in the 12th century, described a haunted house, where the spirit hurled handfuls of dirt at people, as well as tearing their clothes. These accounts created the standard model for poltergeist hauntings—a spirit is tied to a location and seems to target those who enter its space, manifesting largely through physical disturbances.

In the 18th century, Methodist John Wesley recorded persistent poltergeist activity at his childhood home—the Old Rectory in Epworth, England. The spirit was given the nickname "Old Jeffrey" and seems to have been viewed almost fondly, but in general, poltergeists were not seen as benign. In 19th-century Tennessee, the Bell family claimed they were haunted for years by a spirit that jabbed pins into their sleeping children, and, in the 1850s, the captain of the HMS *Asp* claimed he had lost many of his crew members due to the actions of a poltergeist terrifying the men.

Poltergeist theories

Believers do not agree on a single explanation for poltergeist activity. Some hold that the spirits of the deceased are making themselves known, while others believe that a malicious energy is attached to a specific place or, sometimes, a specific person. It has also been suggested that unconscious psychic phenomena can be projected by those who live in a building that is thought to be haunted.

Skeptics point out how easy it is to fake poltergeist disturbances, and many cases, such as the famous Enfield hauntings of the 1970s, involve children and teenagers who have been suspected of creating the evidence themselves. Furthermore, physical evidence can be misinterpreted: in a museum in Manchester, UK, an Egyptian statuette was seen to rotate inside a sealed glass case. However, rather than being haunted by an unruly ghost, it was discovered to be turning due to the subtle but strong vibrational forces created by the traffic on a busy road nearby.

▲ **Poltergeists on film**
The 2016 movie *The Enfield Poltergeist / The Conjuring 2* is based on the reported poltergeist hauntings of two young girls living in Enfield, UK, in 1977. Poltergeists have proved to be popular antagonists in horror films.

◀ **Paranormal phenomena**
This 1958 magazine illustration shows the scene described by a young widow in Milan, who claimed to hear noises in the night and see objects levitating—phenomena that are characteristic of poltergeist hauntings.

SUMMONING SPIRITS
medieval grimoires

▲ Spell in action
In this 14th-century depiction of a grimoire being used, a magic circle protects the magician from the demon he is summoning, while the sun and moon recall the importance of astrology to effective magic.

A grimoire is a book of instructions for performing magic, including summoning and communicating with spirits, drawing magical symbols, and making amulets. The word "grimoire" probably derives from the French word *grammaire* ("grammar"), which was used to denote any book written in Latin. The origins of this early form of spellbook can be traced to the Arab world, with Latin translations reaching Christian regions later. Grimoires were sometimes attributed to biblical figures with magical abilities, such as Moses or Solomon.

Books of wonders

In the 10th century, some Muslim intellectuals began to speculate that magic might influence the cosmos, citing the reputed achievements of the prophet Solomon—for instance, in commanding jinn (see pp. 72–73) or angels—as grounds for its legitimacy within Islam. Many Muslim scholars condemned magic, but works such as the *Shams al-Ma'arif* ("Illumination of Knowledge") and the *Kitāb al-Bulhān* ("Book of Wonders") enticed readers with the possibility of controlling supernatural forces or influencing planetary

activity. The 11th-century *Ghāyat al-Ḥakīm* ("Goal of the Wise"), which incorporated ideas from Hellenistic sources, offered magicians the power to appeal to the stars. The *Reconquista* (reconquest) of Muslim Spain by Christian rulers stimulated interest in Islamic learning—including magic— as Christians encountered Islamic texts. The *Ghāyat al-Ḥakīm* was translated under the title of *Picatrix*, and was soon diffused across Christian Europe.

Merging traditions

Many Jewish people lived under Arab rule in 11th-century Europe, bringing these cultures into close contact. Jews borrowed practices such as spirit-summoning and making astrological talismans from Islamic sources. Islamic magical traditions influenced the Jewish mystic tradition of Kabbalah, which (relying on the occult qualities of the Hebrew alphabet) attempted to deploy "names of power" to compel the obedience of spirits (see pp. 122–123). This composite Jewish and Islamic magic was recorded in the 13th-century *Sefer Raziel HaMalakh* ("Book of the Angel Raziel"). Other texts purported to be of Jewish origin, including *Clavicula Salomonis* ("Key of Solomon"), which was said to have been written by Solomon himself.

In the Christian world, magicians (often clerics) fused Islamic magic with church rituals in texts such as the "Munich Handbook," amending rites of exorcism to summon as well as banish demons.

A range of spirits were summoned by grimoires, from Greco-Roman planetary gods to beings common to Muslim, Jewish, and Christian traditions (with origins in the Qur'an and Bible), such as angels, archangels, demons, jinn, and even Lucifer—the Devil—himself.

◀ Powerful symbol
Grimoires often included sigils, magical signs or diagrams supposed to be imbued with the power to summon the influences of planets, stars, or spirits. This example is from a 15th-century English manuscript.

▲ **Arabic astrology**
This detail from the 14th-century *Kitāb al-Bulhān* ("Book of Wonders") shows the Zodiac sign *al-Mīzan* (Libra). The Arabic grimoire tradition continued long after it had inspired Jewish and Christian versions of magic books, portraying a world filled with miracles.

"Through [the mirror] you will bring together men, winds, spirits, demons, the living, and the dead."

PICATRIX, 13TH-CENTURY TRANSLATION OF THE *GHĀYAT AL-ḤAKĪM*

▲ Expecting a visitor

In this woodblock print, entitled *Welcoming Good Luck*, female members of a family are preparing the household in anticipation of a visitation by Zigu. Folk divination rituals allowed people to ask the goddess for help and advice.

CRY FOR HELP

planchette-writing

China has a long history of communicating with spirits. A precursor of French automatic writing and the Ouija board (see pp.236–237), planchette- or spirit-writing, known as fuji, became popular during the Song dynasty (960–1279) as a form of Chinese folk divination. Transcribing messages received from the spirits was initially unimportant, but the practice slowly evolved to include writing them down, as well as refining an earlier ritual developed during the Tang dynasty (618–907). Tang spirit mediums would invite the deity Zigu ("Lady of the Latrine") to communicate, using a V-shaped wooden device called a ji to write messages in sand or incense ashes. Made of willow or peachwood (for repelling evil), the ji had to be formed from the part of the tree exposed to sunlight, which represents divine wisdom, and painted red. The practice required a medium to "support" the ji—or, later, the planchette (a plate or tray with a pencil as one of its legs), a reader to announce what was written in the sand or ashes, and a scribe to transfer the message to paper.

Answers for everything

Planchette-writing transformed from a folk tradition (folk fuji) to a literary phenomenon (literati fuji) in the 10th century. Over time, the practice expanded to include the summoning of folkloric figures and deities other than Zigu. By the Ming dynasty (1368–1644), it had become an element of Daoism, and members of the male literati were using fuji to predict civil examination questions and results in their pursuit of becoming government officials. An altar dedicated to the ritual was even erected within the Forbidden City by Ming emperor Jiajing, and fashionable clubs sprang up, where educated men could communicate with the spirits.

Women, too, began to dabble in spirit-writing, although it remained largely a male pursuit in the Ming-Qing period (up to c. 1912). A small but growing set of women writers participated in fuji at formal and informal poetry gatherings. Of these, perhaps the best-known is Qian Xi, who produced more than 300 spirit-written poems.

Despite its prohibition by the Qing administration, planchette-writing continued to flourish, helped by the rise of spiritualism in Europe and the US in the late 19th and early 20th centuries (see pp.222–225). Spiritualists tried to invest the ritual with a scientific basis. Similarly, automatic writing became a tool in Freudian psychoanalysis, as a way of exploring the unconscious mind.

Going global

When the first Ouija board was released in the 1890s, planchette-writing became a truly global phenomenon. Instead of the ji and sand tray used in fuji, these "talking boards" had a peeping glass, which moved around the board to spell out messages allegedly received from the spirit world using the English alphabet and Arabic numerals.

Today, planchette-writing has been largely abandoned in China, apart from in folk shrines. However, the practice persists in Daoist temples throughout Taiwan, Hong Kong, Malaysia, and Singapore, where it is used in rituals to produce spirit-written scriptures and converse with the Immortals.

▲ **Rise in popularity**
Featured in the Qing-dynasty illustrated magazine *Dian shi zhai huabao* ("Dian Shi Zhai Pictorial"), this lithograph depicts *fuji* being practiced on a spirit-writing altar.

IN CONTEXT

Lüzu quanshu

Said to have been written by the spirit of Patriarch Lü, one of the eight Daoist Immortals, the *Lüzu quanshu* ("Complete Books of Patriarch Lü") is part of the Daoist canon. It was first published in 1744 in 32 scrolls by the spirit-writing altar society Hansanggong from Wuchang, China. The work forms the basis of Daoist devotional practices and rituals, and is also an indispensable source for studying Qing Daoist communities. Later editions in different numbers of scrolls were compiled at other spirit-writing altars; for example, the *Lüzu quanshu zhengzong*, produced in 16 scrolls by the Jueyuan tan spirit-writing community in Beijing between 1803 and 1805.

The *Lüzu quanshu* contains the teachings of Patriarch Lü, and is one of many Daoist works produced using planchette-writing.

RESTLESS AND UNNAMED
the ghosts of the Roma

▲ Speaking to the dead
In this 19th-century woodcut, a Romani woman summons dead spirits to determine the fate of a woman's soldier husband. Historically, the Roma have been seen as having magical powers, such as the ability to communicate with the dead.

The Roma are traditionally a nomadic people, originating from northern India. Romani groups commonly believe in supernatural forces. Spirits of the dead—*mule*—are both honored and feared. Belief in *mule* may be one of the most ancient Romani traditions, as it is found in almost all subgroups.

The Roma believe that evil powers surround the living, but certain rituals can help keep harmful forces at bay. A minister, such as a Christian priest, is often asked to baptize newborns to protect them from harm, and red ribbons tied to babies' wrists also provide protection. The Roma also turn to clergy for burial rites, believing that the souls of the dead can become restless and will not transition to the next world if proper rites are not observed.

Returning spirits
Most Roma follow set mourning rituals, including a three-day wake attended by family and their community. Many families leave offerings of food and alcohol at the graves of the deceased, and tend to the grave with regular visits.

It is believed that the *mulo*, the ghost of the deceased, can return to haunt the living. When a person dies, their belongings are traditionally destroyed, often by burning. This is to erase all material ties to the dead, so nothing remains to draw them back to the world of the living.

The spirit of a dead person can return for many reasons. For example, if an object that was borrowed from them while living is not returned, the *mulo* might cause trouble until it is given back to their descendants. Mentioning the name of the dead person or being too close to their grave could also disturb them and could cause their spirit to return. While a family will avoid mentioning the name of their own deceased, curses can be invoked using the names of dead from other families.

Mule come mainly at night, either as humans or transformed into animals such as dogs or birds. Their appearance is supposedly accompanied by the barking of dogs or by other animals becoming disturbed. When *mule* are seen, they walk sideways to avoid showing their faces.

The undead
Some spirits can be violent, and the word "mulo" also refers to "the living dead." Some Roma believe that those who suffer untimely deaths due to "evil" influences—for example, dying by murder or suicide—can become not ghosts but vampires (see pp.216–217). These creatures will seek out those who have wronged them to get their vengeance.

▶ Vibrant *vardo*
English Romani travelers, known as Romanichals, traditionally lived and moved around in *vardos*, or horse-drawn wagons, that were elaborately decorated with symbols for luck and wealth. This Reading-style *vardo* dates from c.1870 and features three carved and gilded lion heads.

"[The *mulo*] has been known to appear as an animal, as a human being, or occasionally as merely a head, a hand, an arm or even a finger."

ELWOOD B. TRIGG IN *GYPSY DEMONS AND DIVINITIES* (1973)

▲ **Funeral pyre**
In the 19th century, the *vardo* and belongings of a dead person were burned. Nothing could be sold for fear of offending the dead person's spirit. Today, it is more common to burn a few belongings in a symbolic gesture to tradition.

RUN FOR YOUR LIFE
the Wild Hunt

The Wild Hunt is a nocturnal procession of
supernatural beings in the guise of hunters in
pursuit of prey. This sinister procession travels
across the sky, along isolated roads, or through
woods and fields, usually in the cold nights of
midwinter. Driven by a mythological or legendary
leader, the otherworldly troop may be accompanied
by raging noises and menacing animals such as
hounds or birds. It is both frightening and
dangerous to behold.

Demonic riders

The term "Wild Hunt" comes from the German
folklorist Jacob Grimm, who first recorded the
Wilde Jagd in his 1835 work *Deutsche Mythologie*
("German Mythology"). However, stories of ghostly
cavalcades are much older. One of the earliest
literary references to the hunt comes from English
monks, among other witnesses: 20 to 30 demonic
hunters, accompanied by black dogs and the
call of hunting horns, were reportedly sighted

IN CONTEXT

Jan Tregeagle

In some versions of the Wild Hunt, the quarry is a named person. This could be a historical or legendary figure, such as Britain's King Arthur, or a local person, often one who has lived a sinful life. Jan Tregeagle is Cornwall's example. This 17th-century English magistrate, known for his cruel ways, is said to have gone to Hell following his death. But after his ghost was summoned to testify in court, he refused to return to the Devil's custody. Tregeagle was thus set a series of impossible tasks in penance, with a troop of demons ready to hunt him down across Bodmin Moor should he ever abandon his futile errands.

If Tregeagle tries to escape his eternal duties, demonic dogs hunt him down.

riding their dark horses through the night sky at Peterborough Abbey in 1127. According to the *Peterborough Chronicle*, "The hunters were black and large and hideous and their hounds all black and broad-eyed and hideous, and they rode on black horses and on black bucks [deer]."

Packs and their leaders

Stories of spectral nightly hunts are a widespread phenomenon in folklore. Various versions of the motif appear around the world, from hosts of dead warriors in Japan to the North American Iroquois tale of the brothers who still hunt the Great Bear in the sky. In Europe alone, there are many variants, and the parading specters described range from fairies to the tortured souls of the dead.

In British folklore, the procession may be a pack of supernatural dogs, baying loudly as they cross the sky, a portent of misfortune for anyone who sees them. Alternatively, they may be a parade of dead people who sinned in life and are cursed with wandering the Earth, suffering torments, until their sins are atoned for. In Ireland, meanwhile, the processing figures may be the Slua Sidhe, a fairy cavalcade that takes to the sky at night to wreak havoc for any unwitting humans they encounter. In Scandinavia, *Oskoreia* ("The Terrifying Ride") refers to the hunters or heroic warriors of the god Odin, among them the fearsome female Valkyries, who speed across the sky in pursuit of prey. The supernatural hunters are often led by a single figure, who changes name and nature depending

on time and place. In Scandinavian and Germanic versions, it is often the Norse mythological Odin, or the analogous Germanic Woden or Wotan, god of wisdom, war, and death, who leads the hunt, accompanied by his wolves and ravens. Closely associated with midwinter and Yuletide (the Germanic winter festival, whose traditions were incorporated into Christmas), and often depicted as a bearded figure riding through the night sky on his eight-legged horse Sleipnir, Odin has been interpreted as the precursor to Santa Claus.

▼ **Human prey**
An antlered ghost said to haunt England's Windsor Forest, Herne the Hunter was created or appropriated by William Shakespeare. This etching depicts a scene from William Harrison Ainsworth's 1842 novel *Windsor Castle*, in which Herne captures Mabel.

In Welsh folklore, the Wild Hunt is led by Gwyn ap Nudd, the hunter-warrior ruler of Annwn, the Otherworld. Gwyn ap Nudd is accompanied by the Cŵn Annwn, the red-eared spectral hounds of the Welsh Otherworld, whose hunting grounds include the mountain of Cadair Idris in Gwynedd, Wales. Similarly, in Irish folklore, the Slua Sidhe may be led by their king of the Otherworld, Manannán mac Lir.

Many variants position mythological women as the hunt's leaders, alongside their roles as guardians of beasts. These women include Diana (a Roman goddess), Percht (from Alpine mythology), and the witch queen Herodias, believed in medieval Europe to be the leader of a nightly witches' parade.

Led by the Devil or the damned

The Wild Hunt could also have the Devil at the helm, in pursuit of souls or sinners. Conversely, it could be led by a human, damned by Satan or cursed by a demon to an eternity of nocturnal procession. This was often seen as punishment for hunting on a Sunday and violating the Christian Sabbath. One such sinner, in Cornwall, England, was the priest Dando. In some versions of Dando's tale, he is whisked away to Hell by a mysterious horseman, and his dogs are the ones doomed to an eternity of futile chase. Other British folk stories tell of King Herla and his troop, who were cursed following a

◄ Warrior maiden
In Norse mythology, Valkyries guide the heroic dead to Valhalla and ride with Odin's Wild Hunt. This bronze statue by Stephan Sinding depicts a mounted Valkyrie speeding fiercely into battle.

trip to the Otherworld; while in Westphalia, Germany, the semi-historical huntsman Hans von Hackelnberg is said to have refused to go to heaven after dying on a hunt in the 16th century, so was condemned to keep hunting forever.

Ominous sight

Unpleasant consequences supposedly await those who encounter the Wild Hunt. Witnesses may be whisked away with the hunters, carried miles from home, and then abandoned. Or worse, they may be taken down into the realm of the dead. In some Germanic tales, the hunters enter houses, stealing food and drink and leaving havoc in their wake. Those unlucky enough to meet the Irish fairy troop might be carried away and dropped from a great height. Meanwhile, in northern England, hearing the barks and howls of Gabriel's Hounds (either named for a man so fond of hunting he was buried with his dogs, or for the angel Gabriel pursuing the souls of the damned) means that misfortune and death will surely follow. The hounds' baying may even foretell catastrophe, famine, and plague.

▶ Bizarre beasts
This 16th-century engraving of the Wild Hunt by Italian Renaissance artist Agostino de' Musi depicts the obscure creatures that accompanied the mythical hunters, such as mounted goats and spectral or skeletal horses.

◀ **Charging on**
Hermann Hendrich's 1913 painting *The Ride of the Valkyries* portrays a scene from Richard Wagner's opera *Die Walküre* ("The Valkyrie"), in which they ride across the sky. The opera premiered in Munich, Germany, in 1870.

DYBBUKS, IBBURS, AND GOLEMS
Kabbalistic spirit possession

Originating in 12th-century Spain and southern France, Kabbalah emerged from earlier forms of Jewish mysticism, with new maps of the afterlife and the soul. Kabbalists seek to understand the relationship between the divine and mortal realms. The attributions of God are depicted in diagrams of the Tree of Life of Ten Sefirot (forms of energy, or "emanations"). According to Kabbalists, disrupting this energy produces malign and benign forces, in the shape of dybbuks, golems, and ibburs.

Both the Talmud (the ancient set of Jewish laws) and the 12th-century foundational Kabbalistic text the *Zohar* ("Book of Radiance") describe how the souls of evil people become *mazzikin* (malicious spirits)

◀ **Protecting mother and child**
Copied from the Kabbalistic manual *Sefer Raziel HaMalach*, the symbols on this amulet represent the angels Sanoi, Sansanoi, and Samangalaf, invoked for protection against the demon Lilith during childbirth.

after death. Since spirits of the dead are not believed to have a physical form, they must possess the living.

Possession and animation

The tradition of the dybbuk was developed in 16th-century Safed (in present-day Israel), where students of Rabbi Isaac Luria circulated manuals on exorcising dybbuks. These disembodied ghosts were dead people who had committed acts so bad that their souls could not even enter Gehenna (a place of purification in the Jewish afterlife), removing them from the cycle of *gilgul* (reincarnation).

The first dybbuk case involved a young woman possessed by the soul of an evildoer. The dybbuk spoke through her in his native tongue, and did not recognize his host's Yiddish. She recounted details of the man's life that she should not have known.

Another possessing spirit (albeit a righteous one) was the ibbur, which was said to help humans—for example, by aiding an "incomplete soul" who had not completed all 613 *mitzvot* (commandments of the Torah). Some who aspired to possession would sleep on the grave of a holy or righteous man, a *tzadik*, in the hope that their soul would be "cleaved" (stuck to) by the holy man's spirit.

Jewish mystical spirituality also gave rise to the golem: a body without a soul (such as a clay figure), brought to life through the power of a Kabbalistic ritual. Medieval commentaries on the *Sefer Yetzirah* ("Book of Formation"), a text describing the linguistic secrets of creation, contain the first instructions for creating a golem. They warn of grave consequences that follow from small errors in the magic writing.

▼ **The power of words**
This manuscript contains a diagram from the mystical tradition of the *Sefer Yetzirah*, which describes how God created the universe by combining Hebrew letters. Kabbalists also create golems by using magical powers of language.

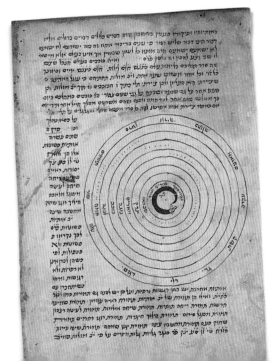

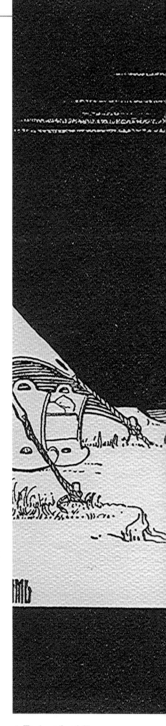

▲ **Tortured spirit**
Condemned to wander, the dybbuk was often the soul of a male sinner who possessed the body of a woman. Moses Cordovero, a 16th-century Kabbalist, called the dybbuk (depicted by Ephraim Moses Lilien) an "evil pregnancy."

"Evil one, speak and say who you are in clear speech!"

COMMAND IN A DYBBUK EXORCISM, MID-16TH CENTURY

The Grim Reaper

The Black Death swept across Europe in the 14th century and, over the course of only five or six years, wiped out at least one-third of the population. To the medieval mindset, this inexplicable plague seemed like divine punishment, and it was from this context of mass mortality that the Grim Reaper emerged—the figure who personifies death.

Art of the time depicted Death in many forms. In the popular *Danse Macabre* works, skeletal figures led people, both young and old, rich and poor, into their tombs and showed how death was indiscriminate and cared nothing for social status. Images of skeletons bearing weapons, such as arrows and swords, also proliferated and emphasized the threat and violence of sudden death.

The Grim Reaper is most often shown as a skeleton robed all in black and carrying a scythe. Greek mythology shaped this image; the infant-devouring god of time, Cronus, was shown as an old man with a sickle, while the god of death, Thanatos, carried a scythe. This tool had resonance in the agrarian society of the Middle Ages and symbolized how, with each swing, it could "reap" thousands of lives. Ravens or crows often accompanied the Grim Reaper and, in mythology, these scavenger birds also represented an omen of death.

> "The self same death am I, that with my syth do cut like hay, All things that live upon the earth …"
>
> **MARCELLUS PALINGENIUS**, *ZODIACUS VITAE* ("ZODIAKE OF LIFE," TRANSLATED BY BARNABE GOOGE, 1565)

▲ **Death and the Miser** (c. 1490) by Hieronymus Bosch shows Death arriving for the soul of a miser, who is being offered both a cr...

MEETING
THE
SPIRITS
1400–1700

Introduction

As people around the world sought to communicate with spirits in their various guises, the authorities began to crack down on sorcery and illicit texts. In the 15th century, Europe saw the rise of the witch trials, which led to the death of between 40,000 and 60,000 people, mostly women, over three centuries. The laws instituted by different European states were concerned not only with supposed witches, but also with "cunning-folk," or popular magicians, whose "good" magic was considered equally diabolic as it encouraged people to put their trust in magic rather than God.

From the late 14th century, the growing number of demonological texts had raised fears among the elite of a grave satanic conspiracy against Christendom. The sense of chaos and threat was compounded by the advent of the Reformation in the 16th century—not to mention the simultaneous print revolution, which helped spread fears about orgiastic Sabbaths, death-dealing witches, and mass spirit-possessions.

The suppression of magic and spirit contact in all its forms was not just a European concern. The Spanish and Portuguese Inquisitions set up tribunals in their American colonies, where thousands of Indigenous people, colonial migrants, and enslaved Africans were tried for their magical and religious practices. At the outset, Portugal dominated the transatlantic slave trade, and its Inquisition archives contain some of the earliest detailed knowledge of the new syncretic religious traditions that emerged along the Atlantic coast of the Americas as a result. Archaeological excavations at the slave market in Rio de Janeiro, Brazil, have revealed many amuletic objects that fell or were stripped from newly arrived enslaved people.

Due to the new technology of the printing press, the once-secret knowledge contained in the manuscript grimoires owned by the medieval clergy could be disseminated more widely. The Vatican issued its *Index of Prohibited Books*, and in Protestant states,

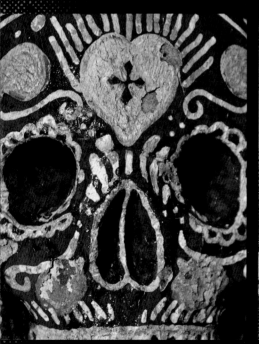

Celebrating the dead *see p.141*

Orgiastic witches' Sabbath *see p.146*

Diabolic sorcery *see p.157*

the printing of magic books was banned. Nonetheless, there was a profitable market for occult books. Among the earliest and most influential were famed magician Heinrich Cornelius Agrippa's *Three Books of Occult Philosophy*. First printed in Germany in the 1530s, the books gave a learned overview of Renaissance magical interests, including Jewish Kabbalah, geomancy, astrology, and alchemy. Agrippa was not in favor of summoning the supernatural, though—yet after his death, *The Fourth Book of Occult Philosophy* was published in his name. This notorious work contained a series of rituals for conjuring spirits.

In Asia, China had its own sorcery scares, notably an investigation instigated by the Qianlong Emperor in 1768 that concerned the crime of *jiaohun*, or soul-stealing. A group of masons and their sorcerer masters were thought to be stealing souls to increase their own spiritual powers by cutting off men's "queues" (braided ponytails). No mass trials and executions ensued, but there were some mob killings. China also saw the rise of an artistic vogue for depicting demon processions— evidence of belief in a pantheon of spirits. The tradition spread to Japan, where demon or *yōkai* encyclopedias flourished as an art form in the 17th and 18th centuries.

"A great many of us, when we be in trouble, or lose anything, we run hither and thither to witches or sorcerers …"

ENGLISH BISHOP HUGH LATIMER, IN A SERMON LAMENTING THE USE OF CUNNING-FOLK OR "WISE MEN," 1552

Venerating saintly souls *see p.164*

Spirit-possession ritual *see p.174*

Summoned specter *see pp.182–183*

▶ **Beaded skull**
The Bamileke of Cameroon exhume and carefully preserve the skulls of ancestors. These precious objects are kept in a special room, and regularly appeased and cared for by a Keeper of Ancestral Skulls. This 19th-century skull is decorated with glass beads and cowrie shells.

SPIRITS EVERYWHERE
African spirits and ghosts

While traditional African religions usually revere a remote Supreme Being, they also include many lesser, more relatable spirits. These entities—nature spirits, ancestors, and other supernatural beings—vary in power, physical form, and gender expression. They are more involved in people's lives than the Supreme Being, mediating between humans and the divine.

Enhancing nature

To believers, Africa's landscapes are enlivened by the nature spirits who inhabit them. The towering peak of Morocco's Jebel Toubkal is home to Sidi Chemharouch, king of the jinn. Away from the Atlas Mountains, people must be wary near water, where the seductive but evil jinni Aicha Kandicha lurks, her long hair and beautiful face distracting from her goat legs.

Animal totems identify and link individuals and clans to each other and to desirable characteristics of different animals. The tingoi of Sierra Leone's Mende people, and similar protective yet capricious water spirits in other belief systems, are thought to populate rivers, lakes, swamps, and oceans. Tree spirits guard village entrances, while bush spirits, credited with teaching African peoples the secrets of civilization, must be treated with care, for fear of abduction. People look to celestial (or sky) spirits, linked to the sun, stars, and wind, for everything from agricultural calendars to architecture. Keeping up respectful relationships with these spirits is vital to peaceful and productive communities, and many rituals and prohibitions help people coexist with nature and its supernatural beings.

Keeping ancestors happy

Ancestral veneration is a defining feature of African worldviews. Ancestors—the spirits of dead relatives and important clan or community members—live in the ancestral realm (see pp.84–85), using their power and wisdom to influence the living and intercede with the Supreme Being and other spirits

◀ **Bird totem**
The unique soapstone-carved birds found in the ruins of the medieval city of Great Zimbabwe depict *chapungu* (the bateleur eagle) or *hungwe* (the fish eagle), both important bird totems to the Shona of Zimbabwe.

in beneficial or harmful ways. Cultivating a good relationship with ancestors is said to lead to happiness and prosperity, while offending them by neglect or breaking ethical codes is likely to have dire consequences. Ancestral veneration includes sacrifices, libations (liquid offerings), sharing food, consulting them through spirit mediums, and following the rules they set for ethical living. Only those who follow these guidelines can become ancestors themselves.

Restless souls

The ghosts of people who died "bad" deaths (by murder, for instance) or were not properly buried are another group of African spirits. These include the *akalogoli* of the Igbo people (Nigeria) and the *jochiende* of the Luo (Kenya). Since they cannot cross over to the spirit world, they linger as wandering ghosts, wreaking havoc and causing illness or misfortune to get attention so they can be properly buried.

▼ **Divination tray**
Nigeria's Yoruba people practice Ifa divination. Diviners called *babalawos* (men) or *iyalawos* (women) use decorated trays like this one to communicate with ancestors and other spirits.

THE WEEPING WOMEN
female ghosts in Central and South America

The people living in Mesoamerica before European colonization had deeply held and elaborate beliefs about the nature of life and death (see pp.88–89). Usually, there was no return from death, so ghosts were seen as a sign of something being terribly wrong. Many of the ghosts from the precolonial folklore of this region take the form of a woman seeking revenge.

Tears and fears

The most famous Latin American ghost is La Llorona, whose name means "the weeping woman." Tales vary, but she is generally pictured as a woman wearing white—her dress wet—and wailing. In the most common telling of her story, she was a woman who drowned her own infants after being abandoned by her lover. Today, she is said to appear as a harbinger of doom and attacker of children.

◀ Weeping spirit
The Mexica fertility goddess Cihuacōātl was said to haunt crossroads and weep for the son she reputedly abandoned. Her story may have influenced similar tales of female ghosts who mourn their children.

The first record of La Llorona dates from the mid-16th century (after the invasion of the Spanish), and many accounts say the tragic ghost was an Indigenous woman who had been deserted by her Spanish husband. However, there are links to earlier tales. A Mexica legend describes how—a decade before the arrival of Spanish *conquistador* Hernán Cortés and his troops—a specter had appeared, crying out that her children would soon be forced to flee. Other sources suggest this warning came from Cihuacōātl, a Mexica female deity associated with childbirth and infants.

Vengeful ghouls

Many of the stories of Mesoamerican ghosts share similar features. The Venezuelan ghost known as La Sayona is said to appear to victims as a beautiful

◀ Controversial figure
A Nahua woman known as La Malinche acted as a consort and translator to Hernán Cortés. The mother of his first son, she may have inspired tales of weeping women.

> "She passed by in the middle of the night, wailing and crying out in a loud voice: 'My children, we must flee far away from this city!'"

NAHUATL ACCOUNT OF A BAD OMEN THAT OCCURRED IN TENOCHTITLAN (NOW MEXICO CITY) IN 1509, PRINTED IN THE *FLORENTINE CODEX*, BOOK XII

woman in white. In life, she allegedly murdered her husband and mother after discovering they were having an affair; in death, she lures men into the jungle to inflict her revenge. Another female ghost seeking retribution on adulterers is the Mexican La Matlazihua, whose name derives from the Nahuatl language and means "the woman who traps."

Mountain guardians

If a man finds himself in the Andes mountains and hears a bloodcurdling scream, he should think twice before he rushes to help. According to

Colombian legend, this is how La Patasola draws in her victims. La Patasola manifests as a one-legged woman, but once a man comes near, she is said to transform into a snake and devour him. Today, she is viewed by some as a protective spirit of the mountains, targeting those who come to strip the land. Similarly, La Madremonte ("Mother Mountain") is a land-guarding spirit said to appear as a woman with glowing eyes, covered in soil and plants that often obscure her face. Those who dare to cross into her wild territory may be struck with disease or become lost in confusion.

▲ **La Llorona**
Depictions of this mournful spirit vary enormously, but—as seen in Alejandro Colunga's *La Llorona con Nino, Fantasmas y Diablos* (1988–1992)—she is often shown as a mother clutching a child, or as a ghostly figure dressed in white.

▶ **Hungry beast**
A wendigo is a skeleton-like monster that craves human flesh. Wendigo stories warn of the consequences to those who abandon their family obligations. More recently, such stories have become powerful Indigenous metaphors for depicting the evil effects of colonialism.

SHAPE-SHIFTERS AND SKINWALKERS

Indigenous American ghosts and monsters

Ghosts and monsters remain central to Indigenous American cultures in the 21st century. Through strong oral storytelling traditions, ghost stories and sacred legends maintain important boundaries between life and death, nature and culture, humans and other-than-humans. For some, the presence of such supernatural beings is unsettling, while for others, they provide spiritual power that may be used to help or to harm.

The question of what happens after death is a longstanding preoccupation. When families bury their dead, they provide ritual offerings of clothing, food, and water—the things their loved ones will need on their journey to the land of the dead. The goal is to let go with compassion and safely manage the boundary between life and death. Indigenous American ghost stories reflect this human desire to reckon with the unknown. In many tales, ghosts appear when people violate taboos—for example, by wearing a deceased person's clothing or disturbing their burial place—since human remains and graves are dangerous and can pollute the spirit of the living. Transgressions can lead to "Ghost Sickness," a condition that includes recurring nightmares, fearful feelings, weight loss, and general weakness.

Shifting shape

The ability to transform from human to animal or bird makes shape-shifters especially uncanny. In Diné beliefs (from the US Southwest), witches are thought to use human remains to transform themselves into skinwalkers, a particularly sinister shape-shifter. In their animal form, skinwalkers attack and even kill victims. The Lakota people (of the Great Plains and Black Hills) tell stories of those who stop to assist a young woman alone on the road, only to discover that she is no ordinary person. People who encounter this "deer woman" describe her as human, but with deer haunches and cloven hooves. To those who respect women and children, she offers fertility and well-being. For those who do not, she inflicts a vengeful death.

Wild men and wendigos

In Indigenous tales, monsters like the ice-hearted wendigo and "Wild Man" lurk on the fringes of human life, where nature meets culture. Wild men are ghostly figures in the beliefs of the Kwakwaka'wakw people of British Columbia. These howling, foul-smelling creatures peer into windows, steal food, and sometimes kidnap people, especially women and children. They tempt humans to eat "ghost food" (empty cockle shells) so that they, too, will become spirits. Described as giant bipeds with large mouths and covered in dark, tangled hair, they are shy but dangerous. If treated with respect, wild men might bestow humans with spiritual power.

Wendigos differ because they once were humans. They became malevolent monsters through acts of selfishness and greed, especially toward their kin. Wendigos are found in the beliefs of Algonquian-speaking peoples, and are associated with winter and times of famine. According to legends, people who committed cannibalism to avoid starvation might transform into a wendigo, cursed to feed on humans but never feel satiated.

▲ **Wild Man of the Woods**
Bukwus, a wild man, is a powerful supernatural spirit that dwells in the woods. He is recognized by his long, matted hair; humanoid face; and wide mouth. A mask depicting Bukwus, such as this one, would be worn by the Kwakwaka'wakw during winter ceremonies.

◀ **Hunting charm**
The Alutiiq people of Alaska fastened ivory sea otter amulets like this one inside their kayaks when hunting. According to Alutiiq belief, the sea otter was once human. Hunters respectfully return the bones of killed otters to the sea so they can be reborn.

▲ A yarn painting from the 1970s depicts Huichol shamans sending "prayer arrows" to communicate with the spirit world.

Shamanic visions

Shamans (see pp.14–17) bridge the physical and spiritual worlds to communicate with spirits during altered states of consciousness. Their powers include the ability to heal the sick and retrieve wandering spirits.

Among the Huichol (or Wixárika) people of northern Mexico, shamanic figures, known as *mara'a kate* or "singers," are central to religious life. They chant and sing ancient Huichol myths, and call on deities who represent particular animals, specific places, and natural phenomena such as planets. Selected by the deity Urukáme to receive shamanic power, *mara'a kate* have hard-earned and specialized knowledge they use for the benefit of the community. When a new *mara'a kame* (the singular form of *mara'a kate*) is first chosen, they become unwell—thought to be the body's reaction to receiving Urukáme's spiritual power. To cure the illness and to complete the process of becoming a *mara'a kame*, the person must journey to the spirit world.

At the center of Huichol beliefs is *hikuri*, or peyote, a cactus plant consumed ceremonially for its hallucinogenic properties. *Mara'a kate* conduct healing ceremonies during which they guide individuals through the visions they receive while in this altered state. Huichol artists create colorful yarn paintings based on these experiences as visual offerings and prayers to their deities, and as commercial art sold to collectors.

> "… the gods will explain things to you in your dream …"

RAFAEL PISANO, HUICHOL MARA'A KAME, ON THE PROCESS OF BECOMING A SHAMAN, 2023

▲ **Wolf dance**
At wintertime ceremonials, people gather to dance, sing, and feast, and invite the animal spirits to join them. This painting by German artist Wilhelm Kuhnert depicts a Kwakwaka'wakw First Nation ceremony at Tsaxis, Canada, in 1894.

GUARDIANS AND GUIDES
Indigenous spirit animals and totems

Among North America's Indigenous peoples, there is a common awareness of the mystery and power of plants and animals. They appear in meals; as guardian spirits in dreams and visions; and in stories, songs, and dances. The relationship between humans and other-than-humans is one of mutual respect and reciprocity. Hunters, for example, may offer prayers and water to the spirit of the animal they have killed to thank them for their sacrifice. Animals, trees, and plants are cherished for their

ability to provide sustenance, warmth, medicines, clothing, and transportation for their human relations. In turn, humans honor them with "first foods" rituals like the Green Corn ceremony of the Eastern Woodlands nations, which takes place when the first corn ripens, or the First Salmon ceremony held by Coast Salish people in early spring.

While sharing his life story, the Lakota elder and holy man Black Elk said, "It is the story of all life that is good to tell, and of us two-leggeds sharing in it with the four-leggeds and the wings of the air and all green things, for these are children of one mother and their father is one Spirit." In other words, plants and animals are more than food—they are family. Relationships are rooted in ancient beliefs about the animating spirit found in all living things.

Animal people

Since time immemorial, Indigenous peoples have gathered to share food, songs, dances, and stories. Animal people, the curious and humorous spirit beings that were created before humans, are often at the center. Humans owe thanks to the animal people, because it is they who readied the world for their "two-legged" younger siblings. In stories shared by tribal peoples of the Intermontane West (the area between the Rocky Mountains and the Sierra Nevada), the trickster Coyote (see pp. 44–45), both a creator and a destroyer, fashioned fishing sites and tamed the north wind. He also tricked others out of their food and is said to be the main reason why humans cannot live forever.

Like humans, Coyote and the other animal people are a mix of bad and good qualities. They are selfish, envious, and destructive, as well as altruistic, wise, and creative. These stories entertain but they also instruct humans, who are imperfect, in how and how not to behave.

As "children of the same Spirit," humans and other-than-humans are understood to be more alike than different. Animal people are able to

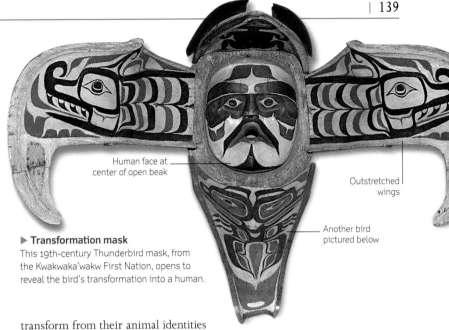

Human face at center of open beak

Outstretched wings

Another bird pictured below

▶ **Transformation mask**
This 19th-century Thunderbird mask, from the Kwakwaka'wakw First Nation, opens to reveal the bird's transformation into a human.

transform from their animal identities into humanlike beings, so in the Pacific Northwest, when Raven removes his cloak of feathers, he is changing into his human persona. Likewise, in the context of religious ceremonies, Indigenous people can be transformed by inviting their animal spirit guardians in to join them.

Cyclical worldview

A common thread in Indigenous belief systems is that the boundaries between spirits and humans, animals and people, the living and the dead, are permeable. Supernatural beings do not have their own world; they exist in the real world. Beings with their origins in the past also dwell in the present and still possess exceptional power to confer gifts to the humans who seek them.

IN CONTEXT

Totems

The term "totem" describes symbols representing a social unit, like an extended family or clan. It comes from the Ojibwe word *doodem*, meaning "one's brother-sister kin." Clans claim special relationships to certain animals. Some see their ancestors as the offspring of human and animal pairings. The animals also symbolize desired traits. Ojibwe Bear clan people, for instance, like bears, are traditional protectors. Clan symbols regulate marriage by clarifying who is not a relative.

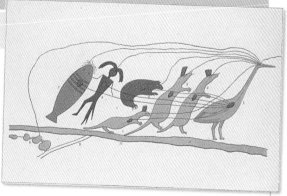

This symbolic petition for land rights, taken to Washington, D.C., in 1849 by Ojibwe leaders, depicts clan symbols.

OFFERINGS AT THE ALTAR
el Dia de los Muertos

The Day of the Dead, or *el Dia de los Muertos* in Spanish, is a Mexican festival that honors deceased loved ones and welcomes the spirits of the dead back to the world of the living. Its uniquely rich symbolism and rituals reveal the deep roots of modern Mexican identity, which maintains a connection with the past through this celebration of the spirits each November.

Through the changing civilizations of Mesoamerica—the Olmec, Toltec, Maya, and Mexica—one idea that stayed constant was a belief in the regenerative symbolism of death within the cyclical processes of the universe (see pp.88–89). Death was to be embraced without fear, and the dead were not mourned, as their essence remained among the living. The Maya believed the souls of the dead lived on mountains, and for the Mexica, souls could be resurrected as hummingbirds or butterflies. The Mexica even dedicated a whole month of their yearly calendar to festivities that honored the goddess of the underworld, Mictēcacihuātl, who was linked with both death and resurrection.

Indigenous and Christian souls

After the Spanish invasion of Mexico in 1521, the colonizers sought to suppress all Indigenous religions and traditions. In response, the native people blended many of their customs with those that were imposed by the Spanish,

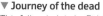

▼ **Journey of the dead**
This folk-art plate by Fidel Avalos Espinosa shows skeletal figures (*calacas*) undertaking the long and arduous journey from the land of the dead, in order to join the living for the Day of the Dead.

◄ **"Lady of the Dead"**
The goddess Mictēcacihuātl, shown in this statue with a grinning skull face, was central to Mexica celebrations of death as a giver of life, and closely resembles images used in the modern Day of the Dead.

in order for their traditions to survive. Many scholars see the Day of the Dead as a continuation of Mesoamerican celebrations, syncretized with European Christian practices.

The Mexica celebrated their festival of the dead in August, but the post-colonial Day of the Dead takes place on November 1–2, corresponding with the three-day Christian observance of All Saints' Eve, All Saints' Day, and All Souls' Day (Allhallowtide; see pp.96–99). This Christian festival honored the dead with feasts and graveside vigils, echoing earlier pagan festivals (see pp.56–57), during which restless spirits were appeased with offerings. These traditions influenced the modern Mexican festival.

Welcoming the dead

The Day of the Dead centers not only on the remembrance of lost loved ones but on a reunion with them. The first night is for the *angelitos* ("little angels")—the spirits of infants who have died. On the second night, the spirits of dead adults arrive and, welcomed into homes as honored guests, join in the festivities with the living. Altars are set up with images of the dead and *ofrendas* ("offerings") of

"Before the Day of the Dead they sell a thousand figures of little sheep, lambs, etc. of sugar paste, which they name *ofrenda* ..."

FRANCISCO DE AJOFRIN, CAPUCHIN FRIAR, 1740s

◀ **Elaborately painted skull**
Decorated skulls (*calaveras*), such as this painted example, feature widely in Day of the Dead celebrations. Skull symbols appear in Indigenous art, representing death and rebirth, and also in Christian iconography, as memento mori.

▲ **Welcome spirits**
This elaborate and highly decorated altar in the historic city center of Oaxaca, Mexico, invites the spirits of the dead by providing them with the food and drink that they enjoyed while alive.

"The Mexican ... is familiar with death, jokes about it, caresses it, sleeps with it, celebrates it; it is one of his favorite toys and his most steadfast love."

OCTAVIO PAZ, *THE LABYRINTH OF SOLITUDE*, 1950

their favorite foods, such as sugar *calaveras* (brightly decorated skulls), to encourage the spirits to return. These may be eaten by the living but, it is thought, will not provide nourishment as the spirits consume the soul of the food.

During the daytime, graves of the deceased are cleaned, repaired, and decorated, especially with orange marigolds. Sometimes called the flower of the dead, their strong color and aroma are believed to help guide the spirits back to their graves. A night vigil is sometimes held beside the tomb of a loved one, with candles lit to draw out the spirits. Roaming mariachi bands and troubadours wander the streets, singing the most popular folk song for the Day of the Dead: *La Llorona* ("the weeping woman"; see pp.132–133), about the vengeful ghost. People also parade through towns dressed as skeletons—a practice which could echo the Mexica, who depicted their gods as skeletal, or the *Danse Macabre* in European iconography of the Late Middle Ages, which depicted people dancing with the dead.

Lovers' reunion

Different cities have their own particular traditions and stories relating to the Day of the Dead. In the town of Pátzcuaro, the ghosts of two dead lovers are said to rise on the Day of the Dead. According to the legends of the Purépecha (Indigenous people of the Mexican state of Michoacán), Prince Itzihuapa was killed by ghosts guarding a treasure at the bottom of a lake. His lover, Princess Mintzita, was heartbroken and died of grief while waiting on the shore for his return. The pair can reunite only once a year, on the night of the festival.

Modern celebrations

After Mexico won independence from Spain in 1821, the Day of the Dead continued to be celebrated, especially in rural areas where belief in the supernatural was strongest. The festival gained its popularity in cities in the 20th century, when it was celebrated as a unique product of the nation and key to Mexican identity. During the Mexican Revolution of 1910–1917, José Guadalupe Posada's image of a skeleton wearing a large European hat, *La Calavera Catrina*, criticized Mexicans who acted too much like Europeans. The image became synonymous with the Day of the Dead, with many of those who dress as skeletons for the day representing La Catrina.

Since the 1970s the Day of the Dead has also become an important part of Mexican-American Chicano identity. In Mexico and beyond, the appeal of a ritual that recognizes human mortality and allows for interaction between the living and the dead seems to grow stronger every year.

▲ **National pride**
La Calavera Catrina by José Guadalupe Posada depicts a skull wearing a European hat (Catrina) to mock high-society Mexicans for hiding their Indigenous cultural roots. The figure is often replicated in parade costumes and figurines as the Lady of the Dead.

IN CONTEXT

Monarch butterflies

Each fall, millions of monarch butterflies migrate from the United States to Mexico and their arrival coincides with the Day of the Dead. Before their migratory route was discovered, their sudden appearance seemed miraculous and symbolic, and the butterflies were believed to be the resurrected souls of the dead returning to Earth. The image of the butterfly is therefore an important cultural symbol in Mexico, and especially significant in the iconography of the Day of the Dead.

Women dressed as monarch butterflies walk in a parade for the Day of the Dead in Mexico City.

HAUNTING THE BOARDS
ghosts in early modern drama

The rediscovery of many classical plays in the 16th century greatly inspired contemporary playwrights, bringing the dead back to the stage. Ghosts appeared in both ancient Greek tragedies and comedies, where they offered advice and delivered prophetic warnings to the living, and also featured in the Roman tragedies of Seneca, where they incited the protagonist to revenge. The dramas of the early modern period (c. 1500–1800) developed from these ancient models.

Heavily influenced by Seneca, the first ghost to appear on the Elizabethan stage was in Thomas Kyd's *The Spanish Tragedy* (first performed in 1592). In Kyd's work, the ghost of Don Andrea, who has recently been killed in battle, is accompanied by the spirit of Revenge, who also provides the theme of the play. Kyd's drama helped spawn the genre of Revenge Tragedy—these plays abound with ghosts intent on avenging their injuries (often with extensive bloodshed).

Of the English plays that survive from 1582 to 1642, specters feature in a staggering 59 of them. Dramas by the French playwrights Molière, Racine, and de La Taille are also haunted by ghosts.

Shakespeare's specters
Ghosts appear 51 times across the works of Shakespeare and have a significant part to play. *Richard III* (c. 1593) is the first of the Bard's works to feature ghosts: at the play's climax, the wicked king is haunted in his dreams by all the victims of his treachery. They command him to "despair and die" and cause him, finally, to reflect on and judge his own wickedness.

▼ **Long-lived spirits**
Shakespeare's ghosts became entrenched in popular culture. In this 1889 lithograph from Ireland, the ghost of a murdered man appears to C. S. Parnell, the leader of the political group linked to the crime. Parnell is portrayed here as Macbeth.

In *Macbeth*, the king is famously haunted by those he has murdered, and yet the play contains an element of uncertainty about whether the spirits are real or simply figments of guilty imagination. Banquo's ghost, for example, is visible to Macbeth but no other guest at the feast. In *Hamlet*, the ghost reveals details of the old king's murder and yet, while this sets the revenge plot in motion, Hamlet is unsure whether or not the ghost is real.

Contemporary theorists were divided on the reality of ghosts. In 1572, *Of Ghosts and Spirits Walking by Night* was published in English and widely read. Written by the Swiss Reformed theologian Ludwig Lavater, it explained how the Protestant rejection of Purgatory meant that ghosts could no longer be visitations by restless souls, but were rather demons sent from Hell. In *Hamlet*, Shakespeare expresses these exact fears, and many other dramatists played on this ambiguity for dramatic effect.

◀ **Ghostly presence**
This 1890 illustration shows the moment at the beginning of *Hamlet* when the specter (named only "Ghost," but seemingly that of the dead king, Hamlet's father) first appears. At the play's premiere, the role was played by Shakespeare himself.

A dramatic entrance

Actors playing ghosts powdered their faces with chalk and often made their entrance from below the stage—contemporary audiences associated this with Hell, provoking instant fear. A 1599 play, *A Warning for Fair Women*, mocked more theatrical ghosts for having high-pitched voices and appearing with flashes of light and gunpowder smoke. However, Shakespeare's ghosts scared the living by looking just as they did in life, with few stage effects needed.

▶ **Real ghost stories**
Audiences' fascination with ghosts coincided with real beliefs in spirits. Penny pamphlets were published in the 17th century, some detailing personal encounters with ghosts.

> "What may this mean, That thou, dead corse, again, in complete steel, Revisit'st thus the glimpses of the moon."

HORATIO IN SHAKESPEARE'S *HAMLET*, ACT I, SCENE IV (1604–1623)

AGENTS OF SATAN
witchcraft and familiar spirits

The witch-hunts of the early modern era (c. 1500–1800) were enabled by beliefs in Satan and spirits. By the 15th century, many theologians believed that so-called witches could make a covenant with Satan for the power to harm their enemies. Some believed Satan gave an "imp," or familiar spirit, often in animal form, to assist the witch in harming people (often children), cattle, and crops. By the 17th century, the idea that witchcraft involved a pact with Satan was widespread throughout much of Europe. The version of the Devil who fraternized with witches was different from the Devil of theology, however, as he took a physical form and was even believed to have sexual relations with his followers.

Witch trials

Between about 1450 and 1700 thousands of people, mostly women, were tried for witchcraft in Europe and North America. Beliefs about witchcraft varied from region to region, making it difficult to define exactly what a witch was supposed to be. In France and Scotland, witches were said to work in covens and worship Satan at gatherings called Sabbaths (or Sabbats), attended by shape-shifting demons; in England, they were usually solitary workers of evil.

The papal heresy investigations of the 14th and 15th centuries spawned the concept of diabolic witches, but it was the birth of secular laws against witchcraft in the 16th century that led to widespread witch trials. The accused were sometimes tried en masse in major hunts, such as those inspired by the work of English "Witchfinder General" Matthew Hopkins in the 1640s. One of the biggest hunts took place in Bamberg (now in Germany) in 1626–1632,

◀ **Diabolical dealings**
French priest Urbain Grandier was accused of seducing the nuns of Loudun and causing their demonic possession. Produced at Grandier's trial in 1634, this pact allegedly contains the signatures of not only Grandier but of Satan, Leviathan, Astaroth, and other demons.

where 1,000 people were executed. In Spain and Portugal, accused witches were investigated by the Inquisition, but with few resulting executions. Taking cues from European ideas, witch trials soon spread to North America, where a cascade of accusations were made in Salem, Massachusetts, in 1692–1693.

Familiar spirits

The imp, or familiar spirit, was central to English witchcraft accusations. Some witchfinders believed that when Satan made a pact with a would-be

▼ **Dancing with devils**
This English woodcut from *The History of Witches and Wizards* (1720) depicts four witches dancing with demons at a Sabbath.

◀ **Around the cauldron**
Based on German artist Hans Baldung Grien's engraving of 1510, this illustration portrays naked women at a witches' Sabbath. These late-night gatherings were imagined as an inversion of everything considered morally acceptable.

▲ Feline familiar

The English pamphlet on witchcraft, *A Rehearsall Both Straung and True ...* (1579), contained various images of the accused women and their animal familiars. More than any other animal, cats were identified as potential familiars—perhaps because they were popular pets.

witch, he sent a demon in animal form to suckle from a special "teat" on her body. This creature then became the witch's familiar, and could be sent out to perform evil deeds such as sucking cows dry of milk or riding horses during the night. During the English Civil War (1642–1651), a Parliamentarian pamphlet claimed that witches in Prince Rupert's army were sending out their familiars to harm their enemies. In East Anglia, Matthew Hopkins identified witches by searching

their bodies for teats (seemingly marks, warts, or flaps of skin), many of which were "found" in the witch's genitals. Hopkins and his associates also believed that if a witch were tied up overnight and watched, the familiar would appear to suckle from her. These familiars could supposedly be shared among witches—accounts from trial records show women lending or bequeathing imps to relatives, friends, and neighbors.

People who kept pets were at particular risk of conviction, since a close bond with a pet could be interpreted as a witch's relationship with her familiar. Some, however, were skeptical: in 1632, King Charles I's personal physician, William Harvey, publicly cut open a toad said to be a witch's familiar, to show it was an ordinary amphibian.

Ghosts or fairies?

Most imps in English reports of witchcraft took the form of animals. Some familiars, though, could shape-shift and take more terrifying forms, such as the cat, Gyles, who was said to serve a witch called Doll Barthram in 1599. Gyles could allegedly transform into "a thick dark substance" that invaded the bodies of the witch's victims. Other imps were humanoid in form. Mary Clowe, tried in 1645, was accused of receiving a familiar in the form of "a little boy," while Elizabeth Hubbard was apparently given three children as imps. Another supposed witch, Ellen Driver,

---

IN CONTEXT

The *Malleus Maleficarum*

The most notorious of all witch-hunting manuals, the *Malleus Maleficarum* ("Hammer of Witches") was the work of the Dominican friar Heinrich Kramer. Published in the Holy Roman Empire in 1487, the *Malleus* argued that women were more prone to witchcraft than men, and explained how demons called incubi had sex with them. The manual has been credited with many of the misogynistic stereotypes that drove subsequent witch-hunts, and it made the case that executing witches was the only way to stamp out the practice of witchcraft.

According to the *Malleus Maleficarum*, witches collaborated with the Devil to commit crimes against good Christians.

"… that which she called Hoult would come first, and then that which she called Jarmara; which did appear in the likeness of a white Dogge, with red spots …"

EDWARD PARSLEY, IN HIS TESTIMONY AGAINST ACCUSED WITCH ELIZABETH CLARKE OF MANNINGTREE, ENGLAND, MARCH 25, 1645

▲ **Broomstick riders**
A cauldron, feline familiars, and broomsticks feature in this 17th-century portrayal of witches flying to a Sabbath meeting. Mass-produced woodcuts helped to reinforce stereotypical views of women as witches.

confessed to bearing two "changelings" fathered by the Devil. It is possible that some women accused of witchcraft imagined that the spirits of children lost in infancy returned to them as familiars; some trial records show these familiars sharing names with deceased offspring.

Accounts of witch trials occasionally identified familiar spirits as fairies. At his trial in 1566, James Walsh from Dorset, England, spoke of white, green, and black fairies, seemingly associating the black fairies with the imps of witchcraft. English folklore is full of stories of fairies turning themselves into animals, so perhaps people accused of witchcraft drew on such tales under torture and interrogation. Elsewhere in Europe, however, witches were associated with incubi or succubi rather than imps: these devils impregnated women with changelings and stole men's semen for use in spells.

KEY

1 This summoning circle is used by a magical practitioner to invoke a demon for the purpose of treasure hunting (see p.159). The circle protects him from being harmed.

2 The demon has typical demonic features—horns, hair, and cloven hooves. Demons—and other evil spirits—were believed to guard buried treasure.

3 A naked man digs for treasure. Nudity was often part of such rituals.

4 Another man cuts the hair from a corpse hanging from the gallows as part of this necromantic ritual.

▶ **Summoning ritual**
Demonologies that depicted the grotesque appearance of demons were popular with some book collectors in the 18th century. The ritual depicted here is from the *Compendium of Demonology and Magic* (1775).

CLASSIFYING EVIL
demonological texts

Demonology is the study of demons. It originated as a branch of theology that tried to make sense of the Christian doctrine of the fallen angels—the idea that Satan rebelled against God, and the angels who supported Satan fell from heaven and became demons. Since magicians and theologians were interested in understanding the nature and activity of demons, demonology also became a branch of magic that speculated about the powers of demons and their hierarchies (like angels, demons were believed to be organized into ranks). Demonology was central to the witch trials of the 15th to 17th centuries (see pp. 146–149), because ideas about demons and familiars underpinned both the witch's pact with the Devil and how witches supposedly harmed people through familiars.

Practical demonology

While some theologians were interested only in the theory of demons, many demonologists sought practical applications for their ideas. Some, such as Italian Franciscan friar Girolamo Menghi, were also exorcists, and believed that understanding demons would help them cast these evil spirits out of the possessed. Others, among them the Jesuit scholar Martin Delrio, were interested in helping the Spanish Inquisition pursue magicians and

witches. Some demonologists were witchfinders, seeking to justify their profession by showing that witches really cooperated with demons.

Describing demons

The 13th-century friar and philosopher Thomas Aquinas laid the groundwork for demonological speculation in *De Malo* ("On Evil"), but later theologians such as Heinrich Kramer (author of the *Malleus Maleficarum*; see p. 148) went into detail about demonic abilities, including the capacity to take physical form, possess people's bodies (see pp. 176–177), and even impregnate women.

The most developed demonological works, such as King James VI of Scotland's *Daemonologie* (1597) and Martin Delrio's *Investigations into Magic* (c. 1600), sought to understand the limits of magicians' and witches' power over spirits. These, in turn, inspired books by magicians themselves, which guided would-be practitioners in recognizing the spirits they might summon and explained how to placate them with offerings (see pp. 156–159). The Church condemned these practices as idolatry.

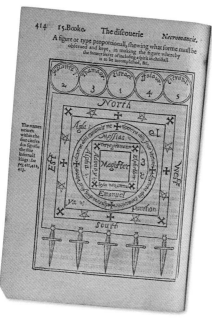

▲ **Necromancer's art**
English skeptic Reginald Scot's *The Discoverie of Witchcraft* (1584) revealed the mysteries of witchcraft and magic—such as this necromantic ritual (one whose magic came from or interacted with the dead)—in order to demystify them and convince readers that magic was just fraud.

IN CONTEXT

Skepticism

Not all demonologists came to the conclusion that demonic activity on Earth was real. Skeptics from around Europe, including Johann Wier, Reginald Scot, Antonio Ferrari, and Samuel de' Cassini, argued that the claims of magicians, witches, and witchfinders were fraudulent in equal measure. They did not usually deny the reality of demons entirely, but suggested that a good God would not allow demons free rein among humans, and associated belief in demonic activity with superstition and credulity.

Dutch physician Johann Wier, a well-known skeptic of witchcraft, is pictured on the frontispiece to his work *De praestigiis daemonum* (1563).

THE DEVIL'S MANY FACES
satanic figures

▼ **Devouring the damned**
Fra Angelico's painting of
The Last Judgment (c 1432)
shows Satan devouring the
souls of the damned after
they have been sent to Hell
as punishment for their sins.
This scene is also described
in Dante's *Divine Comedy*.

The problem of evil is one of the oldest philosophical
issues in human history. For monotheistic faiths,
a way of explaining how evil could coexist with
an omnipotent God was to posit the existence of
a figure, such as Satan, who could be its source.

Zoroastrianism (see pp.26–27), the main religion
of the Persian Empire from the 6th century BCE,
is often considered the world's first monotheistic

faith, because it worships only one god:
Ahura Mazda, the lord of creation. However,
its cosmology also includes a second godlike
figure, called Angra Mainyu, who wields
destructive powers. This figure greatly influenced
the development of the Jewish idea of Satan when,
from 597 to 538 BCE, the Jewish people were exiled
from Judah and forced to live in Babylon.

Although there is no specific satanic being in Jewish belief, a figure referred to as Ha-Satan ("The Satan") appears in the Tanakh—the Hebrew Bible—as an emblem of the *yetzer hara* (evil impulse). Acting in the role of "the adversary" or "the accuser," Ha-Satan tested a person's faith—such as when he inflicted illness, ruin, and misery on Job to see if Job would curse God. In later Judaism, Satan took on a directly oppositional role to God, echoing the dualistic separation between evil and good in the Zoroastrian religion.

Cast out of Heaven

By the time of the Christian New Testament, Satan had become the name of a demonic figure who, as God's chief enemy, was a personification of evil, and whose name was used interchangeably with the Devil. The Book of Revelation gives the longest description of Satan as "the deceiver of the whole world" and depicts him as a red dragon with seven heads. According to the Bible, he was once the angel Lucifer, meaning "Day Star," who led a rebellion against God and was cast out from Heaven. He then waged war on God with the help of a monstrous army, but was defeated and banished to a lake of fire. The gospels say that those who follow Satan will be cast into Hell on Judgment Day. They also relate stories of him tempting Jesus in the desert with promises of earthly power.

In the Qur'an, the enemy of humanity and leader of all demons is called Iblis (see p.73). When Allah commanded the angels to bow before Adam (the first man), Iblis refused and so was cast out of Heaven. In contrast to his Christian counterpart, most Islamic theologians assert that Iblis is unable to create evil, but they do ascribe him agency in tempting humans to perform evil acts.

Early Christian texts also describe the coming of the Antichrist, who is Satan's chief agent at the time of the apocalypse. Similarly, Muslims believe that Dajjal, a false prophet, will arise and, using demonic powers to perform miracles, try to lead the faithful away from Allah before the Day of Judgment.

A pact with the Devil

The idea of making a deal with the Devil—or his intermediaries—can be found in the grimoires of the early modern era, and was a charge levied at accused witches (see pp.146–147). However, as shown when Faust summoned Mephistopheles (see pp.156–157), the results of such a pact were usually considered to be unfortunate, and to lead to an eternity of damnation.

▲ **The pride of Iblis**
This illustration, from a 1415 Islamic text, shows Iblis refusing to bow before Adam along with the other angels, which led to him being cast out of Heaven for his pride.

Showing day and night, the moons symbolize balance

The pentagram; a symbol of the occult

▶ **Horned king**
When the Knights Templar were accused of heresy in 1307, it was said that they worshipped an evil deity called Baphomet, pictured here. Since then, several occult groups have incorporated Baphomet, shown as half-goat, into their spiritual systems.

Poppets, dolls, and effigies

The ancient Egyptians believed that statues and images contained something of the spirit of the thing they represented, and this idea has persisted through the ages. Deriving from the Latin *effingere* ("to form"), an effigy is a figure of a person, god, or spiritual being that has been formed out of materials as a means to connect with otherworldly powers. In England in the Middle Ages, the term "poppet" came to mean the same thing, while the idea that figurines can be receptacles for spirits has given rise to the haunted doll.

An ear of corn represents abundance

Dots of flower pollen show fertility

The Butterfly Girl pollinates the flowers in spring

▶ **This Hopi "Butterfly Girl" spirit doll** (or *kachina*), made for girls, represents the spirit beings who live among the Pueblo from winter solstice to mid-July.

▲ **A rambaramp**, a life-size effigy of clay and plant fibers, is built around the skull (said to house the soul) of a revered male ancestor on the islands of Vanuatu.

▲ **This Kongo spirit doll**, made entirely from iron, resembles a human being and was created to house the soul of a man after his death.

▲ **A wooden effigy** from Nigeria represents an ancestral spirit and symbolizes the forebear's continuing connection with the living.

Encrusted with chicken blood and other liquids

▲ **A New Orleans voodoo doll** connects the *lwa* (spirits) with the living and, contrary to stereotype, is often used to appeal to the spirits for healing and guidance.

▲ **21st-century poppets** are made from simple materials such as burlap and string and are often sold online by New Age stores and crafters. They are used by modern witches in spells for love, luck, and healing.

▲ **This clay effigy** from the 4th century CE was found in Egypt, pierced with 13 bronze needles and buried inside a terra-cotta vase with a binding spell—invoking the spirits of the dead to bind a woman to an infatuated man.

◀ **Annabelle**, the allegedly evil doll locked in a glass case at The Warrens' Occult Museum (see p.257), has been accused of being possessed and moving on its own. In the 1970s, it supposedly clawed its owner's partner, making his chest bleed.

Case decorated with a Christian cross and the Lord's Prayer

▲ **A *nkisi nkondi* statue** (see p.168), known as an African power or "fetish" figure, is ritually created by adding substances and attachments to call forth empowering spirits from the unseen realm of the dead.

▶ **Okiku** is a Japanese doll believed to embody the spirit of a child who died suddenly, at the age of three. Many claim that the doll's hair continues to grow.

◀ **Lily** is a piece of merchandise, mass-produced by a US ghost tour company, which capitalizes on the appeal of haunted dolls and their associated Gothic lore.

WARNING, POSITIVELY DO NOT

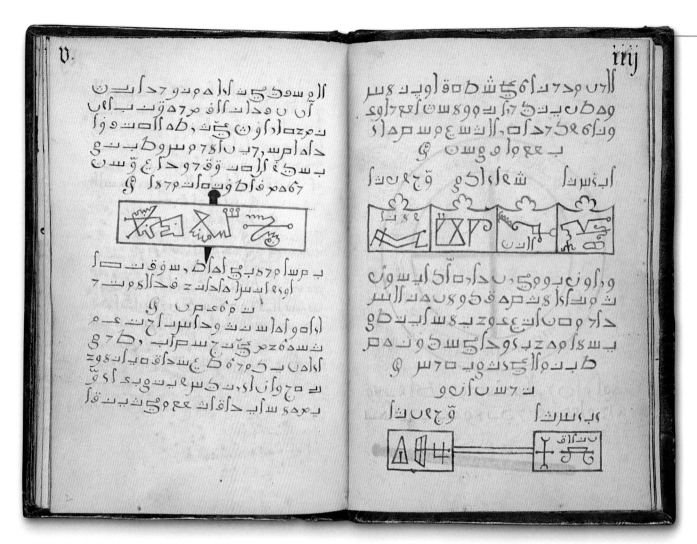

▲ Black magic
Produced in the late 16th century, the "Compendium of Unnatural Black Magic" was written in an invented script based on Arabic. This grimoire was attributed to the medieval Scottish magician Michael Scot.

SPELLBOOKS FOR SUMMONING
early modern grimoires

Popular since the Middle Ages (see pp.112–113), grimoires and spellbooks continued to circulate in the 16th century, albeit mostly in manuscript form, since strict censorship usually prevented the printing of magical books. The Papacy included several grimoires in its *Index of Prohibited Books*, and many were destroyed, meaning that only a few early modern grimoires survive to the present day. Spellbooks that gave instructions for summoning demons, the spirits of the dead, angels, and fairies represented the most dangerous form of magic as far as the authorities were concerned.

A spell for everything

Medieval grimoires, including *Clavicula Salomonis* ("Key of Solomon"), were reproduced in the early modern period. Other grimoires were more haphazard compilations of the spells used by a working magician, such as the English "Book of Magic, with Instructions for Invoking Spirits, etc," now held in the Folger Shakespeare Library, and the *Svarteboker* ("black books") of Scandinavia. These grimoires offered spells for finding lost objects, compelling or retaining a person's love, finding treasure, and even harming enemies.

◀ **Faustian bargain**
Johann Georg Faust was a real person who lived in the 16th century, but his legend soon outgrew him. Faust became the magician *par excellence* who made a pact with the Devil, as depicted in this drawing from a 1741 English pamphlet.

Demonic covenants

The influence of Renaissance magic and Christian versions of the Kabbalah (see pp.122–123) is evident in early modern grimoires, including instructions for making astrological talismans and ascribing special magical power to Hebrew names. Some focused on only one kind of magic—such as the 17th-century German *Höllenzwang* grimoires, which focused on treasure-hunting. The *Höllenzwang* also belonged to the genre of diabolic grimoires, which specifically invoked the Devil (variously called Satan or Lucifer) or one of his senior demons, such as Mephistopheles or Lucifuge Rofocale.

While some grimoires encouraged a covenant with the Devil, most stopped short of summoning him, preferring to invoke more junior demons. Grimoires presented the practice as a demonstration of the magician's holiness and power over spirits (following King Solomon), rather than as a pact with the Devil. This made it easier for magicians to square their acts of magic with the Christian faith—although Church authorities regarded all grimoires as equally forbidden.

Hunting for treasure has long been part of magic and, in an age before metal detectors, magic was often a treasure-hunter's only hope for deciding where to dig. Spirits were believed to guard treasure, but could also be persuaded to reveal its location. Treasure-hunting therefore involved summoning spirits and making offerings. The *Höllenzwang* grimoires were inspired by a tale in the first printed *Faustbuch* (a book of stories about Johann Georg Faust) in 1587, in which the demon Mephistopheles reveals treasure to him.

▶ **Treasure trap**
This diagram from a *Höllenzwang* grimoire shows how to make a magic circle for treasure-hunting. A spirit would be summoned into the circle and compelled to reveal where the treasure was hidden.

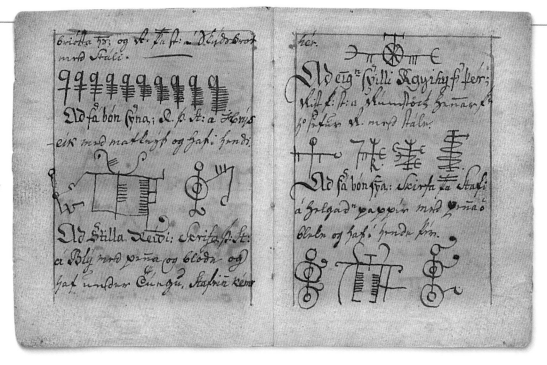

▶ Written in code
Traditional Icelandic magic (*galdr*) dates back to the Viking period and made use of rune-like symbols and magic pictures called *galdramyndir*. A number of spellbooks survive, including this example from c. 1800.

Put into print

Printed grimoires were rare but highly sought after. In 1559, a book attributed to (though probably not written by) notorious magician Heinrich Cornelius Agrippa, *The Fourth Book of Occult Philosophy*, was printed at Magdeburg, in Germany. While Agrippa's first three books dealt with the theory of magic, the fourth offered practical guidance on summoning spirits. An English translation appeared in 1655, after press censorship was lifted during the Commonwealth period (1649–1660).

Magic for the masses

Witchcraft had been decriminalized in many European countries by the end of the 18th century, and it was in this period that grimoires (many of which, as forbidden texts, had already been destroyed) became sought after by collectors of rare books. There was a thriving trade in grimoires, with books often changing hands for large sums. However, this demand also resulted in grimoires being created specifically for the collectors' market, usually with elaborate and grotesque illustrations designed to impress. The notorious Italian writer Giacomo Casanova became, in later life, a librarian to several noblemen because he was renowned for his knowledge of grimoires and occult books. In some cases, collectors believed in the occult and wanted grimoires as a source of power, but many Enlightenment-era collectors had no such beliefs; rather, they were fascinated by the rarity of these books and their sinister reputation. Grimoires became trophies in the libraries of the rich.

In addition to the lavish grimoires collected by the wealthy, the relaxation of censorship laws in France allowed printers to bring out cheap editions of magical books for the first time. Known as *Bibliothèque bleue* ("blue library") publications because

IN CONTEXT

The Grand Grimoire

Also known as *Le Dragon Rouge* ("The Red Dragon"), *The Grand Grimoire* was a spellbook of diabolic magic, inviting magicians to seal demonic pacts. It presented itself as centuries old, but appeared in France in the 18th century and was reprinted as a *Bibliothèque bleue* book throughout the 19th century. *The Grand Grimoire* perhaps drew inspiration from French priest Urbain Grandier's Satanic pact, produced as evidence at his 1634 trial in Loudun, as well as from the Faust legend. Lucifuge Rofocale was said to countersign the pacts.

Lucifuge Rofocale, one of Lucifer's most senior demons, is in charge of the government of Hell, according to *The Grand Grimoire*.

they were small, cheaply printed pamphlets wrapped in blue paper, these early mass-produced grimoires included works such as *Le Dragon Rouge* ("The Red Dragon") and *La Poule Noire* ("The Black Pullet"), names designed to impress and even frighten the reader. These grimoires were popular among "cunning-folk" (professional local magicians) who, even if they were barely literate, would fill their consulting rooms with the books to impress their clients. However, some authorities continued to crack down on the publication of

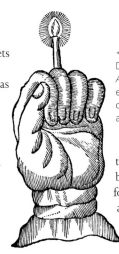

◄ Guiding hand
Described in the 18th-century grimoire *Petit Albert*, the "hand of glory" was the hand of an executed criminal. Prepared correctly, the hand could be used as a candle to light a thief's way at night, while making the thief invisible.

these magical books, calling them blasphemous. The Spanish Inquisition, for example, banned and confiscated as many grimoires as they could in the 18th century, putting them on the *Index of Prohibited Books*.

▼ Collectors' item
During the 18th and 19th centuries the authorities became less concerned by grimoires, so censorship laws were relaxed. Some spellbooks, such as the late-18th-century *Clavis Inferni* ("The Grimoire of Saint Cyprian") were elaborately illustrated in order to appeal to collectors.

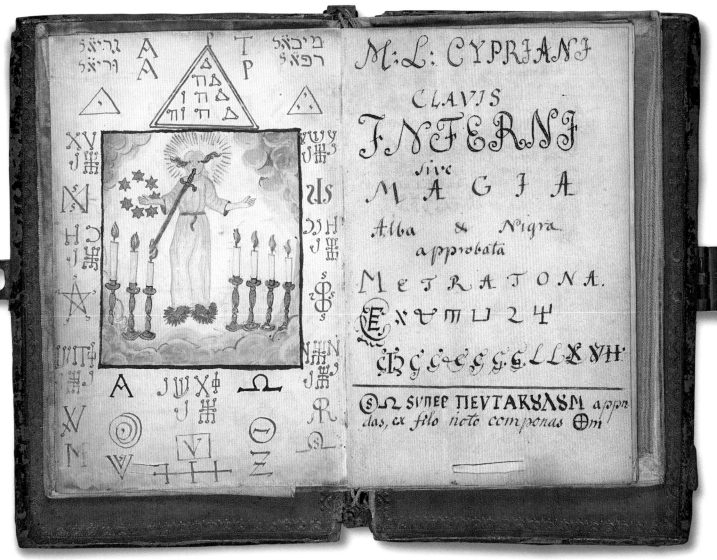

INVOCATION, EVOCATION, AND CEREMONY
Renaissance conjuring

▲ Magical disk
This wax tablet or seal is inscribed with John Dee's *Sigillum Dei Aemeth*, a magical diagram that combined sacred geometry with the names of God, and was used for conjuring angels with a "shew stone," or magical mirror.

The rediscovery of ancient texts during the Renaissance period, which led to a revival of classical learning, threw light on the magical arts that had been a feature of many pre-Christian cultures. The practice of conjuring spirits can be traced back to the Greek Magical Papyri of late antiquity, which contained spells for summoning a spirit "to visible appearance" and constraining it with the use of magical characters. In ancient Rome, the word *evocare* ("to evoke") for conjuring referred to the calling of the *genius loci* ("spirit of the place") into other locations. The term "invocation" meant drawing a spirit into the body, but the two terms were often used interchangeably.

In his *City of God* (c. 413–426 CE), Augustine of Hippo condemned conjuration and the practice of animating statues, claiming that the spirits involved were evil demons known as *goetia* ("howling spirits"). Augustine's characterization influenced many centuries of Western thought, and conjuring was forbidden throughout the Middle Ages, driven into what the historian of magic Richard Kieckhefer has called a "clerical underworld" that copied and proliferated grimoire manuscripts (see pp.112–113).

"White" magic
The Renaissance gave research into occult sciences an intellectual respectability and many scholars pioneered new ideas about lawful forms of magic, often known today as "high" magic. The guiding principle for many a Renaissance magus (magical practitioner) was the Hermetic axiom "as above so below," which held that every object in the material world was a reflection of astrological and spiritual powers, and that a magician could harness astral energies as a means to reveal divine wisdom.

The Italian philosopher and Catholic priest Marsilio Ficino was an early proponent of this principle, and many Renaissance scholars followed suit. These magi admitted the existence of spiritual beings to whom it was possible to address prayers, hymns, or innocent spells. Ficino's *De Vita Coelitus*

IN CONTEXT

Heptameron

This grimoire (book of magic) was falsely attributed to the Italian astrologer and physician Pietro d'Abano (1259–1316), who died in the prison cells of the Inquisition. It is an early example of Christianized Renaissance magic, and includes invocations to angels (one for each of the seven days of the week), rather than spirits, and asks for their assistance in achieving various goals. Angels are seen as powerful spiritual beings who can intercede on the practitioner's behalf, and prayers are included alongside spells. In 1581, the *Heptameron* was placed on the Index of Prohibited Books.

Pietro d'Abano was best known for his medical writings, but also penned treatises on alchemy, astrology, and the human soul.

Comparandi ("On conforming your life to the heavens") Christianized the study of astrological magic and talismans. While his writings did include references to conjuring practices of "spiritual and demonic magic," he stopped short of recommending the conjuration of spirits due to concerns about blasphemy and the danger of summoning demons.

Divine conjuring

Later scholars were bolder about the inclusion of conjuring material. German philosopher Heinrich Cornelius Agrippa included many summoning rituals in his *De Occulta Philosophia* ("Occult Philosophy"), such as magical squares, numerology, and conjuring circles inscribed with divine names. Agrippa proposed a *magia reformata* ("reformed magic"), which was holy and considered the highest of the sciences. This rehabilitated magic could only be accomplished by invoking benevolent spirits.

However, Renaissance conjuring that identified itself with "good" rather than "evil" magic still flirted dangerously close to definitions of religious heresy and associations with witchcraft. In 1600, Italian magus Giordano Bruno was burned at the stake by the Catholic Inquisition and in 1604, John Dee (see pp.162–163) petitioned King James I to withdraw the accusation that Dee was a "Conjurer, or Caller, or Invocator of Divels, or damned Spirites."

▲ **Black arts**
A woodcut from Petrarch's *De Remediis Utriusque Fortunae* ("Remedies for Fortunes," c.1354–1366), shows magicians. One stands in a summoning circle holding a skull, while another practices haruspicy (divination) using the entrails of a goat.

John Dee the conjurer

Sir John Dee cut an enigmatic figure at the court of Queen Elizabeth I of England. Important in early modern science, Dee was a practitioner of Paracelsian alchemy and a magus (person who practiced magic) notorious for claiming he could conjure angels. Dee sought a universal "Enochian" (angelic) language, told to Adam by God, that could heal the "book of nature," and a "real cabala" (occult knowledge) that could manipulate reality. As well as his magical diagram for invoking angels (see pp. 160–161), he designed a sigil, *Monas Hieroglyphica*, which combined astrological symbols into a complex talisman to store astral energies. When decoded, it would supposedly unlock the mysteries of creation.

In the 1580s, Dee became associated with a man named Edward Kelley who, in this 19th-century painting by Henry Gillard Glindoni, is shown sitting behind Dee, wearing a cap to conceal the cropped ears of a convicted counterfeiter. Kelley, who would use an obsidian mirror (a technique known as "scrying") to summon angels, could have been tricking Dee, but both men's diaries reveal Kelley was terrified by the angels, fearing they were actually demons.

Glindoni's painting seems to have originally depicted Dee's occult practices. X-ray scans have revealed that an earlier version had a ring of skulls around Dee, which were painted over in the final version to depict him as a scientist rather than a conjurer of spirits.

> "Herein lie their Names, that work under God upon the Earth."
>
> JOHN DEE, *DE HEPTARCHIA MYSTICA*, 1582

▲ **John Dee performs a scientific experiment** for Elizabeth I's court in this 19th-century painting by British painter Henry Gillard Glindoni.

KEY

1 The Eyüp Sultan Mosque stands on the other side of the courtyard from the tomb.

2 Abu Ayyub al-Ansari's shrine was built on the site where he died in 684 CE. The tombs of holy men and women were popular places of pilgrimage in Ottoman Istanbul, because it was thought that the souls of saints could intercede with Allah on behalf of the living.

3 The Ottoman Empire's longest-reigning ruler, Suleiman I (r. 1520–1566) led his army in many successful campaigns. Sultans were believed to have the power to call on ghostly warriors for military assistance.

▶ **Venerating saints**
This Ottoman illustration shows Sultan Suleiman I visiting the tomb of Abu Ayyub al-Ansari, one of the companions of the Prophet Muhammad.

THE MARCHING DEAD
Ottoman ghosts

In orthodox Islam there are no ghosts. Once a person dies, their soul is believed to travel to Barzakh, a place between life and the afterlife where it remains until it is judged. Most Islamic scholars agree that spirits do not return to the human world. But in the Ottoman Empire from the 14th century onward, the flourishing genre of *aja'ib* or "wonder" literature featured many supernatural tales, ranging from the actions of jinn (see pp.72–73) to ghostly appearances.

Wailing spirits and wicked souls
At its greatest extent, in the 16th century, the Ottoman Empire stretched from present-day Austria to the Persian Gulf. Across its territories, beliefs about ghosts varied widely. For some Sufi scholars, it was possible for spirits to return to the human world: many stories tell of souls being seen to wail beside their own dead bodies. Similarly, the writer Cinânî recorded that when a sick person is on the verge of death, the soul of a dead person may enter their body and speak to reveal their own suffering in the afterlife. Only readings from the Qur'an were said to have the power to drive the spirit out. In some parts of the empire, wicked souls were thought to be able to reanimate corpses, which then became vampires (see pp.214–217), and only driving a stake through their heart or cutting off their head would end the possession.

Ghostly heroes
The Ottoman view of ghosts was mostly positive. Ghosts tended to be the souls of brave soldiers or devout saints who could only act under Allah's authority. Some came in dreams. Evliya Çelebi was visited in a dream by the spirit of the Prophet Muhammad and the souls of devout saints, who encouraged him to set out on his celebrated travels.

Sultans were thought to be able to call on an army of ghosts to aid them in battle. Visible only to those with a special ability, these spirit warriors were known as "the men of the heart" and they attacked the morale of the enemy. At the capture of Hamedan in 1586, a ghostly army made up of martyrs who died in the first years of Islam was said to have appeared to fight on the Ottoman side.

▲ **Marvels and wonders**
Alongside tales of ghosts, writers of the *aja'ib* genre also collected stories of supernatural creatures, such as the dragon fish, al-Tannīn, shown here in a 15th-century illustration from al-Qazwīnī's *Wonders of Creation and Oddities of Existence*.

IN CONTEXT

Evliya Çelebi

Spurred on by a dream featuring the Prophet Muhammad, 17th-century writer Evliya Çelebi traveled throughout the Ottoman Empire, producing a long account of all he saw and heard. His work included stories of witches, jinn, vampires, and unquiet spirits. At times, according to Çelebi, the living soul could leave the body: while Sultan Bayezid II was fasting, he began to hunger for some soup, so his soul emerged from his mouth in the form of a blind weasel and tasted it for him.

While on his travels, Evliya Çelebi wrote more than 4,000 pages.

LINGERING LOVERS
China's waiting women

▲ Pleading for love
This 1618 woodcut print by Zhang Maoxiu (1558–1639) illustrates a scene from *The Peony Pavilion*, when Du Liniang begs the Lord of the Underworld to allow her to return as a ghost and find the man she loves.

Characterized by her protracted lingering in hope of reuniting with a lover, the "waiting woman" is a type of *gui* in the Chinese pantheon. *Gui* is usually translated as "ghost" but can include all supernatural beings. The waiting woman probably originated in the playwright Tang Xianzu's 1598 play, *The Peony Pavilion*. His heroine, Du Liniang, is a beautiful 16-year-old girl, who falls in love with the scholar Liu Mingmei in a dream. She dies pining for him, and her spirit must wait for him to fall in love with her, so she may live again and become his bride. A possible earlier source of this trope is the Tang poem "Woman Waiting for Her Husband," by Wang Jian (767–830 CE), where the waiting woman turns into sentient stone.

Later depictions
The waiting woman also features in Cao Xueqin's classic 18th-century novel, *The Dream of the Red Chamber*. The character Qingwen (whose name means "Bright Cloud" or "Bright Design") is a servant in love with the story's protagonist, Jia Baoyu—he, however, is in love with his cousin. Unjustly slandered for conducting an illicit affair and dismissed from the household, Qingwen dies from an illness soon after, and turns into a *gui*, with little chance of reconciling with her beloved.

Pu Songling's *Liaozhai Zhiyi* ("Strange Tales from a Chinese Studio," 1740) similarly contains an example of a waiting woman. The story "A Supernatural Wife" is about a spirit who is destined to be the otherworldly wife of a man as repayment for his kindness to her in a past life. She must wait until he is afflicted with poverty and terminal illness before she can appear before him and reveal this to him. As a supernatural being, she is able to cure her husband and endow him with wealth. They then live happily until they both magically

disappear into the clouds to be together forever. Notably, Pu innovates the waiting woman lore by having the *gui* actively seek out her betrothed, rather than biding her time patiently and passively.

Modern examples
Today, the waiting woman remains a trope in Chinese fiction. The idea is the basis for *Time Before Time*, a 1997 Hong Kong television drama series focusing on the Buddhist theme of reincarnation; and the award-winning *Rouge*, a 1988 film directed by Stanley Kwan that starred Anita Mui as the titular *gui* and Leslie Cheung as her awaited but ultimately faithless lover. Stylistically elegant and tonally melancholic, the latter is also a powerful commentary on the island state's changing landscape, where the past simultaneously becomes erased by, and continues to haunt, the present.

Variations on the theme
Comparable beings to the waiting woman can be found in neighboring countries, such as the Japanese *kurokami* (black-haired revenant) and the *nangnak* from Thailand—one famous example of the latter being the legendary Mae Nak Phra Khanong, who died in childbirth while her husband was away at war and returned to the home as a spirit to wait for him to come back. However, there are marked differences between these examples and the Chinese *gui*, namely the motif of vengeance associated with the *kurokami*, and the culmination of a reunion only to be separated again forever in stories of the *nangnak*.

▶ Waiting mother
This statue of Mae Nak Phra Khanong and her child is placed in her Bangkok shrine, where people pay their respects and seek her favors, especially those wanting to avoid military conscription.

"I have at length succeeded in my search for you."

MRS. ZHAO TO HER HUSBAND, IN PU SONGLING'S "A SUPERNATURAL WIFE," 1740

▲ **Diligent maid**
This 19th century painting depicts Qingwen, from *The Dream of the Red Chamber*, and fellow servants of the wealthy Jia household taking a brief rest in between chores.

MANIFESTING SPIRITS
possession rituals in African cultures

The belief that spirits can influence or control humans is ancient and widespread across the African continent. A 1973 anthropological study found that 81 percent of societies believed in spirit possession, but with varying names, manifestations, and purposes. Spirit possession beliefs and practices fascinated Christian missionaries and explorers, whose writings provide the earliest record of the phenomenon. Their commentary, however, often suffers from the biases of their own religious beliefs.

Ancestral visitors

Most African people believe that the dead interact with and influence the living in ways that can be beneficial or harmful. Nigeria's Yoruba and Cameroon's Grassfields people, for example, believe that ancestral spirits can possess individuals, clothing, royal stools, buffalo horn cups, and other items, filling them with ritual power. For the Zulu people of southern Africa, possession by ancestors (*ukuthwasa*) marks the calling to be traditional healers or diviners (*isangoma*), who are mostly women. The relatively few male *isangoma* are trained by women practitioners and often adopt a female identity and wear women's clothes. The Zulu differentiate between *ukuthwasa*, *ukuhlanya* (madness), and *amafufunyana* (possession by evil spirits).

Diverse influences

Indigenous African religions are pragmatic and open to sharing beliefs, with adherents always eager to learn about spirit phenomena that address well-being and fear of the unknown. Zār, for example, is a spirit possession practice found across northeastern Africa that may have originated in Ethiopia or even as far south as the

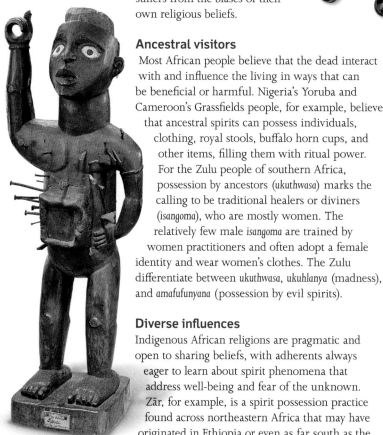

▼ Powerful possession
Nkisi nkondi power figures from the Kongo (present-day Democratic Republic of Congo) are believed to be possessed by a spirit (*nkisi*). This is activated by a sacred substance or "medicine" stored inside them. A *nkondi* is a hunter activated by the substance to track down and punish wrongdoers.

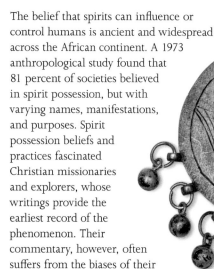

◀ Exorcism through dance
This amulet used in Zār ceremonies depicts the female spirit Sitt Safina as a mermaid. Part of the Throne verse (Qur'an 2:255), recited to drive out evil spirits, is inscribed on the back.

Congo. Zār beliefs and rites involve generally benign spirits, both Islamic jinn and Indigenous northern African spirits. Zār spirits can, however, possess people and cause deviant behavior or illness. To counter this, the possessed take part in a ritual with the spirit. Zār therefore refers to the spirit, to the affliction caused, and to the healing ritual itself, as well as to Zār music, now an art form in Egypt and Sudan, which originates in ritual practices. Zār possession mostly affects women and can confer privileged status in otherwise oppressive conditions. While discouraged by Islamic authorities, the practice is not necessarily perceived as a problem in African cultures.

Among East Africa's coastal Swahili-speaking people, ecstatic dance and musical performances bring forth spirits. *Kipemba* spirits bring blessings and protection from the *rubamba*, their malevolent manifestation. Possession by *pepo* spirits reflects the region's history of contact with inland Indigenous African, Islamic, Asian, and European peoples. *Pepo* are the spirits of strangers—the Arabs, Persians, Indians, and Portuguese who came by sea, and the Nyika, a Swahili term for inland African peoples.

Modern practices

Spirit possession cults in Africa today have similarities in patterns of behavior and ritual that suggest such practices influence each other. An ongoing challenge for Indigenous religions is the prejudice existing in the use of the pejorative word "cult" by outsiders to describe these beliefs and traditions, which have arisen to meet specific communal and cultural needs.

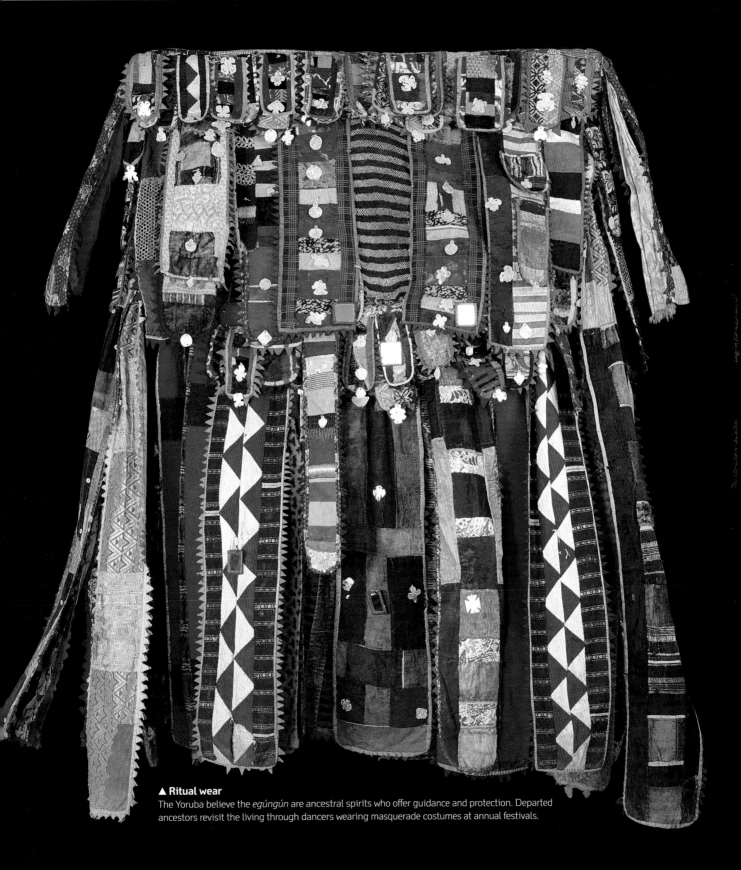

▲ Ritual wear
The Yoruba believe the *egúngún* are ancestral spirits who offer guidance and protection. Departed ancestors revisit the living through dancers wearing masquerade costumes at annual festivals.

▲ **Dogon dancers perform at the** *dama* funeral ritual, ensuring the safe passage of the deceased to the afterlife.

Ritual dance

Dance is a visible and nonverbal means of expressing feelings and thoughts. It uses known, patterned symbols to communicate internal experiences or external events. For African peoples, dance is an interface between the spirit and human realms. When bereaved, African peoples use ceremonial dance to express emotions, give the spirits of the dead a way to communicate, and build the resilience needed to move on.

The *dama* ceremony of the Dogon people in Mali, West Africa, can take place months or even years after a death to mark the deceased's initiation and journey to the realm of ancestral spirits. During performances, the masked dancers embody deities, ancestors, animals, plants, and even objects. These performances depict the history of the world as conceived of by the Dogon. The carved wooden *kanaga* masks pictured here represent Amma, the Creator, and the trembling of the wearer's outstretched arms alludes to the movement of Amma's hands as he created the world. The wearers of the masks usually do not speak, except for shouts that are part of the ritual dance.

The Dogon imbue the masks with meaning through the use of colors representing the elements: red for fire; black for water; white for air; and yellow for earth. The painting of the mask in these colors is believed to bring the mask— and the ancestor it represents—to life, just as Amma brought life to the world through the four elements.

"The sacred dances of Africa bring one nearer the 'time of the gods' on Earth."

FELIX BEGHO, "TRADITIONAL AFRICAN DANCE IN CONTEXT," 1996

SERVING THE SPIRITS
beliefs of the African diaspora

Over many centuries, millions of African people were enslaved and transported to the Americas as part of the Transatlantic Slave Trade. In many places, their religious beliefs "syncretized" with Christianity and Indigenous practices to create a range of "African-derived religions." Nevertheless, these beliefs remain rooted in their African spiritual origins, all of which include invoking spirits, divine and ancestral, for guidance, protection, and well-being.

Protective spirits

Haitian Vodou is a fusion of West and Central African, Taíno, and Catholic religious beliefs. The name evolved from the African Fon word *voudon*, meaning "spirit" or "deity". Vodouists believe in one remote creator God, *Bondye*, but it is the *lwa* (or *loa*)—spiritual beings—who provide humans with assistance and protection in daily life. There are more than 1,000 *lwa*, grouped into many different pantheons but primarily *Rada* and *Petwo*. *Rada lwa* are generally benevolent and creative, while *Petwo lwa* tend to be associated with more volatile tendencies, but the spirits can contain aspects of both. *Ghede*, another pantheon of *lwa*, represent fertility and death—the spirits transport dead souls and can behave irreverently and obscenely.

In Vodou belief, the *lwa* are ever-present—in all nature and in every type of human activity—and are in control of an individual's fate, from birth until death. They are "fed," prayed to, and are believed to be able to manifest in a human body through spirit possession. This is called "mounting," as the person is seen as the *chwal* ("horse") of the *lwa*. It is a core part of Vodou ceremonies because, in this state, spirits are believed to advise, prophesize, and heal. A common Vodou saying is "*sèvi lwa yo*," which means "I serve the spirits."

▶ **Voodoo queen**
The most famous Voodoo Priestess of New Orleans was Marie Laveau, a Louisiana Creole. In her lifetime (1801–1881), she was an activist, philanthropist, herbalist, and entrepreneur.

▲ **Mother spirit**
This Igbo figure depicts Mami Wata, a spirit venerated across West Africa and the Americas. She is associated with wealth and good fortune, and her snake represents both divinity and the art of divination.

▶ **Celebrated spirit**
A Drapo Vodou (Vodou flag) by celebrated Haitian flag-maker Oleyant Antoine (1955–1992) shows Bossou, the sacred bull. A *lwa* of Haitian Vodou, he is associated with soil fertility and male virility.

Dancing with snakes

Louisiana or New Orleans Voodoo merges Haitian Vodou, West African, Indigenous North American, and Catholic beliefs. Reflecting these diverse influences, Louisiana Voodoo includes reverence for Catholic saints syncretized with various African deities; dance ceremonies during which participants channel different deities; and snake veneration. Snakes are a well-known entity and motif in New Orleans Voodoo, since they are connected to Blanc Dani, a Voodoo deity of protection, as well as Haitian Vodou deities like Aida Wedo and Damballa, both serpentine spirits from African Ewe-Fon beliefs.

"There must be feasts for the spirits…"

ZORA NEALE HURSTON, *HOODOO IN AMERICA*, 1931

▼ **Divination drums**
This image depicts Calundu, an old Afro-Brazilian drumming and spirit-possession ritual. Calundu drumming survives in Candomblé and Umbanda drumming and music.

Root working

Birthed on the plantations of the US South, Hoodoo combines influences from West and Central Africa with Indigenous and European folklore. Also known as "root work" or "conjure," it is a system of spiritual healing and protection, created in response to the oppression of slavery. Similar to Vodou, Hoodoo venerates nature spirits and is also renowned for protective amulets, such as "mojo bags"—charms created for the enslaved population. Prayed over by a conjurer and "fed" with ingredients, such as herbs, roots, animal parts, and sometimes grave dirt, these are believed to confer spiritual power on the owner.

South American religions

Candomblé is primarily rooted in the spirituality of the Yoruba, but is also influenced by beliefs from the Ewe-Fon and the Kongo. Originating with enslaved Africans in Brazil, it flowered in the 19th century when the first houses of Candomblé were established in Bahia by three free women: Iya Deta, Iya Kala, and Iya Nasso. As among the Yoruba, the core tenets of Candomblé are recognition of the supreme god, Olórun; divination for one's destiny; and personal and ceremonial devotion to nature deities or deified ancestors called Orixás.

Main Orixás in Candomblé include Exu, Ogun, Yemanja, Xango, and Oxum. The Candomblé equivalent of Vodou "mounting" is called "incorporation." Like other African diasporic religions that focus on the well-being of adherents, Candomblé is a source of community and is essential to healing Banzo—the psychosomatic manifestation of the trauma of enslavement.

Regla Ocha-Ifa or Regla Lucumí (also called Santería) is a Yoruba-derived religion from Cuba. Its tenets include belief in *ashe*—the divine and human power to cause and change—and veneration of a pantheon of Orixás (or Ochas), nature spirits or deities and deified ancestors who mirror those of the Yoruba. Other practices include elaborate initiation ceremonies, divination, ancestral veneration, sacrifice, and trance (also called "mounting"). During initiation, one or more Orixás mounts a devotee who then enters into a lifelong devotional relationship with them. Specific colors, minerals, precious stones, plants, animals, preferred foods and drinks, drum rhythms, and dances are associated with each Orixá. For example, Eleguá, master of paths and crossroads, is associated with red and black, guava, goats, and small rodents called *hutia*. He is given offerings of cornmeal balls, grated coconut, and *Eau-de-vie* (brandy).

Across the diaspora

Many African-derived religions continue to flourish across the Americas, fueled by their emphasis on close relationships with nature deities and ancestral spirits. Whether through the Big Drum Dance of the Carriacou in the Grenadines, or in the wealth of song and dance ceremonies of the Arará from Cuba, the Kumina in Jamaica, or the Winti in Suriname, connection to these spirits provides comfort and guidance, and a welcome counterpoint to the disenchantments of the modern world.

▲ **Sacred altar**
The Yoruba spirits celebrated at this Candomblé altar are Obatalá, spirit of harmony and balance (far left); Oshun, spirit of rivers and love (middle left); Shango, spirit of virility and drums (middle right); and Oya, spirit of whirlpools and lightning (far right).

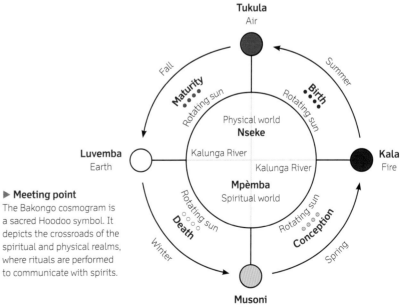

▶ **Meeting point**
The Bakongo cosmogram is a sacred Hoodoo symbol. It depicts the crossroads of the spiritual and physical realms, where rituals are performed to communicate with spirits.

SPIRITUAL INVASION
possession and obsession

▲ Fleeing demon
In this painting by Lorenzo Salimbeni (1374–c. 1420), a man dangles a relic of St. Benedict over the demoniac, while a priest performs an exorcism. A tiny figure of St. Benedict assists, and the demon leaves the victim's body.

The idea that evil spirits can physically and psychologically invade a human body and personality is known as demonic possession. In early Christian belief, possession could result in illness and disability, including seizures and an inability to speak. During the medieval period, a sophisticated understanding of demonic attacks on human beings developed, with possession being the most extreme form of

demonic activity. Demons were also believed to be capable of "obsession" of a person, meaning that a demon "besieged" a person's senses through dreams or apparitions. Obsession could also involve physical attacks on a person, as experienced by St. Anthony, who was repeatedly pushed and pummeled by demons. If someone failed to resist demonic obsession, complete possession might be the result.

A surge in devils

Demonic possession was a marginal concern during the Middle Ages. However, in the 16th century, reports of possession intensified in both Catholic and Protestant areas of Europe. Possessed people, known as demoniacs, were described as displaying unnatural strength, having the ability to speak and understand languages previously unknown to them, and displaying knowledge of events that was impossible by natural means. In addition, their bodies became swollen and contorted, they writhed uncontrollably, and vomited up strange objects. The majority of demoniacs were women and children, and they attracted considerable attention in the first era of print media.

◄ **Mass possession**
In 1632, a group of Ursuline nuns in Loudun, France, displayed symptoms of demonic possession en masse. The local parish priest was executed for throwing a bewitched rose sprig into their garden, but the possessions continued.

Protestant and Catholic exorcists competed to treat alleged demoniacs, in an effort to prove the powers of their "true" religion. Large-scale public exorcisms were common and demoniacs were sometimes encouraged to declare the truth of Catholicism or Protestantism before the spirits were sent away. Demons were believed to have supernatural knowledge, so the demoniac's testimony on behalf of either side was considered invaluable.

Exorcism controversy

Not all senior churchmen approved of the fashion for exorcism, since it handed a great deal of power and influence to the exorcists. In England, the popular exorcist John Darrell was put on trial by the Church in 1598, accused of practicing a "deceitful trade" in "pretended dispossessions." This prompted a furious national debate about beliefs around demonic possession and obsession.

Six years later, in 1604, the Church of England issued Canon 72, which outlawed exorcism altogether, except with a license from a bishop. Such a license was never granted in the nearly 400 years that Canon 72 remained in force. In the Catholic world, exorcisms continued, with a new "Roman Ritual" text published in 1614 (see pp.178–179). However, by the 18th century, under the influence of new Enlightenment medical ideas—which argued that conditions such as epilepsy had a scientific rather than a demonic cause—bishops began to discourage the practice.

▲ **A physical assault**
In this Dutch engraving (c.1658), a demoniac stands on his head as an assembled crowd of Dutch Calvinists pray for his deliverance.

"The child was transformed by the Daemon in to such shaps as a man that hath not beheld it with his eyes, would hardly be brought to imagine."

THE WONDERFULL AND TRUE RELATION OF THE BEWITCHING OF A YOUNG GIRLE IN IRELAND, 1699

Rites of exorcism

For centuries, exorcisms were performed throughout the Catholic world without any organized rules or practices. Methods varied widely—incantations and prayers were recited, water and salt were often used, and many relied on the power of relics, fumigations (using pungent substances such as sulfur and asafoetida), and even physical violence.

However, in 1614, after the reforms of the Council of Trent had created a more centralized Church (focused on the figure of the Pope), the Church published the *Rituale Romanum* ("Roman Ritual"). This set out the rites and rituals that might be led by Catholic priests, and contained the official Latin rite of exorcism. The 1614 rite consisted of a series of adjurations (commands) to the demon believed to be possessing a person's body. The priest would recite the words of the rite, ordering the demon to leave the body of the demoniac (possessed person) and stop troubling God's Church. Many of the specific commands in the *Rituale Romanum* have now passed into popular culture via the film *The Exorcist* (1973), which depicts the rite being—unsuccessfully—carried out on a demon named Pazuzu, who possesses a young girl.

The 1614 rite was superseded in 1999 by a newly approved rite of exorcism, which puts less emphasis on issuing commands to demons, and more on prayer and healing. Unlike the 1614 rite, which could only be spoken in Latin, the 1999 rite of exorcism has been officially translated into many languages, including English.

"The power of Christ compels you."

THE *RITUALE ROMANUM* (1614),
AS QUOTED IN *THE EXORCIST* (1973)

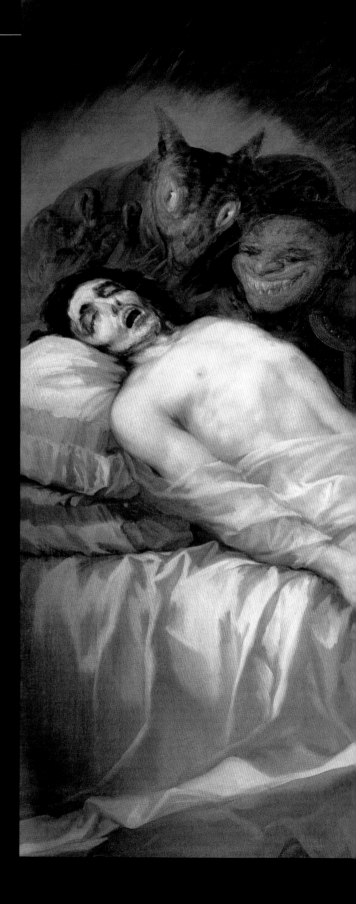

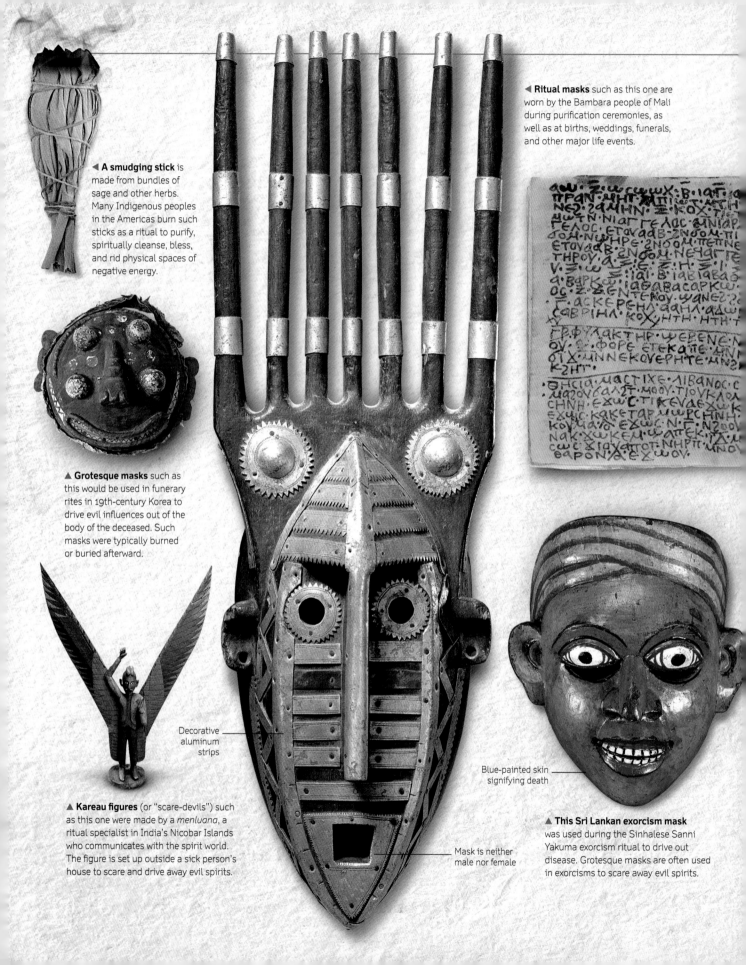

◄ **A smudging stick** is made from bundles of sage and other herbs. Many Indigenous peoples in the Americas burn such sticks as a ritual to purify, spiritually cleanse, bless, and rid physical spaces of negative energy.

▲ **Grotesque masks** such as this would be used in funerary rites in 19th-century Korea to drive evil influences out of the body of the deceased. Such masks were typically burned or buried afterward.

▲ **Kareau figures** (or "scare-devils") such as this one were made by a *menluana*, a ritual specialist in India's Nicobar Islands who communicates with the spirit world. The figure is set up outside a sick person's house to scare and drive away evil spirits.

Decorative aluminum strips

Mask is neither male nor female

◄ **Ritual masks** such as this one are worn by the Bambara people of Mali during purification ceremonies, as well as at births, weddings, funerals, and other major life events.

Blue-painted skin signifying death

▲ **This Sri Lankan exorcism mask** was used during the Sinhalese Sanni Yakuma exorcism ritual to drive out disease. Grotesque masks are often used in exorcisms to scare away evil spirits.

▶ **An aspergillum** is used for sprinkling holy water on a person, thing, or place. In Christianity, and especially in Catholicism, holy water (water blessed by a priest) can play a key role in exorcism.

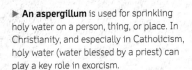

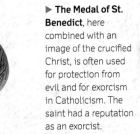
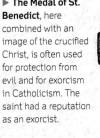

▶ **The Medal of St. Benedict**, here combined with an image of the crucified Christ, is often used for protection from evil and for exorcism in Catholicism. The saint had a reputation as an exorcist.

Coptic Egyptian script

◀ **This 1,300-year-old parchment codex** from Coptic Egypt is a "Handbook of Ritual Power" containing love spells, exorcisms, and spells against a disease called "black jaundice."

◀ **The Bible**, as the Word of God, is believed to have the power to triumph over the forces of evil. For Christians, especially Protestants, reading from the Bible is often a central part of rites of exorcism.

▼ **A dorge** is a Tibetan ritual scepter representing the consciousness of the Buddha, and based on the thunderbolt scepter wielded by the Hindu god Indra. It symbolizes power over spirits.

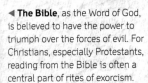

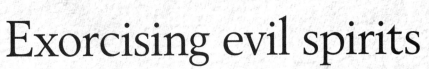

▲ **The tanbura** is a six-stringed lyre used in Zār, an exorcism and healing ritual, originally from Sudan, that involves ceremonial dance, trances, and ritual sacrifice.

Exorcising evil spirits

Across many cultures, exorcism is a dramatic and often physical ritual that involves the use of sacred objects and ritual texts. Exorcism can be multisensory, involving chanting, singing, sacred images, ritual clothing, and suffumigations (the burning of herbs or incense). During an exorcism, sacred texts might play a physical role, such as being placed on areas of the body of a possessed person, while in some cultures loud noises and music produced on a variety of instruments are meant to drive out evil spirits.

UNRULY AND INEFFABLE SPIRITS

Japanese *yūrei* and *yokai*

▼ Skeletal strife
This Edo-period woodblock print by Utagawa Kuniyoshi depicts a mythical scene: Mitsukuni, a royal official, defying the skeleton specter, which has been summoned by Princess Takiyasha (pictured holding a scroll).

Although generally translated as "ghost," the Japanese word *yūrei* is a concept best defined within its cultural context. The idea of *yūrei* is deeply rooted in a cosmology that combines Buddhism and Shintoism, both profound influences on Japanese culture and society to this day. Buddhism provides the notion of the afterlife or *anoyo* ("the world over yonder"), and Shintoism,

a belief in *kami*, the life force residing in every living thing. After individuals die, if *kami* are unable to pass on to *anoyo*, they become *yūrei*, trapped in *konoyo* ("this world here").

Belief in *yūrei* is based on the Japanese idea that the living must care for the dead in return for the latter's protection. Underscoring this symbiotic relationship is the spiritual obligation called *gimu*;

failing to pay *gimu* would recast the dead as *yūrei* threatening the well-being of the living. Other reasons for *yūrei*'s emergence are unfinished business, improper burial and related ceremony, and unnatural death.

Dark souls

The term *yūrei*—with Japanese characters that literally mean "dark soul"—was purportedly coined by the Noh dramatist Zeami (1363–1443). Zeami can be credited with the idea that *yūrei* were visible to the living. However, the historian Koyama Satoko has traced the word's first use to even earlier, in 747 CE, where it appears in a prayer by a disciple of the Buddhist priest Genbō, imploring

that his exiled master be granted Buddhahood. In appearance, *yūrei* can look no different from humans and, in some stories, they are even mistaken for them. Female *yūrei* tend to have long, black hair and to be dressed in a white kimono—the funeral attire for the dead.

Types of *yūrei* include *onryō*, vengeful phantoms who return to seek justice from those who have wronged them; *kosodate-yūrei*, the spirits of mothers who have died in childbirth or shortly after; *funa-yūrei*, ghosts of individuals who died at sea; and *zashiki-warashi*, mischief-loving ghost children. Particularly fearsome are *jibakurei*, cursed spirits that haunt specific places and endanger the living.

The ghost game

Hyakumonogatari Kaidankai ("A Gathering of One Hundred Supernatural Tales") is a Buddhist-inspired parlor game that invites the spirits in. It dates from the Edo period and was initially designed, it is believed, to test a samurai's courage. In one of the earliest written accounts of the game (*Nursery Tales*, 1660), Ansei Ogita describes how 100 blue lanterns were lit in a room to create an otherworldly light, and a mirror placed on a table. Players in an adjoining room, dressed in blue, then each had to recount a ghost story. At the end of each tale, the storyteller had to walk to the room with the lanterns, extinguish a light, and stare at their reflection in the mirror. As the lights went out, one by one, it was believed that the spirits advanced a step closer, and that after the final story, there would be *yūrei* waiting in the darkness.

▲ **Ghosts of Matahachi and Kikuno**

The distinctiveness of different *yūrei* is evident in *yūrei-zu*, a genre of Japanese art that deals with supernatural themes. In this woodblock print by Utagawa Kunisada (1786–1865), two *yūrei* return from their watery grave.

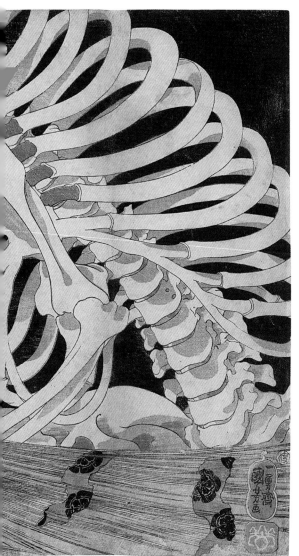

"Unnaturally drained of color, her bloodless skin peeked from her … bone-white burial kimono."

THE GHOST OF OYUKI, JAPANESE FOLKTALE, RETOLD BY ZACK DAVISSON

▲ Night parade
This 18th-century ink-and-color painting by Mochizuki Gyokusen (1692–1755) catalogs 100 monstrous but humorous-looking types of *yokai*, which run amok at night.

The world of *yokai*

Yūrei form a group within a much larger pantheon of supernatural beings known as *yokai*. This word is often translated as "monster" or "demon" and yet the concept is much broader. In the Japanese language, its literal meaning is "alluring mystery" but it can also refer to a dreadful and bewildering experience; a sense of awe and wonder in response to the strange; an unfamiliar sound or smell that begs an explanation; or an inexplicable phenomenon comprehensible only as a supernatural event.

As with *yūrei*, the concept of *yokai* extends from the Shinto veneration of dual-natured *kami* spirits. According to Daoist philosophy, these entities could

IN CONTEXT

Kabuki theater

Originally a form of entertainment in red-light districts, such as Yoshiwara in Edo (present-day Tokyo), Kabuki theater aimed to satisfy the popular appetite for gripping, macabre stories. *Yokai* tales, with their supernatural subject matter and themes of duplicity and death, fitted the bill perfectly. One of the most famous plays is undoubtedly *Yotsuya Kaidan* ("The Ghost of Yotsuya"), by Tsuruya Nanboku IV. Featuring the terrifying *onryō* of the betrayed and disfigured Oiwa, the play immediately gained immense popularity.

Oiwa's disfigured face projects from a lantern in Hokusai's iconic image (c. 1831).

▶ **Striking terror**
This 19th-century carved ivory *netsuke* (button fastener or miniature ornament) shows an *ōni*, a type of ogre or demon believed to dwell in caves or deep in mountains and terrorize the living.

be either yin or yang, with peaceful/positive or negative/angry aspects. *Yokai* also embody this duality and ambivalence, which is illustrated in the liminal or transitional places that many of them inhabit—bridges, crossroads, or the water's edge.

A parade of strange creatures

Yokai appear in many diverse forms, ranging from human (*yūrei*) and were-beast (*kappa*), to animal (*tengu, bakeneko*), demon or ogre (*oni*), and even inanimate household objects (*tsukumoga*). The latter form, a "kami of tool" dating back to the 10th century, included items that gained a soul upon reaching 100 years of age, but could be rendered monstrous through lack of respect.

Always dual-natured, often shape-shifting, and never stereotypical, *yokai* can be friend or foe. Other famous types include the three-legged aquatic creature *amabie*; the trickster *tanuki*, which resembles a raccoon dog; *kitsune*, the Japanese fox; *yuki-onna*, the snow woman; *tsuchigumo*, the giant spider; and *ijin*, a humanoid creature from a land called Ikai, which can cross the boundary separating worlds.

Picturesque monsters

Although *yokai* have been a fixture in Japanese culture since antiquity, one of the earliest examples of *yokai* art is the *Hyakki Yagyo Zu* ("Nocturnal Procession of the Hundred Demons"), a 16th-century illustrated scroll that depicts a well-known idiom in Japanese folklore: a nocturnal parade or riot of 100 demons. The scroll also demonstrates a very real fear of the unknown for the ancient and medieval Japanese.

The *Hyakki Yagyo Zu* inspired the fashion for *yokai* art during the Edo period (17th–19th centuries) and formed the basis for the first definitive *yokai* illustrated encyclopedia, by writer and printmaker Toriyama Sekien (1712–1788). Sekien also produced a series of illustrations known as *Gazu Hyakki Yagyo*, which, together with his other works, represented more than 200 *yokai*—each with its own description and commentary. However, Sekien's cataloging and codifying was a sign of the increasingly rational times. No longer seen as an explanation of the inexplicable, *yokai* started to be depicted in humorous ways, and were largely objects of parody in Edo art (and thereafter).

SYMBOLS AND SECRECY
Rosicrucian beliefs

▲ Written in code
Alchemist Daniel Mögling's 1618 *Speculum Sophicum Rhodostauroticum* ("Mirror of the Wisdom of the Rosy Cross") includes oblique references to a "symbol of Theophrastus" (Paracelsus) and to unnamed "spirits or intelligences" known to Rosicrucian initiates.

As religious wars raged between Catholic and Protestant nations in early-17th-century Europe, a secret society was born. Two manifestos, the *Fama Fraternitatis* and *Confessio Fraternitatis*, were published anonymously in Germany around 1614, followed by a coded mystical allegory called *Chymical Wedding of Christian Rosenkreutz*. These described the origins of a select "Rosicrucian" brotherhood and alluded to obscure mystical knowledge, passed down since ancient times, that only the initiated few could access. In 1623, a mysterious poster appeared in Paris, France, announcing that members of the "Higher College of the Rose-Croix" were in the city. The poster did not reveal their whereabouts, asserting that "the thoughts attached to the real desire of the seeker will lead us to him and him to us."

Shrouded in mystery
According to the *Fama Fraternitatis*, the first priority of a Rosicrucian was to heal the sick, for free. But the manifesto is mostly concerned with the travels of legendary German monk Christian Rosenkreuz, who acquired mystical knowledge from Kabbalists (see pp.122–123) and Spanish *alumbrados* or "illuminists" (followers of a secret society that studied the sciences and practiced a mystical form of Christianity), among others. Allegedly discovered just before the manifestos were published, Rosenkreuz's tomb was a vault, described using sacred geometry and Kabbalistic number-letter codes. Later magical secret societies, such as the

Hermetic Order of the Golden Dawn, used the vault as inspiration for the design of their temples and other sacred spaces used for conjuring spirits.

Elemental spirits
The *Fama* celebrates Swiss alchemist Paracelsus's theory of "elemental spirits," which stated that each of the four classical elements has a corresponding spiritual being: gnomes or pygmies for the element earth, sylphs for air, undines or nymphs for water, and salamanders for fire. Rosicrucians were said to have mystical knowledge that allowed them to see and control these elemental spirits. As the Comte de Gabalis ("Count of Kabbalah") explained in a book published in Paris in 1670, the magical powers that come with esoteric knowledge (available to the chosen few) include command over "all the Invisible People who dwell in the four elements."

The Rosicrucian manifestos may have just been a satire on the part of Lutheran philosophy students, including Johann Valentin Andreae (author of *Chymical Wedding*), mocking the notion of secret knowledge. But some early modern thinkers, spiritual and scientific alike, professed an interest in Rosicrucianism, and the invisible order inspired real secret societies. Henry Adamson's 1638 poem "The Muses' Threnodie" provides an early link between Rosicrucianism and Freemasonry: "We are brethren of the Rosie Crosse, We have the Mason Word and second sight." This "second sight" (clairvoyance) was apparently granted by the Philosopher's Stone—a mythical marvel of alchemy—and allowed Rosicrucians to see the elemental spirits.

◀ Flower of wisdom
A symbol of alchemical and spiritual renewal, the rose cross (a rose on a thorny cross) was adopted as a badge of esoteric wisdom by later Rosicrucian-inspired groups, including the Ancient Mystical Order Rosae Crucis (AMORC), which was founded in 1915.

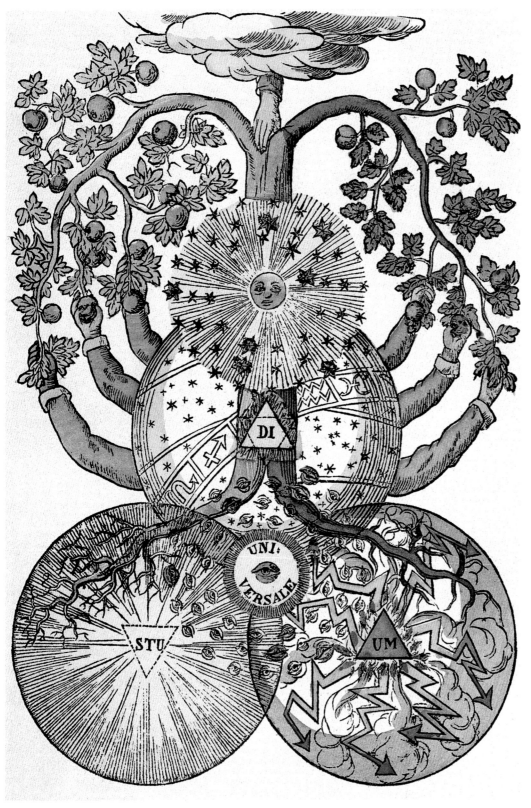

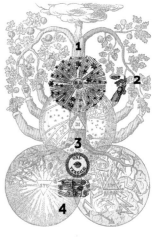

KEY

1 The sun is in the center, rising over good and evil and lighting the way.

2 Human hands reach for different pleasures: fruit, branches, leaves—good or evil. By grasping only for pieces, they are failing to see the whole truth.

3 The eye of wisdom is at the intersection of all three spheres, watching over the visible and invisible worlds.

4 Many other eyes wander freely, wanting to see for themselves but limited by the seeing power granted to them by the eye of wisdom.

◀ **Good or bad?**
Rosicrucian authors created books of alchemical emblems as well as mystical texts, mixing occult diagrams with allegorical and archetypal imagery. This drawing of the Biblical tree of knowledge of good and evil features in a 1785 edition of *Secret Symbols of the Rosicrucians*.

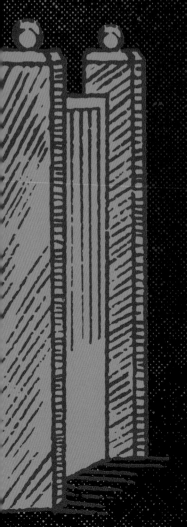

OCCULTISM
AND THE
UNDEAD

1700–1900

Introduction

Following the Reformation, Protestant theologians declared that ghosts were a Catholic fabrication—a superstition—and that there was no Purgatory, from which tortured souls might return to seek assistance from the living. Yet in the 18th and 19th centuries, the continued popular experience of occult encounters undermined the theological position.

Educated Protestants compiled accounts of ghosts as proof that God continued to work miracles in the world. The ghost became a common element in plays as a comedic, scary, or tragic device. And, well into the so-called Age of Enlightenment, some people— especially in parts of Central Europe—continued to argue that witches existed and posed a grave threat. Between 1720 and 1740, about 450 witch trials took place in Hungary, followed by another wave of mass trials around 1755, in which claims were made of vampires attacking people. In German territories, the last of the witch trials were accompanied by

numerous cases of magical treasure-hunting, carried out by bands of men armed with spades and spirit-conjuration grimoires (spellbooks).

The rise of spiritualism in the US and UK during the mid-19th century took many people by surprise. Some were shocked that, two centuries on from the worst of the witch trials, the middle classes were claiming to communicate with the dead. Clergymen wrote in books and pamphlets that such spirit-summoning was the work of the Devil, while some in the nascent psychiatry profession argued that it was a new outbreak of contagious insanity. By the end of the century, what had begun as an exciting parlor-room exercise, to be shared with friends, had become an established religion, with its own meeting halls and churches.

European slavery finally ended during the second half of the 19th century, but colonial plundering of the cultural heritage of the peoples of Africa and Asia continued, whether forcibly or through commerce.

Imagination running riot *see p.192*

Ghostly vessel *see p.201*

Enslaved as a zombie *see p.204*

Thousands of spiritual objects found their way into Western museums and private collections, such as carved wooden *nkisi* power objects from the Congo and amuletic scroll texts created by the holy men of the Ethiopian Christian churches. In North America, similar appropriations of sacred objects and lands took place at the same time as early anthropologists were recording the spiritual beliefs of the Nations that had imbued those objects and spaces with power. Meanwhile, in the Caribbean colonies, French and British authorities tried to suppress the syncretic spirit traditions that had emerged, such as Haitian Vodou.

The expansion of mass-literacy and cheap print gave rise to new forms of popular literature. Newspapers loved to titillate their readers with accounts of hauntings, instances of witchcraft, and the activities of magicians and fortune-tellers. In Britain, Victorian penny dreadfuls fictionalized the lurid newspaper reports of London's Spring-Heeled Jack, a demonic fire-breathing figure said to terrorize women. Novelists created new supernatural beings, such as Dracula, out of old traditions, and by the end of the 19th century, the Haitian zombie had begun to find its way into the growing pantheon of modern, global horror figures.

"… neither man, woman, nor child durst venture beyond the threshold … without a lantern and a thick club stick …"

REPORT OF SPRING-HEELED JACK APPEARING IN HAM AND PETERSHAM, *THE MORNING CHRONICLE*, JANUARY 10, 1838

Spiritualist seance *see p.222*

Victorian dramatics *see p.232*

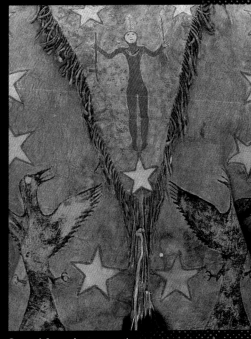

Sacred Arapaho garment *see p.240*

▲ **Graveyard ghost**
In 1804, witnesses reported that a ghost—a tall figure dressed in white—was haunting the Hammersmith churchyard in London and seizing passers-by. Armed patrols were set up, ending in the death of bricklayer Thomas Milward, who was mistaken for the ghost.

FACT OR FICTION?
ghost stories and compendiums

Ghosts were the subject of growing literary interest in the 18th century. Like the "anti-Saduccean" Christian works of the 17th century (see p.94), compendiums of ghost tales, such as Daniel Defoe's *Essay on the History and Reality of Apparitions* (1727), were used to prove the existence of the soul and its immortality. Defoe also wrote one of the first ghost stories. Unlike modern tales, "The Apparition of Mrs. Veal" (1706) is not full of thrills and chills; it tells the sedate story of two women having tea—one of them just happens to be dead. Its aim was to prove life after death, in keeping with the ideas of French Protestant theologian Charles Drelincourt; in fact, the fourth edition of the tale was published in Drelincourt's *Christian Defense Against the Fears of Death*.

Spectral tales

Ghost compendiums often contained a number of common narratives, such as the return of the dead to accuse their murderer, either by haunting the murderer or drawing someone else's attention to them. Another classic narrative was that of the "three-day return": two friends would make a pact stating that the first to die would return to the living to confirm the existence of an afterlife. Such tales usually ended with this confirmation and a warning to live a better life. Stories of people appearing to loved ones across the seas at the moment of their own death also abound. Many of these tropes reappeared in the overtly fictional ghost stories of the 19th century and onward.

"Mrs. Bargrave is the person to whom Mrs. Veal appeared after her death …"

"THE APPARITION OF MRS. VEAL," 1706, A PAMPHLET PUBLISHED ANONYMOUSLY BUT COMMONLY ATTRIBUTED TO DANIEL DEFOE

A TRUE
RELATION
OF THE
APPARITION
OF ONE
Mrs. *VEAL*,
The Next DAY after her DEATH,
TO ONE
Mrs. *BARGRAVE*,
AT
CANTERBURY,
The Eighth of *September*, 1705.

Which APPARITION recommends the Perusal of *DRELINCOURT*'s Book of *Consolations against the Fears of Death.*

The SIXTEENTH EDITION.

While ghost compendiums claimed to have an educational or theological purpose, they were also increasingly seen as a form of entertainment. Appearing in "graveyard" poetry (preoccupied with macabre imagery and death), on the stage (see pp.144–145), and in the emerging genre of Gothic literature (see pp.194–197), ghosts became popular and entertaining literary devices. In the cheap chapbooks of the late 18th and early 19th centuries, "real" ghost tales were printed alongside Gothic stories. The readers of collections like *Tales of Terror, or More Ghosts* (1802) were seeking the "delightful thrill" of terror, not to unriddle the mysteries of the afterlife.

Real ghosts
Ghosts were not confined to the page and the stage. Famous contemporary apparitions were subjects of public interest and acrimonious debate. Belief in

ghosts was rejected by some as "superstition" (often linked to Catholicism) or delusion (associated with "enthusiastic" religious groups such as the Methodists). Methodism founder John Wesley was known for his belief in ghosts due to his stories about "Old Jeffrey," the poltergeist that reportedly haunted his childhood home. On the other hand, those who denied the ghostly (often atheists) could be accused of "fanatical skepticism." As the debate about the existence of ghosts became increasingly polarized, supposed specters like "Scratching Fanny" (see p.282), the Lamb Inn Poltergeist (1762), and the Hammersmith ghost were the subject of inquiries, public ghost hunts, and newspaper wars of opinion in Britain.

▲ **Back from the grave**
"The Apparition of Mrs. Veal" is presented as a true story, and goes into extensive detail about witnesses and their reliability in order to support the tale. It was intended to prove that ghosts exist, rather than to thrill its readers.

◄ **Imagining the afterlife**
The public interest in ghosts reflected a broader interest in life after death. "Byron's Immortality," an illustration from *The Book of Spirits and Tales of the Dead* (c.1827), shows Lord Byron talking to other dead writers riding a cloud. It accompanies a piece of writing imagining Byron's sensations and experiences after death.

CORPSE BRIDES AND HAUNTED CASTLES

Gothic literature and the supernatural

In 1764, British writer Horace Walpole published *The Castle of Otranto* anonymously, passing it off as a translation of a medieval script. His "Gothic story" was an attempt to mix the supernatural adventures of medieval romance and the supposed realism of the modern novel to form a new type of literature. It is a blueprint for many early Gothic novels: a Catholic European location and historic setting; a damsel in distress; a noble hero; a tyrant; a disguised heir; a shady past; and vengeful, providential ghosts.

Terror and horror

The Gothic genre took off in the 1790s. The shelves of circulating libraries were stacked with "horrid novels" (as Jane Austen satirized them in *Northanger Abbey*) and Gothic authors became household names. There were two main schools of Gothic literature: terror and horror. The terror Gothic of

writers like Ann Radcliffe focused on heroines in peril, gave them a happy ending, and used few supernatural elements. Instead, most terror Gothic used the "supernatural explained": heroines encounter unexplained noises and shadowy figures but there is usually a rational explanation. In Radcliffe's *The Mysteries of Udolpho* (1794), for example, the "ghosts" are revealed to be pirates.

The horror Gothic of writers such as Matthew Lewis, on the other hand, featured blood, crime, murder, and supernatural entities that were both realistic and terrifying. Influenced by earlier German ghost stories, Lewis's *The Monk* (1796) tells the tale of the monk Ambrosio, who makes a deal with the Devil and leaves a trail of death and destruction behind him. Horrifying supernatural figures and bloody murderers fill the pages, among them crafty lesser demons, the Devil, and the infamous Bleeding Nun. Young lovers Raymond and Agnes scoff at the Bleeding Nun legend, and Agnes plans to dress as her to escape the castle she is held in. Raymond is dismayed to find the legend is real when he clasps not Agnes but a bleeding ghost in his arms.

▲ **Haunted castle**
The Castle of Otranto is full of paranormal events. Giant helmets fall from the sky and paintings come to life, as seen in this illustration of Manfred's dead ancestor stepping from the frame.

◄ **Bloody apparition**
In this scene from Matthew Lewis's *The Monk*, the hero, Raymond, is tricked into a pact with the ghost of the Bleeding Nun—a murderer whose spirit is trapped in Purgatory.

◄ *Abbey in the Oakwood*
Echoing the settings of early Gothic novels, many 19th-century Romantic paintings, such as this one by Caspar David Friedrich, depicted desolate, ruined, or haunted places. In Ann Radcliffe's *The Romance of the Forest* (1792), the heroine takes refuge in a ruined abbey, the site of a horrifying murder.

In the early 19th century, parodies such as Jane Austen's *Northanger Abbey* (1816) poked fun at Gothic novels. However, the public had not lost its taste for the bizarre, the macabre, and the supernatural. Ghosts crowded the stage, and short, cheap Gothic chapbooks, containing shorter Gothic tales or collections of ballads and stories, were popular. One of the most famous ballads was "Alonzo the Brave and Fair Imogine": this tale of a ghostly soldier returning to drag his unfaithful lover down to Hell was so well known that it spawned a series of parodies—even one by its own author, Matthew Lewis. Romantic poets, too, drew on the Gothic in supernatural poetry. Samuel Taylor Coleridge wrote long poems of supernatural curses, including "The Rime of the Ancient Mariner" (1798), and mysterious vampiric women such as "Christabel" (1816).

The ghost-story contest

Gothic history was made at the Villa Diodati in Switzerland in 1816, when Lord Byron, Percy Bysshe Shelley, Mary Godwin (later Shelley), and Byron's doctor, John Polidori, read German ghost stories and decided to hold a ghost-story-writing competition. Byron never finished his, but Polidori was inspired to create "The Vampyre," a tale of a predatory aristocrat, partly modeled on Byron, who ruins young men and kills young women to drink their blood.

The "Byronic hero" soon became an important part of 19th-century Gothic novels. Noble heroes were pushed aside and replaced with dark, brooding antiheroes in novels such as Emily Bronte's *Wuthering Heights* (1847) and Charlotte Bronte's *Jane Eyre* (1848). The Villa Diodati also gave birth to a different kind of monster. Mary Shelley's *Frankenstein* (1819), written for the ghost-story competition, combines Romantic themes with Gothic motifs and an early version of science fiction.

▼ Looming specters
Commercial Gothic writer Sarah Scudgell Wilkinson wrote more than 100 chapbooks, including *The Castle Spectre; or, Family Horrors: A Gothic Story* (1807), a tale filled with vengeance, lost love, and ghostly visitations.

L. GANIVET, ÉDITEUR.
J. CAZOTTE
ILLUSTRE PAR EDOUARD DE BEAUMONT
LE DIABLE AMOUREUX
SE VEND ICI:
20 CENTIMES LA LIVRAISON.

▲ French fantastic
Similar to later Gothic novels of demonic seduction, Jacques Cazotte's 1772 *Le Diable amoureux* ("The Devil in Love") is a classic tale of the French fantastic where the reader is never sure whether or not the hero is really seduced by the Devil.

A Gothic world

English writers did not hold a monopoly on Gothic fiction. The Scottish Gothic of writers like James Hogg, for example, mixed Scottish history, Calvinist religion, and demonic doubles. Hogg's *The Private Memoirs and Confessions of a Justified Sinner* (1824) features a religious fanatic who believes he is chosen by God but is tricked by the Devil into committing crimes.

Some of the earliest American novels were Gothic, often including the supernatural. In Charles Brockden Brown's *Wieland* (1798), a man murders his family on the order of "divine" voices. Most of the voices are explained, but uncertainty remains: is it madness, demons, or deceit? The American Gothic tradition was developed by writers such as Washington Irving, creator of the famous headless horseman of Sleepy Hollow (see pp. 212–213).

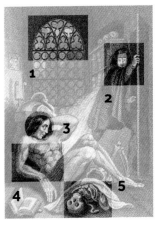

KEY

1 The "dim" light of the moon shines through the window, allowing Victor Frankenstein to behold his creation. Holst added another unsourced light lower down to illuminate the creature for the viewer.

2 Frankenstein flees in disgust and terror from his creation.

3 The first sign of life in the creature is when he opens his "dull, yellow eye."

4 Holst depicted the creature with a handsome face and classical pose. Frankenstein "selected his features as beautiful" but is horrified by the reality of the creature's appearance.

5 The living creature is pictured against skeletal remains, contrasting life and death and hinting at Frankenstein's "unhallowed" work to collect the pieces of his creature.

◄ **Creation of a monster**
In Theodore von Holst's frontispiece to the 1831 edition of *Frankenstein*, the eponymous protagonist Victor Frankenstein beholds his creation and rejects it, afraid and ashamed of what he has done.

MISCHIEF AND MAYHEM
goblins

Mythology and folklore are full of tales about small and ugly humanoids, who can by turns be helpful, malevolent, or mischievous. These wandering sprites are commonly known as goblins and variations on the theme appear in the legends of diverse cultures around the globe.

The word "goblin" possibly derives from the ancient Greek *kobalos*, meaning "rogue"—this became *kobold* in German. In Greek mythology, *kobaloi* were amusing trickster spirits who served the god Dionysus. In the 13th century, Germans carved figures of *kobolds* in their homes to attract useful imps, reflecting a common belief that fairies and goblins could bless a house. The term "hobgoblin" came to refer to a household or "hearth" spirit. Capable of protecting and provoking, the two-sided nature of goblins is a feature of many traditions. The *dokkaebi* of 13th-century Korea, for example, were believed to bring good luck but could also cause mental illness and start fires in the home.

In medieval European folklore, *kobolds* were believed to help with household chores at night. However, in return they demanded respect and, if this was lacking, could turn hostile. Germanic folklore includes the terrifying figure of *Hödeken*, a goblin who was insulted by a kitchen boy and tore him limb from limb.

Dangerous places

In Mesoamerican mythology, the *chaneque* (of the Mexica) and *alux* (of the Maya) were creatures that represented powerful elemental forces and acted as guardians of the natural world. If under threat, they could shape-shift, become invisible, and play other tricks. The word *chaneque* comes from the Nahuatl (Mexica) word meaning "those who inhabit dangerous places," and goblin-like creatures were often associated with underground, dark, or watery locations.

The Hindu holy text *Bhagavata Purana* describes Hara-Bhava, an aspect of the god Shiva, attended to by goblins in the subterranean realms of the universe. In the Central Andes, *muki* were believed to make precious metals appear or disappear and

▼ Little spirit
This wooden statue, carved by a Zulu artist, shows the South African *tokoloshe*, a goblin-like water spirit known for being small and mischievous.

so the miners made deals with them to get rich. In Wampanoag beliefs, *pukwudgies* were believed to lure people toward cliffs, while Japanese *kappas* haunted rivers and streams and pulled humans into their depths. Inhabitants of Flores, Indonesia, tell stories of *Ebu gogo*—small people that lived in the forest—based on ancient humans who really inhabited the area.

▼ Danger to swimmers
The *kappa* is a traditional Japanese *yokai*—supernatural being—that lures people into rivers. This 19th-century illustration shows its reptilian skin and sharp claws.

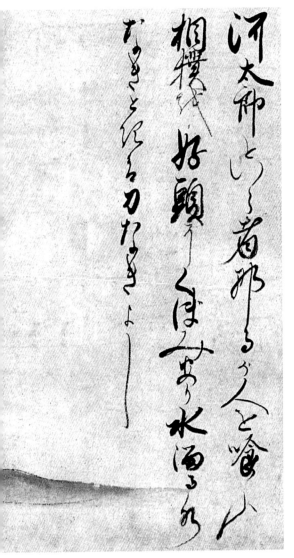

Evil portrayals
Goblins are popular figures in fairy tales, fantasy, and poetry. In J. R. R. Tolkien's Middle-Earth mythos, they represent "evil" in a symbolic battle with the "good"; in literature, the fantasy genre tends to emphasize a goblin's malevolent rather than protective side. The conceptualization of the European goblin has been influenced by antisemitic tropes, many of which are still evident in how goblins are portrayed. German woodcuts of the 15th century, for example, depicted Jewish people with grotesque faces—even today, depictions of goblins often share the same facial features.

▶ Goblin clergy
In this 1799 engraving, the artist Goya satirizes Spanish monks and priests by depicting them as grotesque goblins and highlighting their corruption.

> "Now goblins are cruel, wicked, and bad-hearted. They make no beautiful things, but they make many clever ones."

J. R. R. TOLKIEN, *THE HOBBIT* (1937)

PHANTOM GALLEONS
ghost ships

Appearing and disappearing at sea, so-called ghost ships have been reported since at least the 18th century. In 1786, during a storm off Prince Edward Island, Canada, the wardens of the Seacow Head Lighthouse reported seeing a ship driven toward deadly rocks, but the vessel vanished before it was wrecked. Since that time, many sightings have been recorded along Canada's Northumberland Strait, often just before a storm. Witnesses describe a vessel traveling at great speed, either engulfed in flames or with just the rigging on fire. When one such vessel was spotted in 1900, a rescue boat was launched, but no sign of the ship was ever found.

Strange lights

Many tales of ghost ships can be traced to historical shipwrecks. In 1738, disaster struck when the *Princess Augusta*, also known as the *Palatine* because it was carrying around 340 emigrants from the German Palatine region, ran aground in the treacherous waters off Rhode Island. Locals reported hearing screams and seeing the ship burning, and this ominous sight has been seen many times since—a phenomenon known as the Palatine Lights.

Ghost ships are often described as brightly lit. The Chiloé Archipelago, off the coast of southern Chile, is home to a phantom ship called *El Caleuche*. This galleon sails between the islands, with lights on and sounds of laughter and revelry coming from the deck. Legends differ; some say the ship was made by an Indigenous god to collect the spirits of those drowned at sea, while others claim it is captained by an evil sorcerer, looking to ensnare naive sailors.

No one onboard

The term "ghost ship" can also refer to ships that are physically real but just as mysterious. In 1872, an American merchant ship, the *Mary Celeste*, left New York, bound for Italy, but was discovered adrift a few weeks later, near the Azores. The last log entry had been made ten days previously, the rigging was in a poor state, and the lifeboat was gone, yet the cargo and supplies were still aboard. There were no clues as to why the crew might have abandoned the ship, but they were never seen again.

◀ **Spotted in the fog**
This 19th-century print shows a ghost ship that is said to emerge from the sea mists in Porthcurno, Cornwall, and sail onto the land, before vanishing like smoke.

LE VAISSEAU-FANTÔME

▲ **Abandoned ship**
This 1911 engraving from the newspaper *Le Petit Journal* shows American sailors on board the *Narragansett* discovering the old French warship *Le Richelieu*, adrift off the coast of Ireland with no crew aboard.

IN CONTEXT

Ghost carriages

When the poet Emily Dickinson used the image of Death driving a carriage in her 1890 poem "Because I could not stop for Death," she was drawing on a long folkloric tradition. Many tales were told of a black coach that traveled the roads at night, often pulled by headless or fire-breathing horses, and many believed that to see it was a bad omen—often a foreshadowing of death. Smugglers at Kingskerswell in Devon, UK, exploited these legends to scare locals away. They transported their goods in a hearse and painted this and the horses (but not their heads) with luminous paint.

THE TWO MEN IN THE GIG, or the Great Incendiary, & the G⁺ Man wot destroys Machinery

The Devil and Death driving a carriage are depicted in this satirical print from London, made in 1831.

The *Flying Dutchman*

Inspiring artists, poets, and composers across the centuries, the *Flying Dutchman* is the most famous ghost ship ever sighted. According to legend, the Dutch man-of-war was doomed to sail the seas forever. The first known references to the ship in print appeared in 1790, in Scottish adventurer John MacDonald's account of his 30 years spent at sea. The ship seemed to be associated with storms: according to MacDonald, the weather was so poor that his sailors reported seeing the *Flying Dutchman*.

Many subsequent accounts expand on the story of the spectral ship. Reports from the 18th and 19th centuries often state that the crew of the *Flying Dutchman* had committed some terrible but unnamed crime and, cursed with the plague as a result, were denied entry to any port. Other accounts claim the reckless captain made a pact with the Devil, or that the ship sank after the captain tried to round South Africa's Cape of Good Hope in a storm, damning his crew to an eternity sailing the same route. Legends also reference letters that the ghostly crew tried to pass to sailors, begging for them to be carried home to loved ones. These letters, too, are said to be cursed.

According to sailor's folklore, seeing the *Flying Dutchman* means imminent disaster. In 1881, the future King George V of Britain saw the *Flying Dutchman* as he sailed to Australia. The log book of HMS *Inconstant* records that, soon afterward, a crewman fell to his death from a mast.

> "Who hath seen the Phantom Ship, Her lordly rise and lowly dip …"

ALBERT PINKHAM RYDER, "THE *FLYING DUTCHMAN*," 1879

ETERNAL ENSLAVEMENT
Haitian zombie lore

▼ **Master's bidding**
Haitian Surrealist painter Hector Hyppolite's 1946 work *Vol de Zombis* depicts a grave-robbing *bokor* and his soulless zombies. Fear of never-ending enslavement remained long after colonial rule ended in Haiti.

The brain-eating zombies (see pp.206–207) that now dominate popular culture are not quite the same as those in Haitian folklore. In Haiti, *zonbi* or *zombi* can signify bodiless souls (*zombi astral*) or soulless bodies (*zombi cadavre*), created and controlled by Vodou sorcerers called *bokors*. A *zombi cadavre* is produced when a *bokor* kills and then reanimates their victim with the intention of enslaving them.

The more common *zombi astral* is created when a *bokor* traps a person's spirit in a container and then uses it to enact the sorcerer's wishes.

The origin of the word *zombi* is unclear. It has been linked to Nzambi, the supreme being of the BaKongo people (who now inhabit the Democratic Republic of the Congo), and to the BaKongo practice of creating *zumbi*, bottle fetishes that

capture souls. It may also stem from a variety of West and Central African words that sound like "zombie" and refer to spirits of the dead, corpses, revenants, and so on.

Dying for freedom

In the 17th and 18th centuries, French colonizers put enslaved Africans to work on Haitian sugar plantations. Early colonialist accounts described Haitian beliefs about haunting spirits (almost always in astral form), and the term "zombie" was first used by French writer Pierre-Corneille de Blessebois in his 1697 novel *Le Zombi du Grand Perou* ("The Zombie of Greater Peru"). Haiti's zombie phenomenon is rooted in memories of how enslavement took away people's free will, subjecting them to relentless, inescapable labor. To many enslaved people, death was the only way to gain freedom and return to *Lan Guinée* (Africa) in the afterlife. (Suicide was not an option, as they believed it would leave their spirits trapped in their bodies.)

Fear of eternal enslavement continued to haunt Haitians after slavery ended. Social inequality was still widespread, and labor exploitation returned under US military occupation in the early 20th century. For Haitians, who cherished freedom even if it meant death, zombification was the ultimate nightmare: not alive, nor dead, nor free.

Terrifying tales

Haitian zombies continued to be fodder for wider literature in the 19th and 20th centuries, featuring in Haitian poet Ignace Nau's *Isalina, ou une scène créole* ("Isalina, or a Creole scene," 1836); US journalist William Seabrook's account of Vodou in Haiti, *The Magic Island* (1929; see p.206); and in the memoirs of

US soldiers stationed in occupied Haiti. Zombies remain a disturbing specter in Haiti today, where their existence is supported by the Vodou worldview (see pp.174–175). Fear of a *bokor*'s ability to turn people into zombies is real enough; Article 249 of the Haitian Penal Code explicitly bans the practice. Controversially, zombification has been viewed by some as a means for leaders in Vodou-practicing communities to punish bad behavior, making fear of being turned into a zombie a form of social control. Like other frightening folkloric creatures around the world, tales about zombies are used by Haitian parents to teach their children about acceptable social behavior.

▲ **Forced labor**
This 1749 engraving depicts sugar-cane processing, which remains a major industry in the neighboring countries of Haiti and the Dominican Republic. Poor working conditions continue to fuel anxieties about zombification.

"Although they have no tongues, zombies [can] speak of a particular time and place."

JEAN COMAROFF AND JOHN L. COMAROFF, "OCCULT ECONOMIES AND THE VIOLENCE OF ABSTRACTION: NOTES FROM THE SOUTH AFRICAN POSTCOLONY," PUBLISHED IN *AMERICAN ETHNOLOGIST*, 1999

THE LIVING DEAD
revenants and zombies

▲ Ungodly revenants
These 16th-century frescoes in Kirke Hyllinge church, Denmark, show corpses rising from their graves. Christians believed in bodily resurrection on Judgment Day, but those who returned early or for evil purposes were considered revenants.

Reanimated corpses rising from the grave are a staple of modern popular culture and appear in the folklore of many ancient civilizations. What the dead can do, once animated, depends on the legend.

The first reference to the living dead features in the oldest story to have survived from the ancient world. In the *Epic of Gilgamesh* (from Mesopotamia, c. 2000 BCE), when the goddess Ishtar is spurned by the hero, she threatens to raise the dead, who will "devour" the living and overpower them in number.

The archaeological study of ancient burial sites suggests that fear of the returning dead was widespread. Graves at the ancient Greek necropolis of Passo Marinaro, Sicily, were found to contain bodies that had been weighed down with stones, as if to hold them in place. Other sites show similar precautions taken—bodies buried face-down, or with stakes driven through the chest.

Walking corpses
Revenants, from the French word *revenir* ("to return"), are corpses that come back from the dead and are found in many European folk beliefs from the Middle Ages. They appear in Norse sagas as *draugr*, which stink of death and are immune to weapons. However, in Christian cultures, revenants became a spiritual rather than a magical concern, believed to be animated by demonic powers or due to the dead person's soul being "unclean."

The 12th-century writers William of Newburgh and Walter Map record many accounts of walking corpses, related as a common occurrence and described as a factual event. Revenants show more free will than is usually attributed to a zombie—although in Haitian folklore, the latter can occur either as soulless bodies or as bodiless souls (see

▶ Vodou zombies
William Seabrook's 1929 book *The Magic Island* (see p.205), brought Haitian zombie lore to a wider audience and influenced later representations of the living dead.

▶ Undead steed
This Buddhist art shows the deity Mahakala riding on the back of a *ro-lang* ("risen corpse"). This creature could supposedly be created through spiritual practice.

pp.204–205)—and often seem to target those who had wronged them in life. In an age of rampant disease, revenants were also associated with pestilence, or as an omen of plague, and were dealt with by cutting off the head or burning the body.

Modern horrors
The Haitian concept of zombies was introduced to the wider world after the US occupation of the island (1915–1934) and inspired many Hollywood films, such as *White Zombie* (1932). Some early examples did not use the term "zombie," as was the case in H. P. Lovecraft's story "Herbert West–Reanimator" (1921), in which the protagonist tries to reanimate corpses scientifically. The term was also absent in director George A. Romero's *Night of the Living Dead* (1968), which called its undead beings "ghouls." Nonetheless, Romero's film codified many of today's commonly recognized zombie tropes, and the sequels of the franchise call them by that name.

CURSED BOUNTIES
treasure-hunting in North America

▲ **Guardian ghost**
A motley group of treasure-hunters dig for pirate loot in a colonial cemetery in John Quidor's painting *The Money Diggers* (1832). The hunt is led by a sorcerer wearing a red cape. Quidor captures the moment when the trio spot a pirate ghost on the cliff above them.

Treasure-hunting using supernatural aid (see p.157) had long been practiced in Europe, and was transplanted to North America as a result of European colonization. Life for the early colonists was challenging, between food shortages and wars with the Indigenous population, but the idea of striking it rich, which drew many to the colonies in the first place, gave people hope. Encouraged by tales of European treasure hunts, colonists searched for buried wealth in the land in which they had

settled, convinced that valuable minerals or other bounty could be found using divining rods and other occult techniques of European folk magic.

Treasure-hunters may have consulted almanacs containing astrological and mystical information. Often, these gave common-sense advice, such as the best time to plant crops and perform other activities according to the stars. People from every level of society used such almanacs, from the poorest farmer to the most educated landowner.

However, "money digging" was primarily an activity for the poor or those down-on-their-luck. Finds were rare, but this did not dampen the enthusiasm of the seekers. They used diverse techniques, from rituals and spells to engaging mystics or mediums to lead them in their hunts. People also gazed into gems called "peep stones" or "seer stones" for guidance. Digging was carried out in silence so as not to alert the spirits guarding the treasure.

Pirate booty

Folklore held that coastal New England was haunted by ghost ships, which fostered the belief that pirates had buried their loot in the area. Hunters believed such treasure was protected by guardian spirits, possibly those of sacrificed crew members. One account from the 1820s describes diggers scared off by gigantic ghosts and spirits riding spectral horses. To ward off ghosts, hunters marked the ground with three concentric circles. Another method involved sacrificing an animal at the site. The most famous treasure that was sought belonged to Captain Kidd, a famed pirate. New England became riddled with holes and tunnels created by people hunting for his treasure.

As colonists spread west, stories of pirate treasure gave way to legends of gold buried by Indigenous peoples. The ghostly guards of these troves were thought to be particularly dangerous because of the violent ways in which the government had displaced these peoples from their ancestral lands.

▼ **Legendary loot**
The notorious pirate captain William Kidd watches as his crew bury treasure in this 19th-century engraving. Adventure novels about Kidd further motivated American treasure-hunters in their search for his hoard.

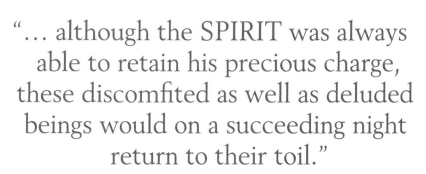

"… although the SPIRIT was always able to retain his precious charge, these discomfited as well as deluded beings would on a succeeding night return to their toil."

NEWSPAPER ARTICLE ON TREASURE-HUNTERS, PALMYRA, NEW YORK, 1831

TERRIFYING TALES
the golden age of the ghost story

Ghost stories became a literary craze in Victorian Britain. Short fictional works with a supernatural element set in a recognizable modern world, they usually included haunted cities, houses, or people, and incorporated new ideas about ghosts from spiritualism (see pp. 222–225). They were written to scare, thrill, inform, or pass on a moral message.

The genre entered a golden age in the mid-19th century, which lasted until the early 20th century. Popular writers such as Charles Dickens, Margaret Oliphant, Elizabeth Gaskell, and Charlotte Riddell produced ghostly tales for magazines or short story collections. Special issues of magazines were often released at Christmas, in keeping with the British tradition of festive ghost stories. The most famous of these is Dickens's "A Christmas Carol" (1843), in which three spirits visit the miser Scrooge and teach him the true meaning of Christmas. Other Christmas tales were more horrifying. Elizabeth Gaskell's tragic "The Old Nurse's Story" (1852) tells of a house haunted by a woman and child murdered by the cruelty of the woman's father and sister.

New ways to scare
There were many types of ghost story. Some tales borrowed from earlier folkloric traditions in which ghosts returned with a specific purpose: to reveal a murderer, for revenge, or to point out a missing treasure. Many, however, were influenced by new ideas linked to the rise of spiritualism, and mediums are common characters. In Rose Terry Cooke's "My Visitation" (1858), an unnamed narrator is visited by the ghost of the woman she loved.

Some writers looked for new ways of creating and exploring fear. Edgar Allan Poe's ghost stories, including "The Black Cat" (1843),

◄ Demonic vision?
In "Green Tea," the reader is left to speculate whether the monkey haunting Jennings is a hallucination from too much green tea, or whether the vicar's occult studies have summoned an unexpected visitor.

in which a cat appears to return from the dead to unveil a murder, relied on psychological terror, mental disintegration, and uncertainty. Henry James, meanwhile, played with open endings. In his masterpiece *The Turn of the Screw* (1898), the reader never knows whether the governess's story of a wicked haunting and a child's death is true, or whether it is based on her own delusions.

Tales of the unexplained
Authors increasingly explored the supernatural beyond ghosts, with weird tales of the inexplicable. One of the best-known writers of the golden age of ghost stories, Sheridan Le Fanu published "Green Tea" in 1872. In this story, a vicar is haunted by a demonic monkey. More famous still, the ghost storyteller M. R. James mixes ghosts with moving mezzotints, demonic manuscripts, well-dwelling creatures, and even vampiric face-eaters.

Golden-age ghost stories continue to fascinate and entertain today, with films and television adaptations ready to scare a new generation all around the world. *The Turn of the Screw* alone has been adapted multiple times, in different languages, producing films like *The Innocents* (1961) and shows like *The Haunting of Bly Manor* (2020).

▶ Fireside storytelling
Ghost stories were not just for reading alone—they were for sharing. Many ghost stories start with a group of friends sitting around a fire. In Alfred Bestall's 1930 illustration *The Ghost Story*, the family are not the only ones listening.

▼ Short but spooky
Ghost stories were usually short, so they could be read in one sitting. First published in 1908, *Tales of Mystery & Imagination* contains some of Edgar Allan Poe's classic tales, including "The Black Cat," "The Tell-Tale Heart," and "The Masque of the Red Death."

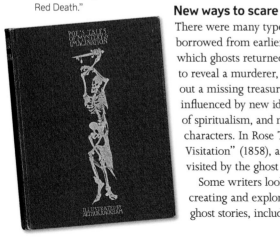

The Legend of Sleepy Hollow

Washington Irving's "The Legend of Sleepy Hollow" (1819) is one of America's most famous spooky short stories. It is the tale of school teacher Ichabod Crane, a newcomer to Sleepy Hollow, New York, who has his eye on the beautiful Katrina Van Tassel and her land. Locally, rumors abound of a headless horseman—said to be a Hessian (German soldier), who fought for the British in the American Revolution (1775–1783) and now rides at night with his head under his arm. One evening, Ichabod is chased by the horseman, and disappears. A smashed pumpkin found at the scene suggests that his pursuer was not a specter, but rather Katrina's favored suitor, Brom Bones, playing a trick on his superstitious rival. But Ichabod is never seen again.

Irving was influenced by his travels in Europe, and especially by German folklore and the headless spirit Numbernips from Johann Karl August Musäus's *Legends of Rübezahl* (1865). Yet Irving created a particularly American myth (albeit a colonial one), taking his ghost from the American Revolution, tying the tale to the Dutch history of the Hudson Valley, and relegating Indigenous beliefs to the postscript. The legend is still popular today, with yearly festivals and numerous reimaginings in fiction and on film.

> "The specter is known at all the country firesides, by the name of the Headless Horseman of Sleepy Hollow."

WASHINGTON IRVING, "THE LEGEND OF SLEEPY HOLLOW," 1819

▲ **Ichabod Crane is pursued by the headless horseman** past the Old Dutch Church in this 1856 painting by William John Wilgus.

▲ **Piercing the heart**
The usual method of dealing with suspected vampires was a stake through the heart.
They were often said to scream as the blow was struck.

BLAME IT ON THE DEAD
vampire panics

The vampire rose to infamy in the 18th century, after a series of cases gave rise to vampire panics in some parts of Europe and, later, the US. Bodies were exhumed and mutilated as friends and family members tried to come to terms with unexplained deaths. There are many possible reasons for the vampire panics: a lack of knowledge of bodily decomposition, epidemic disease, or malnutrition. But no one can be quite sure of the ultimate cause.

Detecting vampires

In 1725, a Serbian peasant called Peter Blagojević was accused of killing eight people after his death. Before dying, the victims all reported that Peter had visited them in the night and strangled them. Accompanied by the local priest and Imperial Provisor Ernst Frombald, an Austrian official, the villagers exhumed Peter's body and found all the signs of a vampire: he had not decomposed, had long hair and nails, and had fresh blood on his mouth. They staked his corpse and blood erupted from his ears and mouth. Frombald sent his report to Austria, where it was published in a newspaper and circulated widely. Suddenly, vampires were the subject of scientific and theological inquiry.

A similar case occurred in Medwegya, Serbia, in 1731, and investigators were sent in to determine the reality of these vampiric claims. The military doctor who went to investigate witnessed the dying victims and opened graves, and returned an official report that sided with the locals, confirming the existence of vampires.

Have no mercy

The first known vampire scare in the US happened in June 1784. Many people at the time were dying of tuberculosis, which was believed to be caused by vampires. In a letter to the editor of a local paper, Moses Holmes warned readers about a foreign doctor who was advising people to dig up and desecrate the corpses of their relatives. To find a vampire, corpses would be exhumed and examined to see if they were fresh and contained liquid blood—if so, they would be burned. Various New Englanders carried out the doctor's ritual, including Isaac Burton, who dug up his first wife in 1793, believing her to be causing the sickness of his second.

The most famous New England "vampire" is Mercy Brown, who died of tuberculosis in 1892. When Mercy's brother Edwin fell ill, her body was exhumed and found to be barely decomposed. Her liver and bloody heart were burned and made into a tonic for her brother, but it did not save him.

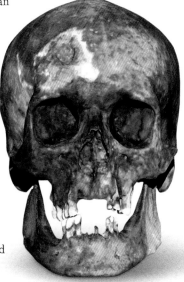

▲ **Desecrated victim**
The skeleton of suspected vampire John Barber, who died in 1855, was found in Griswold, Connecticut, in 1990. The head and legs had been removed, and the rib cage ripped open to extract the heart.

IN CONTEXT

Vampire chronicles

Augustin Calmet was a French Roman Catholic monk who is most famous today for his *Dissertation on the Apparitions of Angels, Demons, and Spirits, and on the Revenants and Vampires of Hungary, Bohemia, Moravia and Silesia*, published in 1746. He applied scientific and theological reason to vampire cases and came up with potential natural explanations or logical flaws in the stories. In the end, though, he concluded that "we must keep silence … since it has not pleased God to reveal to us either the extent of the demon's power, or the way in which these things can be done."

Calmet's revised edition of his best-selling work in 1751; the newly titled treatise featured spirits, vampires, and revenants, but no longer covered angels.

TRAITÉ
SUR LES
APPARITIONS
DES ESPRITS,
ET
SUR LES VAMPIRES,
OU LES REVENANS
de Hongrie, de Moravie, &c.

Par le R. P. Dom AUGUSTIN CALMET,
Abbé de Sénones.

Nouvelle édition revûe, corrigée & augmentée
par l'Auteur.

TOME I.

A PARIS,
Chez DEBURE l'aîné, Quai des Augustins,
à l'Image S. Paul.

M. D. CC. LI.
Avec Approbation & Privilege du Roi.

BLOODSUCKING MONSTERS
vampires

People have long told stories of terrible beings that prey on the blood of the living. In ancient Mesopotamia (see pp.22–25), the demon Lamashtu was believed to kill children; drink the blood of men and eat their flesh; cause miscarriages; and bring its victims nightmares. In Assyria 4,000 years ago, a mother wrote a protection spell against the *ekimmu*—angry vampiric spirits thought to drain the life from sleeping children and possess the dead bodies of victims. Ancient Greek *lamiae* were ravenous female spirits who seduced men and then consumed them. Later, in medieval England, William of Newburgh recorded tales of walking corpses, the bodies of unholy men, spreading pestilence by lying on top of their victims. He calls one of them a *sanguisuga*, meaning "bloodsucker."

Living dead
The "vampire" comes from Central and Eastern European folklore and mythology: the Romanian *strigoi*, Slavic *upir*, Greek *vrykolakas*, and Serbian *vampir*. These diverse but connected traditions of the living dead coalesced into the 18th-century idea of a vampire—a corpse reanimated by demons or unable to rest due to some crime committed while alive—and spawned panics across Europe and the US (see pp.214–215).

Vampires were said to prey on those they knew in life, gradually sucking their blood and life away. Their victims seemed to die of a mysterious and untreatable illness, so vampire cases are often linked to outbreaks of disease. People developed ways of dealing with suspected vampires, such as burning them, removing body parts, or thrusting a stake through the corpse's heart.

▼ **Femme fatale**
Polish Surrealist artist Boleslaw Biegas used vampiric creatures as an allegory for the battle between the sexes. In *A Vampire in the Form of a Lizard* (1916), a naked man is overpowered by a large reptilian vampire with wings and the head of a woman.

▲ **Unquenchable thirst**
In Filipino folklore, the word *aswang* describes a whole host of mythical creatures, all of which love to feast on human blood and flesh. They are often depicted with long, pointed tongues, which they use to suck up blood and viscera.

Other bloodsuckers
Vampire-like creatures feature in legends from around the world. In Ewe folklore of Togo and Ghana, the *adze* turns into a firefly to pass through keyholes and suck the blood of its victims. The Caribbean *soucouyant* is an old woman by day, but at night strips off her skin and enters people's homes as a fireball before drinking their blood. A vampiric creature from Peruvian tales, the *pishtaco* often comes in the guise of a white man and feeds not on blood but on the fat of its victims. Meanwhile, in the Philippines, the *manananggal* can split her body in two, with her torso growing wings to help her hunt. Her usual victims are pregnant women and she uses her long tongue to suck out the heart of the unborn child.

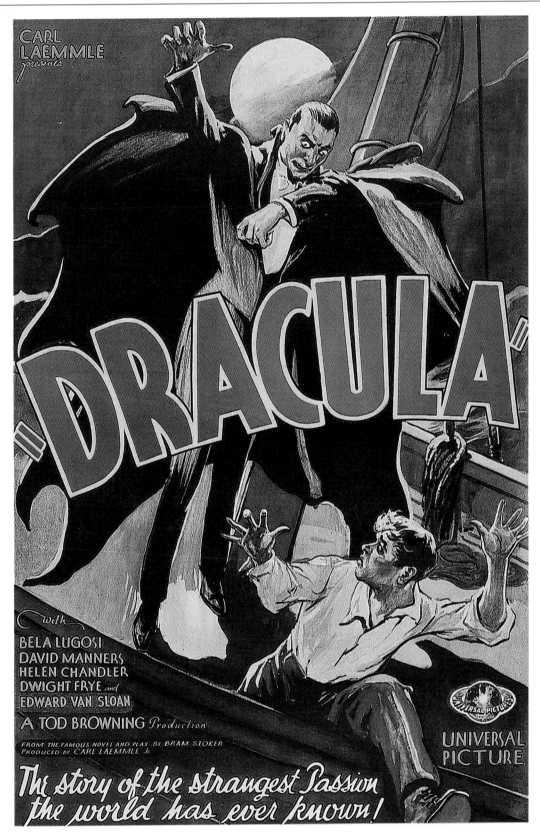

◄ **Cursed count**
Bram Stoker's 1897 novel
Dracula inspired some of the
first horror films, including
this 1931 adaptation. Stoker
was inspired by previous
vampire tales like Sheridan
Le Fanu's *Carmilla* (1872),
by "real" cases of vampirism,
and by Vlad of Wallachia—
also known as Vlad Dracula
("Son of the Dragon")—who
famously impaled his victims
on spikes.

Incubi and succubi

Demons have long been supposed to come to humans in their sleep. Both nightmares and night terrors were thought to be caused by demons, visiting sleepers during the hours of darkness, when a person's spiritual defenses were believed to be at their weakest. Two of the most feared examples of these demons were named in medieval times as incubi and succubi.

The male incubus was thought to seduce women while they were sleeping. Its name derives from the Latin *incubare*: "one who lies on top." Some versions of the British legends of King Arthur claimed that the wizard Merlin was fathered by an incubus and there was a common belief that human-demon couplings resulted in half-demon offspring.

The succubus was described as a beautiful female demon who seduced sleeping men. Its name also comes from Latin—in this case, *succubare*: "one who lies under." According to Jewish folklore, Adam's first wife, Lilith, who deserted him, returned as a succubus and haunted men with sexual dreams.

In the Middle Ages, when chastity was prized in general, and particularly by those in religious orders, these demons were considered a threat to salvation. Succubi and incubi were believed to work together, by stealing semen from a man and impregnating a sleeping woman. According to King James I of England, they even took bodily fluids from the dead to create their unnatural children.

"Incubus and Succubus devils have always existed."

MALLEUS MALEFICARUM, A TREATISE ON WITCHES, 1486

▲ **An incubus crouches with an air of menace** on top of a sleeping woman in Henry Fuseli's 1781 painting *The Nightmare*.

SOULS RETURNING HOME

Māori *kehua* and spirits

▼ **Phantom canoe**
This painting by Kennett Watkins depicts a *waka wairua* (spirit canoe) gliding across the North Island's Lake Tarawera in 1886. Māori witnesses to the ghostly apparition saw it as an omen of disaster when, 11 days later, on June 10, 1886, Mount Tarawera erupted, killing many and causing devastation to the area.

The Māori of Aotearoa (New Zealand), like other Polynesian peoples, believe they came originally from an ancient homeland called Hawaiki where their *atua* (ancestral spirits) reside. Māori spiritual beliefs have been passed on orally, through stories and songs. They believe in guardian ancestral spirits, various ghosts, and fairylike beings, but such beliefs are considered a *tapu* (sacred or taboo) subject, not to be discussed with outsiders.

The Māori believe that a person's *wairua* (spirit) remains near the corpse of the deceased until burial. Eased by the *tuku wairua* ritual, in which chants of farewell are made and relatives cut off locks of their hair, the *wairua* travel to Cape Reinga, or Te Rerenga Wairua ("the leaping place of the spirits"), at the far northern end of the North Island. There, spirits descend to Rarohenga (the underworld), a place of light and peace, by sliding down the roots of an ancient pōhutukawa tree. From Rarohenga, spirits return to Hawaiki, the land of the ancestors.

Some *wairua* do not succeed in returning to Hawaiki, either because their burial rites were incorrect, they were stillborn, or their deeds in life were so evil that the underworld refused

to take them. They become *kehua* (ghosts) who appear in dreams or to *tohungas* (priests), who act as mediums to communicate with dead spirits. Not intrinsically evil, *kehua* can appear in *kehua atua* (spirit processions) that portend disaster, as was reported at Mount Tarawera in 1886. They may also inhabit the bodies of the *kakariki*, a bright green lizard that makes a sound like malicious laughter. *Kikokiko*, the *kehua* of evil people, can cause disease or possess the living.

Shy spirits and sea fairies

According to oral tradition, the landscape of Aotearoa was populated by supernatural beings when the Māori first arrived. *Patupaiarehe*, shy fairylike creatures with light skin and red or fair hair, who sometimes kidnapped Māori women, lived in forests and on high mountaintops. They built their houses from vines or swirling mist and ate only raw forest produce or fish. Cooked food drove them away, as they could not abide its smell. The *maero* were more feared. Huge, with bodies covered in dark hair, they wielded stone clubs and attacked any humans who entered their domains. They had lived in Aotearoa before the Māori and resented their displacement.

The *ponaturi*, sea fairies with red hair and white skin, dreaded daylight but came on land at night, slashing human victims with their long, razor-sharp claws. One story tells of a Māori hero, Tāwhaki, taking revenge on *ponaturi* who had killed his father by trapping them in his house until dawn. He then opened all the windows and doors, flooding it with light, which killed them. As with the *kehua*, however, the Māori believe it is better to respect such creatures and avoid angering them—or to have a holy man perform rituals to dispel them.

▲ **Ancestral home**
Canoes prepare to depart the ancestral homeland of Hawaiki in search of new lands in this 20th-century engraving. Hawaiki is important as the place where every Māori returns after death. It is also the place where the supreme being Io created the world.

▶ **Forbidden touch**
A woman feeds a *tohunga* (priest) with a long fork in this c.1920 photograph. The hands of Māori holy men were considered *tapu* (sacred or taboo) because of their association with *atua* (ancestral spirits) and ghosts. This prohibited them from feeding themselves or being touched.

"If I die you must snatch my spirit, as it will surely pass this way on its journey to Te Rerenga Wairua."

TŌHĒ, CHIEF OF THE NGĀTI KAHU TRIBE, INSTRUCTING HIS PEOPLE ON WHAT TO DO IF HE DIED ON THE JOURNEY TO FIND HIS DAUGHTER

CROSSING THE VEIL
spiritualist beliefs

Modern spiritualism began in the United States in 1848 when two sisters, Kate and Maggie Fox, claimed that they were communicating with spirits. The spirits, they said, answered their questions and requests with rapping sounds. This was not the first incident of "ghost rapping": the supposed "Cock Lane Ghost" (see p.282) in 1762 had communicated in the same way. However, this earlier case was revealed as a hoax at the time.

The conceptual groundwork for a new interpretation of the rapping phenomenon had been laid by the work of Emanuel Swedenborg and Franz Mesmer. Swedenborg, a Swedish mystic, had asserted that spirits revealed the spiritual world to him. In it, there was a series of hells and heavens through which spirits moved, and an intermediary location known as the "world of spirits." Spirits, he claimed, could communicate with the living.

"Mesmerism," also called "animal magnetism," held that there was an invisible force in all beings that connected them and could be used for healing as well as inducing trances. Influenced by the work of both Mesmer and Swedenborg, Andrew Jackson Davis—who became known as the "Poughkeepsie Seer"—wrote his 1847 book *The Principles of Nature, Her Divine Revelations, and a Voice to Mankind* while in a trance. In it, he stated that spirits could converse with each other in and out of the body. It became an important spiritualist text. Davis welcomed the Fox sisters' claims as proof of his theories and invited them to New York City, which led to their growing fame and the rise of spiritualism.

The movement spreads

Spiritualism grew quickly, arriving in Britain in the 1850s and spreading globally by the 1860s. There was no rigid set of beliefs or practices. Instead, believers congregated around spirit mediums and their meetings. All spiritualists, however, held beliefs in a spirit world, a continued existence after death, the possibility of communication with spirits, and the reality of spiritual development after death. Spiritualist journals like *Banner of Light* (1857–1907) provided a way of sharing ideas and beliefs.

By the 1870s, spiritualist churches had appeared, and many spiritualist congregations still exist around the world today. There is no centralized hierarchy, but most churches usually belong to at least one of the large associations, such as the Spiritualists' National Union (UK), the National Spiritualist Association of Churches (US), and the International Spiritualist Federation. These societies support the work of spiritualists and offer guiding principles for spiritualist beliefs. In Britain, for example, the Spiritualists' National Union, founded in 1902, promotes seven key principles of spiritualism. Historically, it played an important role in defining the legal position of mediums, who were liable to prosecution under the Vagrancy Act (1824) for "fortune-telling" or the Witchcraft Act (1735), which was occasionally used to prosecute spiritualists as frauds.

▲ **Spirit communication**
An image of the "spiritual telegraph" from Andrew Jackson Davis's book *The Present Age and Inner Life* (1853) shows communication between spirits and the living via a telegraphic cable-like line.

IN CONTEXT

The Fox sisters

The Fox sisters were central to the rise of spiritualism in the mid-19th century. Kate and Maggie were young girls when they claimed that the rapping in their bedroom came from a murdered peddler. After being invited by Andrew Jackson Davis to New York City, they began charging people to see their demonstrations. With their older sister, Leah, they became professional mediums and apparently dedicated spiritualists. In 1888, Maggie, who had left the movement earlier, revealed that the "rappings" were a hoax created using apples on strings and later by cleverly cracking their toe joints.

Celebrity sisters (left to right) Leah, Kate, and Maggie Fox helped spark the growth of spiritualism in 19th-century America and Europe.

A popular movement

Spiritualism rose to prominence against a background of changing beliefs. At its epicenters in the US and the UK, spiritualism provided an alternative to traditional Christian beliefs that emphasized the impossibility of communication with the dead and a bleak afterlife of eternal punishment for sinners. Spiritualism instead offered the possibility of communing with lost loved ones. It is no coincidence that spiritualism became popular during the American Civil War (1861–1865), a conflict that saw mass casualties on both sides.

Spiritualism may also have offered comfort to parents who had lost their children. In the mid-19th century, 20–40 percent of children in the US died before the age of five. "Spirit children" (dead children who continued to grow and mature

◀ **Print boom**
Spiritualist texts proliferated in the late 19th century. This example, *Art Magic; Or Mundane, Sub-Mundane, and Super-Mundane Spiritism* (1876) was edited by the English spiritualist writer Emma Hardinge Britten and her husband.

in the afterlife) became central to the practice of some mediums who claimed to communicate with them, and they appeared to their parents at mass seances.

Spiritualist influences

Other belief systems developed from spiritualism. Spiritism (see pp.230–231), which was particularly popular in Brazil, was based on the work of Allan Kardec in the 1850s. Some spiritualist communities grew out of societal pressures rather than alternative beliefs. In the US, Jim Crow laws—which enforced racial segregation—prevented Black Americans from joining white spiritualist congregations. This led to the formation of the National Colored Spiritualist Association of Churches. Many Black spiritualist churches absorbed beliefs from forms of Christianity or from the syncretic religions (see pp.172–175) practiced by the community.

A variety of different practices emerged from spiritualism, including psychic surgery, which developed in Brazil and the Philippines in the 20th century. In psychic surgery, the practitioner lays their bare hands upon the affected body part and supposedly can remove growths (without an incision) or otherwise heal through spiritual guidance alone. The practice has been decried by medical professionals and led to legal trials for fraud. Other, less controversial, ways of communing with the spiritual world include practices such as spirit painting and psychography (automatic writing; see p.228). In both of these examples, practitioners seemingly have their hands guided by spirits while in a trance.

▼ **Community leader**
Mother Catherine Seals was a spiritualist healer and leader who founded the Temple of the Innocent Blood in New Orleans in 1922. Mother Seals, depicted here c.1925, was mentored by Leafy Anderson, founder of the Black American spiritual church movement.

"It is a truth that spirits commune with one another while one is in the body and the other in the higher spheres …"

ANDREW JACKSON DAVIS, *THE PRINCIPLES OF NATURE* (1847)

▲ **Guided glory**
Victorian medium and artist Georgiana Houghton believed herself to be in contact with spirits that included Renaissance artist Titian. She made abstract watercolor drawings guided by these spirits, such as *Glory Be to God* (c. 1868).

An occultist's cabinet

Fascination with the occult appears in the earliest historical records and divination techniques, such as crystal gazing, were practiced as far back as 3000 BCE. As occult traditions evolved over time, practitioners acquired many implements to assist them in their rituals. In the 19th century, the rise of spiritualism (see pp.222–225) coincided with a golden age of invention, which led to a boom in the development of instruments for making contact with the spirit world and transcribing messages ostensibly sent from the dead to the living.

▲ **Writing slates**, such as this 19th-century example, were used by mediums, who manifested messages from the dead through psychography (see p.228).

▼ **This "sorcerer's mirror,"** with inset convex lenses, reflects an unstable image in order to conjure visions in the mind's eye or confuse and repel evil spirits.

▲ **This handcrafted board** (see pp.236–237), with Arabic letters and symbols, was made by Beth Dereli in 2015. Boards can be personalized according to the practitioner's needs.

▶ **Spirit rapping hands** were used in the 19th century as a medium's prop during seances (and were often manipulated with secret devices).

▶ **The Telepathic Spirit Communicator**, a planchette (small board) on a track with an alphanumeric dial, was built by watchmaker W. T. Braham (c. 1900) to relay the words of "spirit people."

▲ **Crystal balls** have been used for millennia for fortune-telling, clairvoyance, or communication with unseen realms.

Convex bubble mirrors distort the image

◀ **This "luminous trumpet"** is a cardboard spirit trumpet made by The Two Worlds Publishing Co. in the 1920s. It served as a megaphone for amplifying spirits' voices.

▲ **The Dial Planchette** (or psychograph) was developed in the 1880s by spiritualist Hudson Tuttle as a cheap, lightweight, mail-order talking board.

Horseshoe outline behind dial, to attract "magnetism"

For resting the fingers or hands

▲ **This planchette**—a heart-shaped piece of wood, mounted on wheels, with a hole for a pencil—was created in 1853 for psychography.

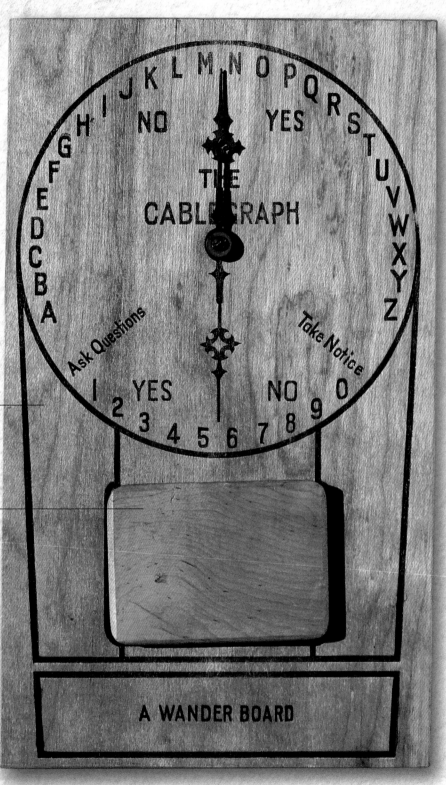

▲ **The Wander Board** (or cablegraph), designed by G. F. Pearson in 1900, replaced the Dial Planchette's pulley and rope with a lever and gears for smoother action.

LIFE AFTER LIFE
Spiritism

▲ Calling the spirits
This photograph from 1977 of an Umbanda ceremony shows spirit mediums singing, dancing, and drumming as part of a ritual that they claim leads to possession by spirits.

In the 1850s, French educator Hippolyte Rivail became interested in seances—meetings where the spirits of the dead communicate with the living via a psychic medium. Impressed by what he saw, he posed a series of questions to several mediums and recorded the responses the spirits gave. From these, Rivail produced *The Spirits' Book*, writing under the name Allan Kardec. The book became the foundation of Spiritism.

Spiritual rebirth
Aided by answers from spirits, in particular one he called Zephyr, Kardec revealed what he believed was the true nature of the universe. Kardec proclaimed that God was the sole perfect being, known as the Supreme Intelligence, and that He had created spirits with free will. These spirits could be found in living beings, or they could be discarnate (without a physical body) but able to speak through mediums. According to Kardec's Spiritist doctrine, when a person dies, their spirit becomes discarnate but can be reborn into a new body. Over many reincarnations the spirit is able

to improve itself through acts of charity and become stronger. Kardec also claimed that there were other, invisible worlds in the cosmos where spirits could be reborn. When he died in 1869, the central belief of Spiritist teaching was carved on Kardec's tomb—that to be reborn and progress spiritually was the ultimate law.

Regional variation
The Catholic Church in Europe opposed Spiritism, despite Kardec preaching that Jesus was the moral guide for humans. In 1861, when 300 copies of Spiritist texts arrived in Barcelona, Spain, they were seized by Bishop Palau and publicly burned. Nevertheless, Spiritism remained popular in Europe until the 1917 Code of Canon Law explicitly forbade its practice among Roman Catholics.

In South America, Spiritism continued to spread, helped by the region's long history of religious syncretism, which saw folk beliefs incorporated into Catholic worship. Today, there are 3.8 million active Spiritists in Brazil, and many schools and psychiatric hospitals are run by Spiritists. Similarly, Macumba, a magical practice involving spirits, and Umbanda, a folk religion, combined animistic beliefs brought to Brazil by enslaved Africans with elements of Kardec's Spiritism.

IN CONTEXT

Psychography

Spiritists believe that spirits can communicate by writing. The spirit is thought to take over the hand of the medium in a process called psychography, or automatic writing. In Brazil, such messages have been widely influential. Medium Chico Xavier (1910–2002) produced many poems, books, and films, which he claimed were written by spirits. The family of deceased poet Humberto de Campos sued Xavier for breach of copyright on poems the medium said were channeled from de Campos, but they lost the case.

Believers say that psychography works through direct control of mediums by spirits, as depicted in this illustration from 1863.

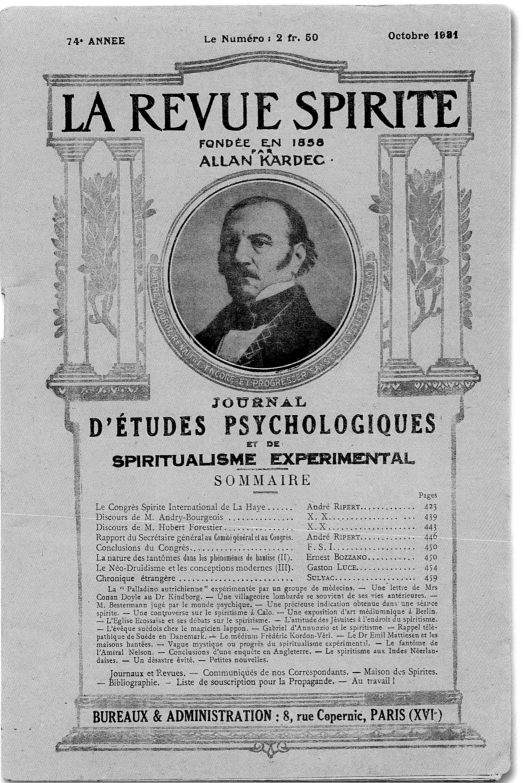

74ᵉ ANNÉE   Le Numéro : 2 fr. 50   Octobre 1931

LA REVUE SPIRITE

FONDÉE EN 1858
PAR
ALLAN KARDEC ·

JOURNAL
D'ÉTUDES PSYCHOLOGIQUES
ET DE
SPIRITUALISME EXPÉRIMENTAL

SOMMAIRE

La " Palladino autrichienne " expérimentée par un groupe de médecins. — Une lettre de Mrs Conan Doyle au Dr Kindborg. — Une villageoise lombarde se souvient de ses vies antérieures. — M. Bestermann jugé par le monde psychique. — Une précieuse indication obtenue dans une séance spirite. — Une controverse sur le spiritisme à Calo. — Une exposition d'art médiumnique à Berlin. — L'Eglise Ecossaise et ses débats sur le spiritisme. — L'attitude des Jésuites à l'endroit du spiritisme. — L'évêque suédois chez le magicien lappon. — Gabriel d'Annunzio et le spiritisme. — Rappel télépathique de Suède en Danemark. — Le médium Frédéric Kordon-Véri. — Le Dr Emil Mattiesen et les maisons hantées. — Vague mystique ou progrès du spiritualisme expérimental. — Le fantôme de l'Amiral Nelson. — Conclusions d'une enquête en Angleterre. — Le spiritisme aux Indes Néerlandaises. — Un désastre évité. — Petites nouvelles.

Journaux et Revues. — Communiqués de nos Correspondants. — Maison des Spirites. — Bibliographie. — Liste de souscription pour la Propagande. — Au travail !

BUREAUX & ADMINISTRATION : 8, rue Copernic, PARIS (XVIᵉ)

◀ *La Revue Spirite*
The French monthly magazine for discussion of Spiritist beliefs was founded by Allan Kardec in 1858 and is still published today. It has featured articles by authors Victor Hugo and Arthur Conan Doyle, and by various scientific luminaries.

A VICTORIAN FASCINATION
celebrity and the occult

The Victorian era (1837–1901) was a time of rapid technological and scientific development in Britain and beyond. New scientific and medical discoveries led people to question accepted beliefs, such as the authority of religious scripture, traditionally used to define and explain the world. Alternative approaches to the spiritual and supernatural developed—ones that seemingly offered proof of their claims. These included spiritualism (see pp.222–225), Spiritism (see pp.228–229), and even Mesmerism (see p.223).

Victorians started to take investigation into the paranormal seriously, not just to debunk deceptions. In *The Night Side of Nature* (1848), English author Catherine Crowe combined a compendium of supernatural incidents, including ghostly visitations, with a challenge to readers to investigate occult phenomena for what these might tell them about the world. In 1882, the Society for Psychical Research was set up—an organization dedicated to exploring "psychical" phenomena like hypnotism, thought-transference, hauntings, and mediumship.

▼ **Parlor-room show**
Seance attendees sit around a table, their hands placed palms down, waiting to communicate with the dead in this woodcut from c. 1850. Seances were a popular form of entertainment at parties.

> "August 27—strong evidence felt of spirit-power. The table, after a gentle vibration, became unmanageable, and was lifted two feet high from the floor …"

CATHERINE BERRY, A MEDIUM DESCRIBING A PRIVATE SEANCE IN HER DIARY, 1876

◄ Crystal-gazing
A poster publicizes a stage performance by Alexander the Crystal Seer, an American magician who answered questions from the audience with the help of a crystal ball.

▲ Stage trickery
Hungarian-American illusionist Harry Houdini fakes an expulsion of ectoplasm in this 1925 photograph by holding a fine cloth between his teeth, to debunk the phenomenon.

A popular way of exploring the supernatural was the seance. Seances could be exclusive gatherings in the home or large public displays by celebrity mediums like Helen Duncan. At seances, mediums acted as intermediaries between the living and the dead. They would work in different ways, including entering into trancelike states and channeling spirits. Many mediums had "spirit guides" which were their point of contact with the spiritual realm.

Over time, mediums found increasingly striking ways of performing or practicing, with spectacles such as listening for knocking, automatic writing or the use of spirit boards (see pp.236–237), and table-turning or tipping. In smaller seances, attendees would often be asked to sit around a table holding hands in the dark to aid spiritual communication (conditions that also made it easier for mediums to use trickery). Some seances featured elements such as full-body materialization: the seemingly physical manifestation of a spirit. In Duncan's case, this also involved the medium's body producing a visible substance—so-called ectoplasm. Other mediums appeared to levitate their own bodies or tables and other objects.

Occult entertainment

Seances were not the only popular occult practice during this period. Fortune-telling was fashionable, along with renewed interest in crystallomancy (use of crystal balls), cartomancy (telling the future with cards), and palmistry (based on marks and patterns on the palms of the hand). Some mediums, including Daniel Dunglas

KEY

1 Mrs. Daffodil Downey, a medium, performed her "Light and Dark Seance or a Clever Capture" to crowds in London for at least six years.

2 The spirit of a beautiful woman levitates a man into the air. The diaries of Harry Houdini suggest that the performances actually did include such an apparition.

3 A disembodied hand plays the violin. Such illusions were praised in a contemporary advert, which wondered "where man's ingenuity crosses and art magic begins."

4 Another disembodied hand holds a dowsing rod (see p.259).

▶ **Pulling in the crowds**
A poster for Mrs. Daffodil Downey's seance at London's Egyptian Hall in c.1885 features common "illusions" used to draw large audiences. Advertisements for occult performances helped nurture the cult of celebrity around mediums.

EGYPTIAN HALL.

MASKELYNE & COOKE'S ENTERTAINMENT.

MRS. DAFFODIL DOWNEY'S SEANCE,

INCLUDING **Mr. MASKELYNE'S** RECENTLY ADDED

MARVELLOUS ILLUSIONS !

EVERY EVENING AT EIGHT, & TUESDAY, THURSDAY & SATURDAY AFTERNOONS AT THREE.

Home, generated dedicated followings. A Scot who honed his alleged psychic powers in the US, Home made his name conducting seances in the light rather than in the standard darkened room. His sessions included trance speaking (where the spirit speaks through the medium), direct voice (where spirits speak somewhere in the room), objects moving, and clairvoyance. He was also renowned for levitating. One report stated that he levitated out of a window and back in again.

Some celebrity occultists were associated with secret societies. Moina Mathers (née Bergson), whose performance of *The Rites of Isis* at a Paris theater in 1899 thrilled audiences by invoking ancient Egyptian spirits, was a key member of the Hermetic Order of the Golden Dawn.

Debunking psychics

Not everyone believed the claims of mediums and many specialized in debunking them. Perhaps the most famous of these was the Hungarian-American illusionist Harry Houdini, who, in the 1920s, used his knowledge of stagecraft to expose performers' tricks. He even testified to US Congress in 1926 in favor of a bill to criminalize "any person pretending … to unite the separated."

Houdini believed that mediums preyed on desperate people's grief. His best-known "debunking" case, that of Margery Crandon, illustrates how seriously mediumship was taken at the time. In 1924, *Scientific American* offered a large cash prize for a proven case of a medium's claims. Crandon was the leading candidate, an upper-class psychic renowned for her incredible manifestations while in a trance. Audience members were pinched and heard whispers from invisible sources, and objects floated, but Houdini was able to show how these tricks worked.

British researcher Harry Price (see p.255) also exposed fraudsters. He revealed the "ectoplasm" produced by Helen Duncan to be cheesecloth that she had ingested and regurgitated. Criticism grew, pointing to all the ways in which common seance practices made it easier to deceive people, while scientific explanations, such as the ideomotor effect (see pp.236–237), showed how objects might seemingly move on their own.

▲ **Spoofing spiritualism**
A satirical print from *Punch Almanack* in 1877 shows a spiritualist gathering having called up a ghostly orchestra. While popular, spiritualism was also the subject of widespread skepticism.

IN CONTEXT

Florence Cook

British medium Florence Cook was famed for the materialization of her spirit guide "Katie King." During sessions, Florence would manifest Katie physically while she herself was bound to a chair. She had an ardent defender in scientist William Crookes, who investigated her for months in his own home. But not everyone was convinced, and she was accused of fraud many times. When Florence came back from retirement in 1880 with a new spirit, "Marie," Sir George Sitwell grew suspicious during a seance. Seeing corset stays under Marie's robes, he grasped hold of them, and when the lights came on, he was holding not Marie but Florence herself. She still had defenders, but this incident discredited her.

This picture was used by William Crookes to prove that Katie King was not simply Florence Cook (leaning on the chair) in disguise.

The seance

World War I (1914–1918) had a devastating impact. Millions of people were killed, and even more lost loved ones in the great influenza pandemic of 1918–1919. It was against this backdrop that interest in contacting the dead grew in popularity in Europe and the United States during the 1920s. People attended seances (see p.231) in private homes and public places in the hope of communicating with spirits via a medium. Newspapers reported strange events at these gatherings, including unearthly voices, lights, and physical apparitions. Learned advocates of spiritualism (see pp.222–225) gave the seance social legitimacy.

Rising literacy rates spread the practice of seances further, helped by popular books like *The Earthen Vessel* (1921) by Lady Glenconner. People could also watch spirit communication in action on the stage and screen. In the silent movies of the 1920s, seances were accompanied by eerie music composed to heighten the experience, while special effects gave the audience a glimpse of ghosts. Films such as *Whispering Shadows* (1921) and *The 13th Chair* (1929) used the seance as the centerpiece of their plots.

In director Fritz Lang's classic *Dr. Mabuse* film series (1922–1960)—a scene from which is pictured—seances were portrayed as the work of charlatans trying to deceive people. This skepticism toward spiritualist practices grew as researchers sought to discredit fraudulent mediums (see pp.254–257) who profited from people's trauma.

> "A large, strong hand then rested upon my head … and I felt and heard a kiss just above my brow."

SIR ARTHUR CONAN DOYLE, DESCRIBING A SEANCE COMMUNICATION WITH HIS SON IN 1919

▲ The German silent film *Dr. Mabuse the Gambler* (1922) mocked those who attended seances as victims of deceit.

ASKING OUIJA
talking boards

Spiritualism (see pp.222–225) grew rapidly in the US in the mid-19th century. After the American Civil War (1861–1865), many grieving loved ones turned to mediums, who sometimes used alphabet boards to contact departed spirits. From the 1880s, people began to acquire their own "talking boards," which became the most popular way to talk with the dead.

A harmless game?

The first talking board was produced in 1886 by the W. S. Reed toy company in Massachusetts; they called it a "witch board." Users placed their fingers on a planchette (pointer) that moved, it was claimed, under the influence of spirits. It pointed at letters and numbers marked on the board to spell out messages. Then, in 1890, Elijah Bond patented a design that became known as Ouija in 1901. When manufacturers asked the board what they should call it, it gave the name "Ouija," which it said meant "good luck." Sales of Ouija boards soon soared. Lavishly decorated boards were produced, as well as cheaper versions for the mass market.

▲ Trusty board
Although Ouija is now a trademark of the Hasbro corporation, many companies made their own early versions. This 1920s example from Massachusetts has all of the usual features of a talking board: the letters of the alphabet, numbers up to 10, "yes," "no," "goodbye," and a planchette to point to them.

Early marketing for the Ouija board described it as both a parlor game and a spiritualist tool for those with no training. Makers of the board presented it as a fun and harmless pastime for lovers, because it gave an excuse for their fingers to touch on the planchette. Ouija boards became an American sensation and featured in films, such as *The Bat Whispers* in 1930, and in popular songs.

Negative reactions

After the release of the 1973 horror film *The Exorcist*, in which a girl becomes possessed after using a Ouija board to communicate with a spirit, opinions changed. Ouija boards were seen as a potentially dangerous tool that invited demonic forces into the home and they were explicitly condemned by Christian groups and churches.

Scientists had a different view—since 1852 they had been able to explain the phenomenon of spirit writing by the ideomotor effect: unconscious muscular movements made by users. Research has shown that when users are blindfolded, the messages of the board become gibberish.

▶ "Weegee Weegee Tell Me Do"
This song from 1920 features lyrics declaring that most homes had a Ouija board—"a game played by nearly every family" in the US "to see what the future days may bring."

IN CONTEXT

Mrs. Curran and Patience Worth

Pearl Curran was a St. Louis housewife who became a literary star thanks to a 17th-century spirit she channeled via a Ouija board. Curran's contact with Patience Worth began in 1913 and resulted in the publication of seven books attributed to the spirit. Curran gave public performances with her Ouija board, during which Worth's dictated words were recorded by Curran's husband in shorthand. The spirit had supposedly communicated almost 4 million words by the time of Curran's death in 1937.

Patience Worth's first novel about one of the thieves crucified with Jesus received rave reviews on its publication in 1917.

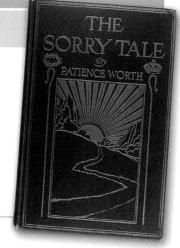

Bellows, which
could be extended
to focus the image

Camera lens

▲ **This 1906 Instagraph
Bellows camera** is the same
model that was used by English
photographer William Hope. He
faked his spirit photographs by exposing
images of the deceased onto photographic
plates before his sessions.

Front extension
frame (for when
bellows are in use)

▲ **A medium during a seance**
is depicted in this 1901 picture,
taken by John K. Hallowell in
Chicago. There are a number
of similar photographs of
spiritualist mediums with
their spirit guides.

STEREOSCOPIC GROUPS AND PORTRAITS

Entered according to Act of Congress by L. M. MELANDER
the office of the Librarian of Congress at Washington

Spirit photography

In the 19th century, new technologies were used to explore the supernatural.
Spirit photography claimed to capture pictures of ghosts. American
photographer William Mumler was the first to claim he had caught a spirit
on camera, after he accidentally used an old plate that had not been fully
cleaned, leaving a ghostly impression on the developed photo. Often linked
to spiritualism (see pp.222–225), spirit photography remained popular into
the 20th century through the work of photographers such as William Hope.

▲ **This 1876 stereograph**, created using a long exposure time, shows a woman placing money in a church box, watched by a ghost.

▲ **Taken by William Hope** around 1920, this image shows a family with a faint ghostly form and a blurred aura for dramatic effect.

▲ **William Hope** used marked plates to create this image of a woman, two boys, and a "ghost." Harry Price (see p.255) exposed the hoax.

▲ **This William Hope image** depicts an older couple with the veiled figure of a young woman. Such images gave comfort to grieving families.

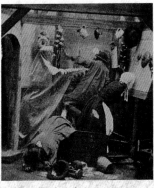

▲ **A hand-colored stereoscope image** depicts ghostly havoc. Such pictures often featured protective spirits or famous ghost tales.

▲ **A London Stereoscopic Company** image from 1865 features a young girl kneeling for prayers, watched over by a ghostly figure.

▲ **This William Mumler image**, created using double exposure, depicts Robert Bonner with a female ghost behind him.

▲ **William Mumler's most famous** picture shows Mary Todd Lincoln being comforted by her husband, Abraham Lincoln.

Card produced by L. M. Melander & Bro., Chicago

◄ **"The Haunted Lane"** shows a ghost scaring a man and boy. Stereograph cards contained two identical images; looked at through a viewer, they became one dynamic photo.

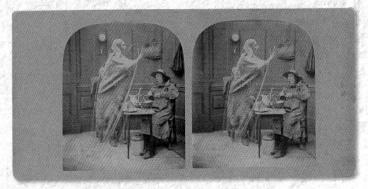

▲ **The London Stereoscopic Company** used photographic trickery for ghostly entertainment in hand-colored stereograph cards between 1854 and 1890, before spirit photographers claimed to capture real ghosts.

VISIONS OF DEATH
the Ghost Dance movement

In the fall of 1869, as Paiute people gathered in what was now eastern Nevada for the annual pine nut harvest, a man named Wodziwob shared prophetic visions. He had sent his spirit to the land of the dead, where he saw his relations happily hunting. Wodziwob told people that if they washed and painted their faces daily and performed round dances, the dead would be resurrected.

Wodziwob's prophecies offered hope at a time when there was little to spare. In 1872 he died, and the Ghost Dance movement he had initiated faded. But on New Year's Day in 1889, during a full solar eclipse, another Paiute prophet, Wovoka, shared new visions. He had traveled to Heaven, met God, and learned that through the Ghost Dance, the dead would return to the living, white people would vanish from North America, and life as it had been before colonization would be restored.

◀ **Sacred protection**
Arapaho people created ceremonial shirts and dresses, painted in yellow and blue and trimmed with sacred eagle feathers. Dancers believed these special garments could prevent bullets from penetrating them.

Revival and suppression
The Ghost Dance movement of 1870 and its revival in 1890 following Wovoka's visions are examples of revitalization movements. These gained traction because they offered two things: relief from trauma, and the restoration of long-established Indigenous cultures. Indigenous peoples in the 19th century faced waves of deadly epidemics, the expansion of railroads across their lands, threats to their natural resources, and growing numbers of settlers.

In the years following the American Civil War (1861–1865), Indigenous peoples experienced brutal campaigns of forced assimilation that further eroded their land bases and threatened their families. In 1867, the federal government sent missionaries to live on reservations to force acceptance of Christianity, while Indigenous agents employed by the government were granted authority to punish people for resisting assimilation policies.

Fatal reaction
The widespread resurgence of the Ghost Dance in 1890, with its message of hope, was fueled by the cataclysmic changes imposed by the US government. The Hunkpapa Lakota leader Sitting Bull was murdered by government-hired tribal police after being falsely accused of Ghost Dancing. Days later, his half-brother Big Foot lay dying of pneumonia at Wounded Knee Creek while his people danced

▶ **Winter count**
The Indigenous peoples of the Great Plains kept pictorial calendars called winter counts to record auspicious events. Yellow Nose, an Ute raised among the Cheyenne, painted this depiction of the Ghost Dance on an animal skin in 1891.

around him, hoping to resurrect their dead and restore a world untouched by settlers. Within hours, US soldiers had surrounded the camp and begun firing on its Indigenous occupants.

In the months leading up to the Wounded Knee Massacre, newspapers printed incendiary stories claiming the Ghost Dance was a violent movement, and US troops responded with force. The holy man Black Elk

later reported seeing cavalrymen indiscriminately kill men, women, children, and infants in arms. These atrocities, however, were minimized by the press at the time.

Among the Lakota, the Ghost Dance movement had been dealt a forceful—though not fatal—blow. In the 1890s, the dance was adopted by other Indigenous peoples hoping to revive their traditions.

▼ Peaceful dance
American ethnologist James Mooney traveled to South Dakota in 1890 to interview survivors of the Wounded Knee Massacre. He hoped that his report would counter misrepresentations by the press of the Ghost Dance (pictured here) as a violent movement.

"The people went on and on and could not stop, day or night, hoping ... to get a vision of their own dead."

A LAKOTA SIOUX, ON THE GHOST DANCE

▲ Recharged
Those seeking a cure using Mesmer's animal magnetism technique were invited to sit on his *baquet*, or tub, which had been charged with an invisible fluid. They then had to press their body parts against the tub's metal rods.

"The title of this book embraces all transmissions of thought and feeling from one person to another, by other means than through the recognized channels of sense ..."

EDMUND GURNEY, INTRODUCTION TO *PHANTASMS OF THE LIVING* (1886)

MIND OVER MATTER
parapsychology

Interest in the supernatural boomed in the 19th century, with the rise of spiritualism (see pp.223–225), Spiritism (see pp.228–229), and similar movements, and spirit mediums became global celebrities (see pp.230–233). But the many reported cases of spirit contact and ghostly apparitions were accompanied by growing calls for proof.

Parapsychology was developed to investigate all manner of purported psychic phenomena. These range from mental abilities—such as telepathy, telekinesis, and precognition—to spiritual matters—including ghost sightings, seances, and near-death experiences. Parapsychologists explore the possible causes for events that seem to go beyond the normal understanding of science and nature.

The first investigations

In the mid-18th century, German physician Franz Mesmer used "Mesmerism," or "animal magnetism," to treat his patients. His methods were based on his theory that an invisible fluid permeated the universe and could be directed by scientific means. Mesmer's claims were investigated by scientists, including Benjamin Franklin and Antoine Lavoisier, who found no evidence to support them. Despite this, Mesmerism spread, influencing later spiritualists.

Formal study

Early studies of psychic phenomena looked into whether spirit mediums could contact the dead. While initial results suggested they could, later researchers pointed out flaws in the experiments. For example, one researcher declared that table-tipping during seances was due to spirit interference, but others pointed out that participants' knees could have produced the effect.

In 1882, the Society for Psychical Research (see p.230) was founded in London to investigate claims of paranormal events. A book published by the society soon after, called *Phantasms of the Living*, contained hundreds of cases of alleged hauntings. Research carried out by members of the society found that a large proportion of the population claimed to have seen an apparition, suggesting that seeing a ghost was not caused by mental illness. The society also sought to test whether or not there were natural explanations for ghost sightings.

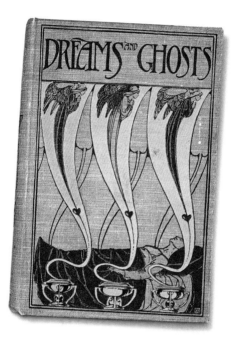

▲ **Dreams and ghosts**
Published in 1897, *The Book of Dreams and Ghosts*, by psychical researcher Andrew Lang, aimed to bring together accounts of ghosts and spirits and explore the reality of the experiences people claimed to have.

Phantasms of the Living

In 1886, Frederic Myers, Edmund Gurney, and Frank Podmore published a two-volume work called *Phantasms of the Living*, which brought together accounts of 701 cases of ghosts making contact with the living. Many people were impressed by the level of detail collected in the authors' research and their attempts to verify aspects of hauntings. Detractors, however, felt that real evidence was lacking, and that many of the accounts could be explained as hallucinations. Even so, the work proved influential in establishing the methods used by many later parapsychologists to conduct experiments.

As well as written accounts, *Phantasms of the Living* contained intriguing pictures gathered from witnesses.

▲ Experiment in action
The parapsychologist Joseph Banks Rhine helped set up the first parapsychology laboratory, in the US. He also created many of the tools used to probe claims of telepathy and precognition in a scientific way.

When Frederic Myers, one of the founders of the Society for Psychical Research, died in 1901, several practitioners of automatic writing began to receive messages, apparently from his spirit. These were fragmentary and sporadic, but when pieced together, they seemed to contain information known only to Myers and other dead figures. This, in turn, led to claims that the messages proved the existence of the soul after death.

A new science

In 1930, a Parapsychology Laboratory was created at Duke University, in the US, to explore psychic phenomena scientifically. Researchers at the laboratory focused on extrasensory perception, using Zener cards (see opposite page), for example, to test claims of telepathy. One participant in an experiment

would look at a randomly chosen card, decorated with different shapes, and another on the other side of a barrier would attempt to perceive which card it was. Statistical analysis of the results allowed researchers to ascertain the validity of claims.

The laboratory's modern successor, the Rhine Research Center, produces a peer-reviewed journal where the latest research in parapsychology is published for academic study. Similar facilities have been set up around the world to investigate whether any parapsychological effects are genuine, and research in this area remains a growing field.

Psychic phenomena

Parapsychologists today study two types of phenomena. Cognitive phenomena are those that exist within the mind of a subject, such as the ability to perceive events before they happen (precognition), or the sensory experiences of mediums who claim to be able to communicate with the dead. Cognitive phenomena include near-death experiences and astral projection (see pp.262–263), which see a person's mind leave their body. Physical phenomena, by contrast, occur outside the body. Some claim that these include apparitions, since ghosts may be seen outside of the mind—by multiple witnesses at once, or detected by scientific tools.

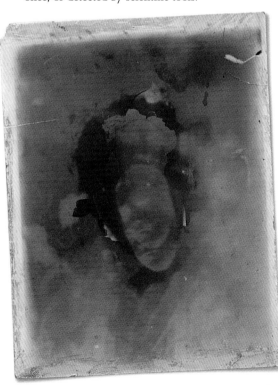

▶ Photographing thoughts
Several psychics claimed to be able to project pictures from the mind onto photographic film. In many cases, the images could be explained by the chemical treatment of film, double exposure, or other manipulations—but some researchers asserted that not all examples were fraudulent.

Many parapsychology researchers prefer to refer to "apparitional experiences" when looking at hauntings. They record what people who see ghosts experience, rather than attempting to document the actual haunting. This is because ghosts tend not to leave physical evidence behind after a sighting. By collecting accounts of hauntings and exploring common themes, researchers can try to understand what triggers the experience of seeing a ghost.

Skepticism

Not all scientists agree that parapsychology is a valid field of research. Many consider it to be a pseudoscience, making claims that cannot be tested according to the scientific method. This is partly due to the discipline's inability to replicate its experiments. Without using the same participants in the same situation, it is impossible to perform the exact same test.

Many of the results of research into the parapsychology of ghosts and hauntings have been criticized as anecdotal and subjective. Likewise, cognitive bias may lead researchers to see patterns where none exist, due to the subjective nature of haunting accounts. Such extraordinary claims require extraordinary evidence—but parapsychologists will continue to search for answers.

▶ **Zener cards**
This 1965 cover of *Science Digest* magazine shows the cards used in extrasensory perception (ESP) tests. Using these standardized images allowed for a larger pool of results and for statistical analysis and comparison between different experiments.

The science news monthly
SCIENCE DIGEST
NOVEMBER 1965   35 CENTS ICD

E.S.P.
Which card is on page 63?

SCIENCE GETS SERIOUS ABOUT EXTRASENSORY PERCEPTION—A 10-PAGE REPORT

Also:
12 ways to handle the stress of modern living
Psychiatrists analyze the L.A. riots
How electricity in the air affects your moods
Now—a drug that 'cures' drug addicts

"… the fact of our seeing no probable cause to account for such divination [in dreams] tends to inspire us with distrust …"

ARISTOTLE, *DE DIVINATIONE PER SOMNUM* (*ON DREAMS*), 4TH CENTURY BCE

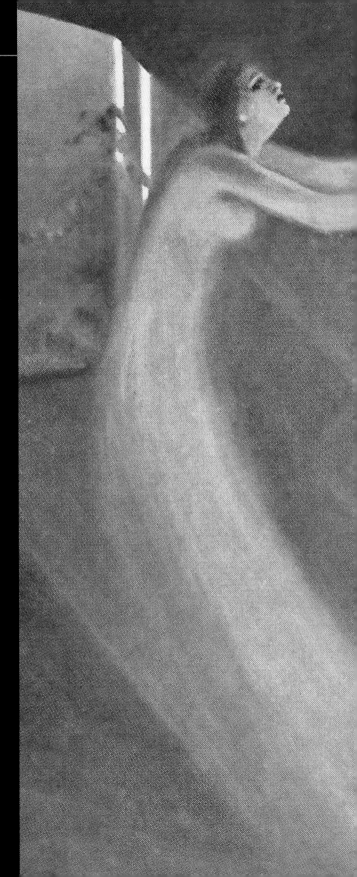

Chopin's ghosts

In the winter of 1839, Polish pianist and composer Frédéric Chopin was staying in a ruined monastery on the Spanish island of Mallorca with his lover, French novelist George Sand, and her two children. Chopin and Sand had gone to Mallorca for his health, hoping that warm weather would help him, but the weather was bad and his health was failing. The couple had been forced to seek refuge in the monastery after they were ejected from their lodgings due to fears the composer had tuberculosis. Both felt trapped, and Chopin was under an enormous amount of stress.

That winter, Chopin experienced a terrible shock. He had, he said, been visited by the ghost of a monk. This terrifying event was not the only time he would experience a haunting. Chopin was plagued by death: he lost a sister at an early age to tuberculosis and his native Poland was crushed by Russia after a failed rebellion. He often described himself as like a corpse and thought about his loved ones dying, once even calling Sand herself a ghost. His hauntings affected his compositions, with sadness and fear manifesting in his music as repeated melodies played in a minor key.

Some have suggested Chopin's ghost in Mallorca was actually Sand's daughter, Solange, who had fought with Chopin, in disguise. Others think temporal lobe epilepsy, which can cause hallucinations, was the cause of both Chopin's ill health and ghost sightings.

> "For him, the cloister was full of phantoms and terrors."
>
> GEORGE SAND, MY LIFE, 1855

▲ **Chopin is visited by apparitions** at his piano in this early-20th-century postcard.

REVISIONISM
AND
REVIVALS
1900 ONWARD

Introduction

It was not long after the invention of the camera that people deliberately started to re-create images of ghosts and spirits using double-exposure techniques, so it is no surprise that some of the earliest moving pictures also tried to capture the essence of a ghost. In 1898, English cinematographer and showman George Albert Smith shot a one-minute comedy called *Photographing a Ghost*. Meanwhile, in France, magician and film director Georges Méliès created some of the most extraordinary scenes of the supernatural and horror in cinema's history.

World War I had a profound collective impact on ways of grieving and the commemoration of the dead. Although there are surprisingly few reports of soldiers seeing ghosts on the battlefield, the conflict produced many accounts of divine battlefield visions and miracles. Prophecy literature predicting the beginning and end of the war boomed, as did the trade in protective talismans and mascots. Spiritualist

mediums did a roaring business in divining the fate of soldiers. Best-selling books were written purporting to be a record of conversations with young military men who had been killed and gone to the "other side." After the war, there was a greater acceptance of spiritualism in wider society, and of fortune-telling. By the 1930s, the newspapers that had once decried astrology as humbug started to introduce horoscope columns. Paranormal investigators became public figures.

At a more esoteric level, the early 20th century saw the growth of new middle-class occult movements. The Theosophical Society—with its theology based on Westernized notions of Eastern religions, including the belief in reincarnation—became a global organization. Helena Petrovna Blavatsky, who had founded the society in 1875, claimed that her wisdom derived from remote thought communications with a group of spiritual masters, known as the Mahatmas, who resided in the Himalayas and Egypt. Similar groups

Enduring practices *see p.265*

Demonic possession imagined *see p.267*

Explaining hauntings *see p.274*

included the anthroposophy movement, founded in Germany by one-time theosophist Rudolf Steiner, who set out in "scientific" terms the personal development of one's inner being necessary to engage with the spiritual plane of existence. Britain's Hermetic Order of the Golden Dawn, meanwhile, was an overtly magical fraternity that drew inspiration from old grimoires, Egyptian religion, and Christian mysticism.

Out of this esoteric milieu arose the modern Pagan movement during the latter half of the 20th century – first with the birth of Wicca and modern "witchcraft," and then with the creation of many diverse magical practitioner movements. This led to a renewed practical interest in the Indigenous animistic and spirit religions of Asia, Africa, and South America.

Today, the world of supernatural beings is as relevant and as interwoven into human lives as it ever has been. People around the world continue to perform rituals to commune with spirits; television schedules are replete with ghost-hunting programs; cinemas worldwide project horror films that play with the supernatural; and the internet has spawned its own contemporary legends for those enticed by the excitement and fear that the idea of ghosts inspires.

"I see dead people ... Walking around like regular people. They don't see each other ... They don't know they're dead."

COLE SEAR, *THE SIXTH SENSE*, 1999

Peace offering *see p.284*

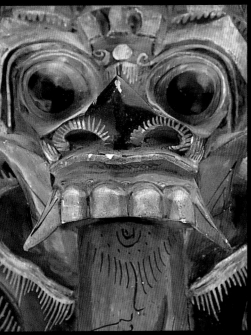

Balinese spirit leader *see p.289*

Ghost people *see p.296*

STRENGTHENED BY SPIRITS
the Boxer Rebellion

Folk religion in China has a long history of spirit possession. Shamans known as *tongji* or *jitong* ("child diviner" or "divining child") believe that they are able to give control of their bodies to deities or spirits. Through them the spirit delivers divine messages and offers guidance while the shaman remains in a trance. Some perform elaborate dances said to date back thousands of years. Toward the end of the Qing dynasty, in the late 19th century, these ideas were treated with suspicion by the Confucian literati and many Chinese Christians because of their potential influence over peasants.

Rising discontent

China had remained isolationist for centuries. Foreign traders were only allowed to use a single port, in a bid to reduce their influence on Chinese culture, and Christian missionaries were viewed as a threat. However, China was forcibly opened to Western powers following the First Opium War of 1839, and the imposition of unfair treaties stoked a growing resentment of foreigners. Many Chinese people looked to ancient folk traditions for help.

Fear of Christianity was heightened by its role in the Taiping Rebellion (1850–1864) against Qing rule. The rebel leader Hong Xiuquan declared himself the younger brother of Jesus, and two shamans, claiming to be possessed by the spirits of God and Jesus, issued orders to the rebels. By the time the rebellion was quashed, 20–30 million people had died.

▼ **Shamanic possession**
Manchu shamanism is one example of Chinese folk religion. Traditionally, shamans wore feathered caps, which denoted their perceived ability to fly to the spirit world, and used bells and drums to create trancelike states for spirit possession.

Rebellious spirits

The Boxer Rebellion of 1899–1901 arose from local groups that practiced traditional martial arts (called "Chinese Boxing" by Westerners). These groups had emerged in China not only to protect villages from bandits and warlords but also to fight the growing influence of Christianity. One group, the Big Swords Society, taught that training could render its members invulnerable to bullets. The group was involved in the murder of German missionaries in 1897.

"Revive the Qing! Destroy the foreigner!"

BOXER SLOGAN, 1899–1901

六月廿八日圖
民倜巢出隊
經英法陸軍
曁各國之兵
興蘭民開彼我

兵大國各法英

英法陸軍與團民廝戰圖

戰大陣對軍兩

Increasing European demands for territory led to calls for a strengthening of the Chinese imperial system and expulsion of all Europeans. The *Yihequan*, or Society of Righteous and Harmonious Fists, was formed in 1899. This society of Boxers (as they were called by Europeans) brought together folk religious practices and local martial arts training groups. The Boxers held distinctive ceremonies, during which paper charms were burned and the ashes mixed with water. This mixture was then drunk, and the Boxers prayed for a spirit to possess them.

Sword over spirit

The Boxers believed that anyone could claim the power of a spirit or deity. Under divine inspiration, they went into a frenzy while in a trance, and a possessed Boxer was thought to be able to withstand a sword blow. Bolstered by popular support, and claims of summoning an army of spirits from heaven, the Boxers attacked Europeans. Backed by the powerful Dowager Empress Cixi, and with some assistance from the Chinese Imperial Army, they laid siege to Peking (now Beijing)—and especially the European diplomatic quarter. The siege lasted just 55 days, until a coalition of Western forces arrived. The rebels were violently suppressed; their spirits did not protect them from European guns and swords.

▶ **Spears and flags**
This photograph, which was probably staged during the rebellion, shows a Boxer carrying a pike (spear)—the traditional weapon that many Boxers carried and that proved inadequate against European artillery on the battlefield.

HUNTING FOR GHOSTS

paranormal investigations

◄ Demonic drummer
This image depicting the celebrated demon drummer of Tedworth appeared as the frontispiece to the 1700 edition of *Saducismus Triumphatus*, a book on witchcraft by Joseph Glanvill.

Throughout history people have sought out ghosts and supernatural apparitions to learn about them. Such ghost-hunting—or paranormal investigation—has become even more popular in recent years.

Early ghostbusters

Ancient Mesopotamian tablets (see pp.22–25) record elaborate rituals and spells that were used to capture and drive out specters. Around 100 CE,

Pliny the Younger wrote a letter (see pp.86–87) describing an investigation in Athens, where a man followed a ghost to find its buried bones.

During the medieval period, European references to ghosts were usually tied to the idea of anguished souls in Purgatory. With the Reformation, ghosts were dismissed as Catholic "superstition" by Protestant theologians. But sightings continued to be reported. In 1681, a book called *Saducismus Triumphatus* (see p.94) described the case of the Drummer of Tedworth. The owner of a house in Tedworth (now Tidworth), UK, was plagued by drumming noises in the night. Visitors who came to investigate reported hearing the sounds, as well as mysterious scratching noises.

Scientific investigations

Investigating the nature of ghosts became a popular pastime in the 19th and early 20th centuries. The first modern ghost hunt took place in 1834 at Bealings House in Suffolk, UK, when owner Major Edward Moor, a member of the Royal Society, was disturbed by the violent ringing of bells. He investigated but found no natural explanation.

This period saw a move toward studying ghosts more scientifically. Scholarly societies like the Ghost Club and the Society for Psychical Research were established in England to search for and evaluate evidence of the paranormal using scientific methods. The Ghost Club led hunts at locations such as Glamis Castle and Culross Palace, both in Scotland. Psychologist Nandor Fodor, a member of the Ghost Club, suggested that ghosts had a physical reality but were emanations of the human brain.

Modern ghost hunters

The arrival of the motor car in the 20th century allowed people to travel farther and investigate ghost sightings for themselves. Hunters such as

Irish writer Elliott O'Donnell and British-American investigator Hereward Carrington were called on to lead inquiries into ghost sightings. O'Donnell was the first researcher to call himself a "ghost-hunter." Carrington was a paranormal investigator who was generally skeptical but maintained that some sightings were genuine and worthy of study. He invented several devices to detect ghosts.

The most influential ghost-hunter of the 20th century was Harry Price, who investigated celebrated cases such as Gef, the Talking Mongoose, which supposedly haunted an Isle of Man farmhouse.

▲ **Mongoose spirit**
This drawing by George Scott depicts Gef, the Talking Mongoose, which allegedly haunted a farm in the 1930s and was investigated by Harry Price. Gef was believed to sing, speak several languages, and steal objects from nearby farms.

IN CONTEXT

Harry Price

British psychic researcher Harry Price made ghost-hunting famous in the 20th century. He used his training as a magician to debunk fraudulent accounts but also supported those he believed to be genuine. After joining the Society for Psychical Research in 1920, he developed a scientific methodology for investigating the paranormal. Published in 1936, *Confessions of a Ghost-Hunter* was Price's own account of the investigations he undertook in his career. It features facts about his debunking of fraudulent spirit photography (see pp.238-239) and his high-profile investigations into Borley Rectory and Gef, the Talking Mongoose. As well as ghosts, Price examined the evidence for spiritualists, telepathy, hypnotism, poltergeists, and other phenomena.

Price used this image of himself with a "spirit" to expose the spirit photographer William Hope in 1922.

▲ **Most haunted house**
Soon after ghost-hunter
Harry Price lived at Borley
Rectory, shown in this
painting, it was gutted by
a fire—an event that Price
claimed was predicted
by a spirit during a seance.

"Although I have investigated many haunted
houses before and since, never have such
phenomena so impressed me as they did on
this historic day. Sixteen hours of thrills."

HARRY PRICE, WRITING ABOUT THE EVENTS AT BORLEY RECTORY ON JUNE 11, 1929

Price found it likely that the spirit in the form of a mongoose was a fake. In any case, the next owner of the property where Gef was seen claimed to have shot the mongoose—a very literal case of ghost-hunting.

For a year Price lived at Borley Rectory, reputed to be the most haunted home in Britain. A phantom coach and horses was said to appear, unexplained footsteps were heard, and objects hurled about. Observers were hired to tour the grounds of the rectory to record any and all spirits and apparitions that made themselves known. Price wrote two books about the spirits at Borley.

Amityville and beyond

In the United States, husband-and-wife ghost-hunters Ed and Lorraine Warren founded the New England Society for Psychic Research in 1952. Calling themselves "demonologists," they studied many of America's most sensational ghost sightings, including at the Amityville house in Long Island. In 1974, the house was the site of a mass murder, and in 1975, when the new owners claimed that it was possessed, the Warrens were the first to investigate and declare the house haunted. They also visited Enfield, in London, UK, to examine evidence of a poltergeist (see pp.110–111) said to move furniture and cause the children to levitate. The Warrens collected haunted objects from their hunts in a basement museum at their home.

◀ **Amityville horror**
Parapsychologist Hans Holzer stands in front of the infamous home at 112 Ocean Avenue, Amityville, in 1980. Holzer believed that Ronald DeFeo Jr. was possessed by demons when he murdered his family there in 1974.

Today ghost-hunting is mostly viewed as a pseudoscience, but it remains popular with the general public. The broadcast of *Ghostwatch* (UK), a BBC mockumentary, in 1992 created controversy for its depiction of a fictional haunting that was presented as real. It did, however, pique public interest in ghosts. In 1996, Andrew Green, author of *Ghost Hunting: A Practical Guide*, invited members of the media to observe his search for ghosts at the Royal Albert Hall. None were spotted.

There has been a recent resurgence of interest with television shows such as *Ghost Hunters* (US) that follow paranormal investigators as they search for evidence of hauntings (see pp.294–297). The internet allows people to share evidence of supposed supernatural activity with millions of others, while the ability to record ghostly experiences on mobile phones has encouraged amateur ghost-hunters to seek out and document hauntings. Visiting haunted places is known as ghost tourism (see pp.282–285) and many historic sites—such as the Ohio State Reformatory in the US—run regular ghost hunts for the general public.

◀ **Demonologist duo**
Ed and Lorraine Warren are pictured here in 1986 outside the Smurl family's Pennsylvania home, which the couple claimed to be haunted by a powerful demonic presence.

▲ **A barograph** measures barometric (air) pressure, which is believed to change when spirits are present. Designed around a metal cylinder (sensitive to pressure) that is linked to a pen arm, the pen traces a graph on a slowly rotating drum—thereby showing pressure changes over time.

▲ **An electroscope** measures electric charge (invisible to the naked eye) in an attempt to detect the static electricity of any unseen ghostly presence.

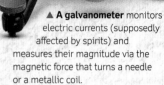

▲ **A galvanometer** monitors electric currents (supposedly affected by spirits) and measures their magnitude via the magnetic force that turns a needle or a metallic coil.

Box housing 65-ft (20-m) strips of 35 mm film

▲ **A thermograph** records temperature over time (a pen, attached to a sensor, traces a line on a roll of graph paper) and is used to identify "cold spots"—inexplicably low temperatures that are said to occur as a result of a haunting.

Electrical signal waveform appears here

▶ **An oscilloscope**, formerly known as an oscillograph, detects electrical signals (thought to be generated or manipulated by spirits) and shows them graphically (X-axis: Time, Y-axis: Voltage).

▲ **The cinématographe** (a celluloid film camera/projector) was developed by the Lumière brothers in the 1890s. Lightweight and relatively portable, it was used by early investigators hoping to catch ghosts on film.

A lens with an adjustable aperture

Wood "neutralizes" external energies

◀ **Dowsing rods** are divining tools, used by ghost-hunters to find paranormal energies. The rods turn inward and outward as a "yes/no" response to interrogations.

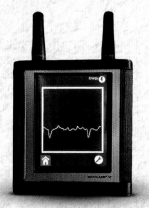

▶ **A spirit communication tool**, the Ovilus deciphers ghostly messages. Electromagnetic field changes activate a "word bank" database, which relays words and sentences.

▲ **A spirit box** is a ghost-scanner radio that rapidly and continually scans through AM and FM frequencies to pick up incoming "spirit messages."

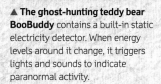

▲ **The ghost-hunting teddy bear BooBuddy** contains a built-in static electricity detector. When energy levels around it change, it triggers lights and sounds to indicate paranormal activity.

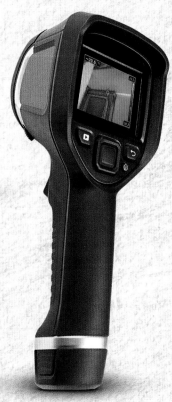

▲ **Thermal-imaging cameras** detect changes in infrared light (invisible to the human eye) and re-create them as a thermal image on the camera itself. They are used to identify mysterious hot and cold spots.

▶ **Electromagnetic field and infrared meters** detect spikes in electromagnetic energy (indicated by the multicolored lights), which many believe signifies paranormal activity.

Paranormal investigation

Throughout history, people have sought to probe reports of supernatural activity by applying the rigors of scientific inquiry to ghost-hunting (see pp.254–257). The spiritualist movement (see pp.222–225) of the early 19th century led to a boom in field-based research and the development of a variety of tools and gadgets to monitor such things as energy fields, atmospheric pressure, and "cold spots." In recent years, more high-tech equipment has been added to the ghost-hunter's arsenal in the hope that infrared meters and thermal-imaging cameras might finally capture undeniable proof of "something there."

Soldiers hold their ground as their dead comrades watch over them in *Backs to the Wall*, a 1918 painting by Scottish artist Robert Gibb.

Ghosts of war

World War I (1914–1918) created unimaginable horrors. Soldiers saw close friends and comrades killed in front of them. Millions died and millions more endured years of fighting under the constant risk of bombs, bullets, and poison gas. The psychological pressures left many suffering shell shock—what is today called post-traumatic stress disorder. In the chaos of battle many soldiers claimed to have seen ghosts, spirits, and angels.

Several soldiers credited ghosts with saving their lives. One said he was told to move by the spirit of his dead brother. A bomb soon struck where he had been sleeping. Others saw recently dead comrades who identified hidden dangers. At Ypres, in Belgium, Lt. William Speight's ghostly comrade pointed to an area that turned out to be mined with explosives. The timers had 13 hours left on the clock.

Sightings of ghosts were reported in the media, and some fictional accounts were even taken to be real. Inspired by accounts of a British victory "against the odds" a month earlier at Mons, Arthur Machen wrote "The Bowmen" (1914), a short story in which spectral archers who had fought at the Battle of Agincourt in 1415 came to the rescue. Many readers took Machen's tale as fact. Some of the art and literature produced by former soldiers also featured ghosts, as a vehicle for exploring the futile slaughter of the trenches, or the hope that dead comrades were not gone forever.

> "The dead officer came once more and, after pointing to a spot on the floor of the dug-out, vanished."
>
> LT. WILLIAM SPEIGHT AT YPRES, BELGIUM, 1915

SOUL TRAVEL
traversing the astral plane

▲ Soul takes flight
Made for Tashakheper, the daughter of an ancient Egyptian priest, around 650 BCE, this coffin painting shows the deceased on her deathbed while her *ba*, depicted as a bird with a human head, flies onward to the afterlife.

Humans have long debated whether or not the spirit can leave the body and explore on its own. According to occult teachings of the 19th and 20th centuries, it is possible: during "astral projection," or an out-of-body experience, a person's inner self can transcend their physical body and travel through the astral plane.

To believers, the astral plane is just one of the planes of the universe, beside the realm of everyday material objects that human consciousness normally interacts with. This notion that other realms exist is a very old one. The ancient Egyptians believed that the human soul was made up of many parts; of these, the winged *ba* (see p.32) was able to leave the body. In many Indigenous religions, shamans were and are thought to be able to project their spirits into other worlds to consult with the gods. The *Mahabharata*, one of the ancient texts of Hinduism, includes a story about a man leaving his body to go in search of his son.

Mind over body
The 18th-century Swedish theologian and mystic Emanuel Swedenborg thought that a human was simply a spirit held in a physical body. Over the course of his life, he experienced several out-of-body experiences that supported this view. Helena Blavatsky, founder of New York's Theosophical Society in 1875, considered Swedenborg one of the greatest "seers" and built on his theories.

According to theosophy (and various earlier traditions), humans have an "astral body" that exists on a different plane to the physical body. Spiritual masters are believed to be able to connect with this astral body. Others might be able to access alternative planes by means of practices such as meditation or lucid dreaming.

Aleister Crowley, a theosophist and one of the most important occultists of the 20th century, developed the theory of "the body of light" (his term for the astral body). Through magical practice and discipline, he claimed that a person could move this body of light into ever-more subtle planes of existence and learn from the beings that lived there. Today, New Age faiths teach that the spirit can leave the body spontaneously during near-death experiences and dreams, or consciously, with practice. Skilled practitioners assert that they can communicate with the spirits of the dead.

Back to the brain
Scientific research has yet to find any evidence to corroborate the idea of astral projection. Though some people claim to have vivid experiences of leaving the body, research shows any disruption to the link between body and brain—for instance, when falling asleep or during trauma—can create a feeling of floating away.

▶ Engulfed in energy
This illustration, from a 1622 theological work by Geronimo Velasquez, shows the spiritual body of a woman surrounded by flames. Believers in astral projection claim that the spiritual body moves as pure energy.

▲ Astral art
Swedish painter and theosophist Hilma af Klint created many abstract works from 1906, after being told by a voice during a seance to paint "on an astral plane." Spirits apparently directed 193 of her works, which predate the abstract art movement by decades.

SPIRIT JOURNEYS
neoshamanism and pagan spirits

▲ Famous witch
Dubbed "Britain's most famous witch" by the BBC, Sybil Leek (1917–1982) advocated for a revival of "our ancient Celtic form of Witchcraft." Here, she introduces one of her familiars, a jackdaw, to another, a boa constrictor.

Inspired by Indigenous and pagan practices for contacting spirits, the term "neoshamanism" encompasses a number of new religious movements. These include New Age spirituality, neopaganism, and Druidism.

The birth of neoshamanism is linked to early studies of Indigenous cultures. In the 19th century, British anthropologist Edward Tylor's theory of animism described Indigenous beliefs that animals, plants, and even rocks were animated by spirits as a sort of primordial "first religion." In the 1950s, Romanian historian of religions Mircea Eliade theorized that shamanism was the essential core of "primitive" religion, and said that shamans used "techniques of ecstasy" such as drumming, chanting, or vision quests, to access the spirit world.

An alternative approach

While the early studies, and later theories, have been criticized for stripping cultural context from a wide variety of distinct religious practices, they inspired interest in a more direct experience of nature. The counterculture movement of the 1960s led many people to reject mainstream religions and seek an alternative worldview. Anthropologist

Carlos Castaneda's books about his supposed encounters with a Yaqui practitioner named Don Juan, who taught him how to access a "Separate Reality" of spirits and magical power, were a hoax, but they inspired a generation of followers. Another exponent of neoshamanism was Michael Harner, who published *The Way of the Shaman* in 1980. Harner applied psychological theories of altered states of consciousness to propose a "Core Shamanism" (also called Urban Shamanism) of techniques and ideas such as drumming, power animals, and visionary journeys.

Though controversial, the work of Harner and other anthropologists led to the development of rituals such as *seidr*, used by North American and British neo-heathens. Inspired by spiritual practices described in the Poetic Edda, a collection of Old Norse sagas that record pre-Christian Scandinavian myths (see pp.104–107), *seidr* ("binding") magic is performed by a *völva* (seeress) with knowledge of "spinning charms" that recall the "threads of fate" spun by the Norns (deities). In a guided meditation, the *völva* goes into a trance and consults spirits in order to answer questions from the group.

▶ Beat of the drum
A shaman wearing traditional garb practices drumming, an "archaic technique of ecstasy" for entering trance states and communicating with the world of the spirits.

▶ Summer solstice
Inspired by the Celtic religion first recorded by Roman statesman Julius Caesar, 1970s Druid reconstructionists meet at Stonehenge to practice their craft and celebrate solstice holiday rituals.

FRIGHTENING FOOTAGE
Hollywood and the horror genre

The medium of film allows for specters to be summoned up at will through special effects and so, almost since the creation of motion pictures, ghosts have appeared on movie screens to delight and terrify audiences. Some of the phantoms are based on well-known stories, while others have been created by writers from their dark imaginations.

Early screen spirits

In 1896, Georges Méliès released what is now commonly thought of as the first horror film: *The House of the Devil.* It lasts for just three minutes but shows a host of sheet-clad ghosts appearing out of nowhere in a way that could never be achieved on stage. Another film, released in 1898, showed men attempting, but failing, to capture a ghost on camera. The spirit throws chairs at the men, then vanishes. These early films were generally intended to amuse viewers with their effects, rather than to elicit fear.

Modern horror films developed around 1910, when popular macabre fiction, such as *Frankenstein* (see pp.194–197), *The Strange Case of Dr. Jekyll and Mr. Hyde,* and the works of Edgar Allan Poe were committed to celluloid. The feelings of menace and dread now associated with the genre emerged in the German Expressionist movement of the 1920s: films such as *The Cabinet of Dr. Caligari,* *The Golem,* and *Nosferatu* used exaggerated visual effects to create unease.

◀ **Innovative cinematography**
German Expressionist film *The Cabinet of Dr. Caligari* (1920) departed from the common realist style of cinema to create a vivid external world shaped by humans' innermost fears.

◀ **The march of the undead**
Despite never using the word "zombie," *Night of the Living Dead* (1968) birthed the zombie genre, which has continued to be popular with fans of horror films.

The invention of the "talkies" in the 1930s heralded the integration of music and sound to build tension in films and the horror genre came into its own. In 1931, the movie *Dracula* was an enormous success. Dubbed a "horror movie" by audiences and critics, it proved there was a hunger for supernatural tales.

An evolving genre

Ghosts were a mainstay of cinema in the middle of the 20th century, sometimes in surprising ways. Comedy films, such as *The Ghost Breakers* (1940), made use of specters to move their plots forward, and ghosts could be portrayed as being helpful and kind. However, they remained figures of horror, too. British production company Hammer Films was founded in 1934 and became synonymous

▼ **"Scariest movie ever"**
The 1973 film *The Exorcist,* about a young girl possessed by a demon, created fear by bringing the action within the domestic sphere and showing the effects of invisible forces.

▲ **Friend or foe?**
The cartoon ghost Casper, first drawn in the 1940s, made his cinematic debut in the 1995 animated film *Casper the Friendly Ghost*. The young ghost is pictured here with his uncles, the Wicked Trio, who are more interested in scaring and playing tricks on the living.

with Gothic horror for decades. During this period, many pioneering directors worked in the genre. Alfred Hitchcock was especially influential in devising cinematic techniques to create suspense.

Competition for audiences in 1950s cinemas led horror showings to include a number of gimmicks. Some movies were shown in theaters with vibrating seats to startle viewers, some offered life-insurance policies in case of death by terror, and some featured skeletons that flew over the heads of the audience. However, the expense of these tactics made horror a less profitable genre and this began to drive a trend toward low-budget productions.

In 1968, George Romero produced *Night of the Living Dead* on a budget of slightly more than $100,000, and this film proved pivotal for the horror genre in various ways. Its low-budget aesthetic and political and social commentary reshaped horror tropes and, despite never actually using the term "zombie" (see p.206), it launched the zombie (and survival) subgenre.

In general, by the 1960s and 1970s, ghosts had fallen out of favor and been replaced with human villains or demonic possession. Hitchcock's *Psycho* opened the door to bloody "slasher films" and ethereal spirits could not match their bloodshed.

"You best start believing in ghost stories. You're in one!"

CAPTAIN BARBOSSA, *PIRATES OF THE CARIBBEAN: THE CURSE OF THE BLACK PEARL* (2003)

Haunted houses

One of the first haunted house movies was *The Uninvited* (1944). In the plot, a brother and sister acquire a house for a suspiciously low sum of money, only to find a spirit already inhabits it. In *The Amityville Horror* (1979)—based on a real case in Long Island (see p.257)—a family moves into a home that was the scene of a mass murder. The father claims "houses don't have memories," and yet they are tormented by supernatural forces. Both films were huge commercial successes and helped establish a horror subgenre and its conventions. These stories tend to follow a familiar pattern: a family moves into a new home and experiences psychic and physical attacks, which drive them to the edge of sanity. However, instead of fleeing from the house, they remain trapped there.

These movies play on the fear that people are not safe, even within their own home and, by placing the horror in a realistic setting, the events are made even more relatable and terrifying. The genre also extends to other haunted structures, such as boats, planes, and even starships, and continues to be a hit with audiences. In 2007, *Paranormal Activity*—a found-footage film about a couple being haunted in their home—was made with just $15,000. It grossed $194 million, and spawned a franchise.

Many television shows also employ the haunted house motif. Ryan Murphy's *American Horror Story* explores many different haunted locations, while Netflix's *The Haunting of Hill House* and *The Haunting of Bly Manor* adapt the 1959 novel by Shirley Jackson and Henry James's *The Turn of the Screw* (1898) respectively.

Diverse hauntings

Ghosts have permeated all forms of cinema. In the children's animation *Coco*, ghosts return to the earth on the Day of the Dead (see pp.140–143), and in the *Ghostbusters* franchise they are used for comedic effect. They even appear in romances, such as the 1990 movie *Ghost*. Supernatural subject matter, both petrifying and amiable, looks set to haunt movie screens for many years to come.

▲ **Spooky setting**
The 2018 Netflix show *The Haunting of Hill House*, loosely based on the horror novel by Shirley Jackson, explores the trauma of a family forced to flee the mansion they are renovating due to paranormal activity.

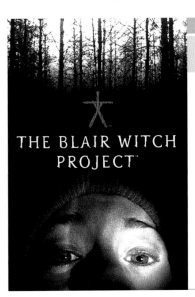

IN CONTEXT

Found-footage films

For a horror film to be scary, it has to convince the audience that it might be real, so many filmmakers choose to label their stories as "found footage," as if they are merely presenting the genuine recordings of a "true story." Often shot amateurishly—quickly and with simple cameras—found-footage films have become a staple of the horror genre. The promotional campaign for *The Blair Witch Project* (1999) went further than most to lend itself an aura of truth. It created a website that presented the evil force shown in the film as a historical fact, and even pretended that the film's actors (deliberately cast as unknown stars) had gone missing and were "presumed dead."

A promotional poster for *The Blair Witch Project* shows Heather Donahue, one of the film's lead actors, looking into a handheld camera.

Krampus

In the Christmas traditions of many cultures, St. Nicholas or Santa Claus is a kindly figure who rewards good behavior. In Germanic folklore, he is paired with a far less benevolent character, who punishes bad behavior. This character, or race of creatures, goes by various names, but is widely known today as Krampus (plural: Krampusse).

The precise origins of this being are unclear, but the German word *Krampus* means "claw," which fits this folkloric bogeyman, who is represented as a horned, demonic beast and is visually similar to the pagan Devil. On *Krampusnacht* (December 5), Krampus was said to chase naughty local children and beat them with a stick, in stark contrast to the gift-giving of his benevolent counterpart St. Nicholas.

Over the centuries, the Christian Church failed in its many attempts to ban Krampus, which had become an integral feature of Christmas. From the late 19th century, instead of Christmas cards, people sent *Krampuskarten*—postcards decorated with "Greetings from Krampus" and often showing children being stuffed into a sack.

In the 21st century, *Krampusnacht* has been revived, and Krampus has entered wider popular culture due to its appearance in a string of horror films. Many places in Austria, Germany, the Czech Republic, Hungary, and Slovenia (as well as some parts of the US and UK) host a yearly Krampus Run, or *Krampuslauf*: a procession of Krampusse dressed in fur suits and horned masks, ringing cowbells, wielding sticks, and (good-naturedly) threatening nearby children.

"As he had for thousands of years, Krampus came not to reward, but to punish."

DESCRIPTION IN THE FILM *KRAMPUS* (2015)

▲ **Men dressed as Krampus** take part in a procession in Börwang, southern Germany, to mark the Christmas season

Ghosts on screen

The supernatural provides a perfect subject for cinema. Films have often been described as a form of dreaming and, with the horror genre, they can portray the audience's most compelling nightmares or, with comedy, highlight the absurdity of these fears. From the early days of experimentation to the present day, many filmmakers have tapped into this rich source material and created haunting tales of the uncanny for the big screen.

▲ *The Haunted Castle* (1897, France), a silent short film, was the first horror movie ever made.

▲ *The Ghost Breakers* (1940, US), a comic take on the supernatural, inspired *Ghostbusters*.

▲ *The Innocents* (1961, UK), a critically acclaimed adaptation of Henry James's *The Turn of the Screw*, perfectly captured the novella's atmosphere of spiraling psychological terror.

▲ *Carnival of Souls* (1962, US) is a cult horror film revered for its eerie portrayal of Purgatory.

▲ *The Changeling* (1980, Canada) contains an iconic scene—a toy ball bouncing down the stairs.

▲ *The Shining* (1980, US) is a renowned and haunting adaptation of Stephen King's novel.

▲ *Poltergeist* (1982, US), with its suburban setting, was a sequel-spawning horror blockbuster.

ビデオに殺されるなんて。

リング

▲ **Ghostbusters (1984, US)** blended spooky tales with quirky humor and broke box-office records.

▲ **The Sixth Sense (1999, US)** is the memorable tale of a boy who claims he can see dead people.

▲ **Spirited Away (2001, Japan)** is a children's animated film about a girl who enters the spirit realm.

▲ **The Devil's Backbone (Spain, 2001)** is Guillermo del Toro's take on Spanish Civil War ghosts.

▲ **Ring (1998, Japan)**, an adaptation of Kôji Suzuki's 1989 novel, merged supernatural events with urban legend to create a genuinely disturbing film, and led to many Hollywood remakes of Japanese horror.

▲ **A Tale of Two Sisters (2003, Korea)** led to an influential horror boom in Korean cinema.

▲ **The Woman in Black (2012, UK)**— this classic remake became the top-grossing UK horror film.

▲ **A Ghost Story (2017, US)** focuses more on existentialist disquiet than jump-scares and suspense.

▲ **La Llorona (Guatemala, 2019)**— weeping ghosts seek revenge against a genocidal leader.

▲ **Spectral spectacle**
Here, a ghost tour actress wanders down Mary King's Close in Edinburgh, Scotland. Visitors to this "haunted" alleyway reported phenomena that researchers have since linked either to low-frequency noises or low humidity in the area.

DEBUNKING GHOST STORIES
science and skepticism

Most cultures have some history of belief in ghosts, spirits, and the supernatural. While many today dismiss these beliefs as fantasies, significant numbers of people still claim to have seen a ghost. Scientific research is helping to shed light on how and why paranormal experiences occur.

Explaining the paranormal
In the 20th century, the term "Stone Tape theory" was coined to explain sightings of ghosts. The theory claimed that some places or materials (such as stone) had the ability to record ("tape") a person's actions and "replay" them in the future. It drew on the ideas of scholars such as Charles Babbage, who suggested that all speech remained in the air as inaudible echoes that some people can perceive, and the parapsychologist T. C. Lethbridge, who claimed that ghosts were remnant energy fields.

Studies have proven that certain environmental conditions can provoke ghostly sensations. In one case, the low-frequency vibration produced by a fan caused shivers and visual apparitions. When the fan was turned off, the "haunting" stopped. The 20 Hz vibration is now known as the "fear frequency."

"People assume that if they can't explain something in natural terms, then it must be something paranormal."

CHRISTOPHER FRENCH, PROFESSOR OF PSYCHOLOGY AND HEAD OF THE ANOMALISTIC PSYCHOLOGY RESEARCH UNIT AT GOLDSMITHS, UNIVERSITY OF LONDON, 2014

Today, ghost hunters (see pp.254–257) often use electromagnetic (EM) detectors, as they believe that ghosts produce measurable EM fields, but it may be that EM fields themselves produce sensations of hauntings. A research study in 2000 used magnetic fields to stimulate the brains of participants. This caused them to feel fear and "see" an apparition that researchers dubbed "a synthetic ghost."

Haunted brains

The human brain has to process a vast amount of data and this may explain how people experience hauntings. The brain organizes the senses to produce useful patterns, but it sometimes gets it wrong; for example, when people see objects in the shapes of clouds. Similarly, when people hear ghost voices in white noise, it might be the brain attempting to create order from chaos. The ability of the brain to generate images is well known. Many people suffer frightening hallucinations while falling asleep or waking up that feel real, but are products of the transition to and from dreaming.

Research into the science and psychology of hauntings is ongoing. However, no matter what research discovers about the paranormal, it is unlikely to stop people from believing in ghosts.

▲ **Making meaning**
These red sandstone formations in the Valley of Fire, Nevada, are often perceived as ghostly faces. Pattern recognition is key to the brain's function, but means that we sometimes "see" specific objects or patterns where there are none—a phenomenon called pareidolia.

IN CONTEXT

Ghostly presence

Not all hauntings involve visual ghost sightings. It is more common to report a presence felt close to the observer. In a 2014 study, researchers used a robot to induce sensorimotor conflict (disagreement in the brain as to what the body is doing) in subjects that caused them to experience a "ghostly presence." Subjects reported feeling something behind them or touching their back. Two participants were so spooked that they wanted to stop the experiment.

Olaf Blanke's robotic device confused people's senses and generated the feeling of a haunting.

Aura photography

According to some spiritual beliefs, every human, animal, and plant is surrounded by an energy field, or "aura." Some people claim to be sensitive to auras, and to be able to see their colors. Since at least the 1880s, researchers have attempted to capture auras on photographic film.

The most famous photographs of auras were taken by Soviet inventor Semyon Kirlian in the mid-20th century. He achieved the effect by passing an electric current through objects placed on photographic paper. Kirlian photographs show living things radiating sparks, which are thought to represent a mysterious, possibly psychic, field of energy that cannot otherwise be seen.

In the US in the 1980s, Guy Coggins created the Auracam, which produces an image of a subject surrounded by a field of colorful energy. Aura photographers believe the colors can be interpreted to show the state of a person's psyche. Conceptual artist and author Christina Lonsdale, with her traveling project Radiant Human, has amassed more than 46,000 aura images. She reports that the color red shows, among other qualities, strength, physicality, and a person facing new beginnings; purple, on the other hand, indicates unconventionality, playfulness, and a visionary perspective. The places that these colors appear on the photograph have different meanings. Colors on the lower left represent the energy of a person's internal state, while colors on the lower right show the energy they put out into the world.

"It's pretty far out!"

WEBSITE FOR AURLA SMARTPHONE AURA CAMERA APP, WHICH USES A PROPRIETARY BIOFEEDBACK ALGORITHM TO CREATE AND ANALYZE AURA PHOTOGRAPHS

FALLING FOR MONSTERS
paranormal romance

Romance novels with at least one supernatural protagonist, paranormal romances came to prominence in the late 20th century, but there is a long history of stories in which people fall in love with monsters and supernatural beings. Examples include the merrows (green-haired mermaids) of Irish folklore and the elfin knights of ballads such as "Scarborough Fair," who set their human lovers impossible tasks.

These tales inspired paranormal romance authors, but none more so than Gabrielle-Suzanne Barbot de Villeneuve's 1740 tale *La Belle et la Bête* ("Beauty and the Beast"). This tells the story of a beautiful princess and a cursed beast, where only her love can make him human again. Paranormal romances often tell a similar tale of redeeming love and a dangerously alluring "monster."

The paranormal romance genre evolved out of 20th-century Gothic romances. These novels, often modeled on the earlier *Jane Eyre* (a "beauty and the beast" narrative itself), usually feature strong, enigmatic male leads who may or may not pose a threat to the heroine. After the Gothic romance genre's heyday, different imprints started to diversify to maintain their audience—including, in some cases, by making the dark masters of dark houses (a Gothic trope; see pp.194–197) literal vampires or demons.

Vampire lovers

The development of paranormal romance is also tied to the changing depiction of the vampire (see pp.214-217): from reanimated corpse in 18th-century accounts to beguiling if ruthless aristocrat in John Polidori's "The Vampyre" (1819); to vicious

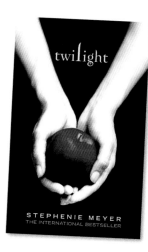

twilight

STEPHENIE MEYER
THE INTERNATIONAL BESTSELLER

◀ **Young Adult phenomenon**
Stephenie Meyer's *Twilight* series gained massive international popularity. The trilogy sees Bella, a human teenager, choose between her two loves: Edward, a vampire, and Jacob, a werewolf.

but tragic lover in Sheridan Le Fanu's *Carmilla* (1872); to amoral but intriguing protagonist in *The Vampire Chronicles* of Ann Rice (1976–2018); to sparkling heartthrob in *Twilight* (2005). The vampire moves from simple predator to complex antagonist to attractive outsider. The US TV show *Dark Shadows* (1966–1971) was a major influence on this shifting perspective. The popularity of the show's vampire, Barnaby Collins, led to tie-in novels and paved the way for the vampire as romantic lead.

Supernatural variety

While some of the most famous paranormal romances feature vampires, today it is a diverse and prolific genre. Readers can encounter romances with supernatural beings of almost every description: ghosts, fairies, werewolves (and every other type of were-creature), and even zombies.

◀ **Beastly manners**
In the original story of *La Belle et la Bête*, the beast is not described in detail, leaving room for the reader's interpretation. While commonly depicted with attributes of bears and lions, in this historical illustration, he is a kind of beaver or walrus.

▼ **Dangerous attraction**
Anne Rice's novel was made into the film *Interview with the Vampire* in 1994, featuring Brad Pitt and Tom Cruise as complex, attractive vampires.

HUMAN BEASTS
were-creatures

▲ Olmec were-jaguar
Jaguars were important in the religion of the Olmec people, the earliest-known major Mesoamerican civilization (c. 1200–400 BCE). They left many statues like this example: the hands are tightly curled into fists, as if becoming feline paws.

Creatures with mixed human and animal forms (known as "therianthropes") are found around the world, dating back to prehistoric times. In Indonesia, cave art has been discovered from 44,000 years ago that depicts human figures with beaks, tails, and other animal characteristics. In Germany, a 40,000-year-old statuette was excavated of a figure who is half-lion, half-man. Early written accounts also recount belief in were-creatures. In Greek mythology, the god Zeus appears in the guise of many creatures, from swans to bulls. In the 1st century CE, Chinese philosopher Wang Chong recounted stories of were-tigers.

Becoming human

Were-creatures are an almost universal global phenomenon, with forms often based on local wildlife, and the more dangerous were-creatures representing local apex predators (those at the top of the food chain). In some legends, were-creatures are animals who can assume human form, like the mischievous Japanese *bake-danuki*, a raccoon dog who can become human. However, in other traditions, were-creatures are spirits who can assume both human and animal forms. In the folklore of Orkney and the Shetland Islands, the tangie sea spirit can take the form of a horse or an old man, and uses both to lure humans into the water in order to devour them.

In many fables, were-creatures are human shape-shifters. Some have control over their transformation, such as the Somali Qori-ismaris, who rubs himself with a stick to become a "hyena-man." Others have less control or are, by nature, a were-creature. In Hawaiian mythology, Nanaue is the son of a shark god and a mortal woman, whose first taste of meat makes him transform into a shark and leads to a perpetual hunger for human flesh.

Werewolves

The mythological ability of a human being to transform into a wolf (lycanthropy) features in the folklore of many diverse cultures. The first recorded account appears in *The Epic of Gilgamesh* (c. 2100–1200 BCE), when the titular hero rejects the goddess Ishtar, in part for changing a shepherd into a wolf. Werewolves are common in tales from the Middle Ages. In the Viking *Völsunga Saga* (c. 1270), Sigmund and Sinfjötli become trapped temporarily in wolf form after putting on cursed pelts. Medieval tales often present a more sympathetic monster than later stories. In tales like Marie de France's *Bisclaravet* ("The Lay of the Werewolf"), the creature is a wolf with a rational soul, capable of loyalty and eager for vengeance. Beliefs about werewolves evolved over time, with the idea of the "evil" werewolf becoming standard in Europe during the early modern period. Many "werewolf trials" took place, such as that of German farmer Peter Stump in 1589: he was accused of making a deal with the Devil, killing and eating children, and lycanthropy.

Today, werewolves thrive in popular culture, where they can be threatening (in horror films) or sympathetic (in paranormal romance, see pp.278–279). They are often used to explore ideas of the "animal within."

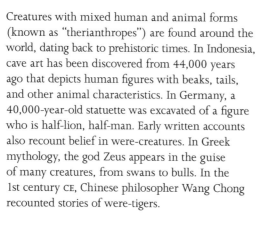

◀ Man in wolf's clothing
As seen on this vase, wolf-men abound in Greek mythology. Zeus transforms King Lycaon into a wolf for killing his son. The term "lycanthropy" also comes from Ancient Greek: *lykoi* ("wolf") and *anthropos* ("man").

◀ **Man or beast?**
Medieval tales often illustrate
the thin separation between
savage beast and civilized
man. This woodcut from the
Nuremberg Chronicle (1493)
depicts a "monster" with two
heads—one wolflike dog,
the other human.

EERIE EXPEDITIONS
ghost tourism

Ghosts can make popular tourist attractions. Ghost tourism—visits to places specifically because they claim to be "haunted"—can take many forms. At haunted hotels, like Jamaica Inn in Cornwall, UK—made famous by the novelist Daphne du Maurier—guests can pay a premium for a room with a resident ghost. Emphasizing the eerie has also proved a successful way to attract tourists to historical sites. For example, at Newstead Abbey, in the UK—the Gothic ancestral home of the Romantic poet Lord Byron—special events offer workshops that teach the basics of paranormal investigation, and there is always the possibility of meeting the ghostly Black Friar, immortalized in Byron's poetry.

Ghost tourism is a booming industry. Ghost walks, which take visitors around multiple sites, often at night, are especially popular. In England, the Original Ghost Walk of York claims to be one of the world's oldest, running since 1973, while Bath's Ghost Hunters Silent Disco Tour offers a less traditional option. Similarly imaginative attractions can be found around the world: ghost tourists can visit the Minxiong Ghost House in Taiwan; go on a haunted and haunting tour of Salem, Massachusetts, home of the infamous witch trials; take a Mystery Ghost Bus round Johannesburg, South Africa; or visit a haunted bathroom at the old Manly Quarantine Station in Australia.

Pull of the paranormal

While modern ghost tourism is a relatively new phenomenon, made popular by ghost tours in the 1980s and 21st-century television shows such as *Most Haunted* (UK) and *Ghost Hunters* (US), ghosts have a long history of attracting tourists. In 1762, the story of the "Cock Lane Ghost"

◄ Spooky souvenir
York ghosts, sold in numerous designs, are popular purchases for visitors to the British city. They are inspired by medieval "ghost-making"—the creation of tokens that pilgrims bought to take to shrines.

gripped London. A young girl, Elizabeth Parsons, reported knocking and scratching from "Scratching Fanny," identified as the ghost of a previous lodger who claimed she had been murdered. People flocked to the house to witness these supernatural signs and were duly charged for entry. The case was revealed as a hoax, but not before the house and its "haunting" had become an early form of monetized ghostly experience.

In 1809, the Paris Catacombs (see p.71) were opened to the public by appointment. Visitors toured the bone-lined tunnels by candlelight and, at the exit, were invited to record their impressions in a register. Their comments prove how popular the catacombs were at the time with both locals and

◄ **In the tunnels**
This 1825 aquatint engraving is a copy of an illustration credited to Victor Auver from "A Tour Through Paris." It depicts a group of eager tourists visiting the catacombs by candlelight.

▼ **Ghost bus**
The site of historic battles, brutal enslavement, and disastrous epidemics, Savannah, Georgia, is considered one of the most haunted cities in the US. Tours take in the darker history of Savannah and uncover its ghosts.

tourists, and today they remain one of the city's main attractions. Tales abound of hauntings—from disembodied voices to sightings of the ghost of Philibert Aspairt, who lost his way in the labyrinth in 1793 and supposedly still roams the tunnels.

Tourists also flocked to other sites throughout the 19th century, including Medmenham Abbey, UK, where locals charged visitors for tours of the home of the infamous "Hellfire Club," founded by libertines in 1749. In the 20th century, paranormal investigator Elliott O'Donnell toured Britain and published popular guides to its most haunted sites. Ghost tourism might only have become big business in the late 20th century, but it has been around for hundreds of years.

▶ **Dolls of the dead**
Mexico has an unusual tourist attraction known as *Isla de las Muñecas* ("Island of the Dolls"), where Don Julian Santana Barrera, a hermit, spent 50 years hanging up more than 1,000 dolls to appease the ghost of a drowned girl who he believed was haunting him.

▼ **Ghost parade**
Every year in November, since 1956, Campbelltown, Australia, holds the Fisher's Ghost Festival. Fred Fisher disappeared in June 1826 and his ghost supposedly appeared a few months later to point to the site of his shallow grave.

Over time, different forms of ghost tourism have developed. Some offer ghostly thrills, while others promise proof of the paranormal. Yet ghost tourism can also function as an act of remembrance; in Salem, Massachusetts, ghost tours serve to bring the stories of those persecuted in the witch trials to life. At times, the line between remembrance and entertainment is blurred. Visitors go to Mexico's *Isla de las Muñecas* not only to remember the girl who died there, but also to be thrilled or spooked by tales of moving dolls and strange noises.

The dark side

Ghost tourism can overlap with other forms of macabre tourism that are not necessarily directly linked to the supernatural. These include "dark tourism," centered on sites associated with violence, murder, and suffering, and "Gothic tourism," focused on eerie or macabre sites or experiences. Events like the annual festival of Fisher's Ghost in Campbelltown, Australia, mix tragic histories with exuberant Gothic entertainment: tens of thousands of visitors descend on the town to see the ghost of the murdered Fred Fisher—who disappeared in June 1826 but whose ghost reportedly appeared a few months later to point to the site of his shallow grave—and to take part in a week of spooky parades and activities.

Exploited tragedies

While exploring ghost narratives can reveal hidden histories, accuracy is sometimes sacrificed for the sake of a good story, and tragedy exploited for entertainment. For example, the Lizzie Borden House in Fall River, Massachusetts—the site of a double murder committed in 1860—was bought in 2021 for $2 million by an entrepreneur hoping to profit from its grisly history. The attached museum's gift shop sells a "bloody ax" (the weapon Lizzie allegedly used to murder her parents) as a souvenir.

Sites of suffering are often associated with hauntings—and prisons and asylums with brutal histories are common ghost-tourist destinations. Philadelphia's Eastern State Penitentiary (see pp.286–287) hosts interactive "haunted houses" for Halloween, offering a live horror experience in the place where prisoners were tortured. Examples like these raise ethical questions over the responsibilities tourists and tour operators bear toward the dead, and how to engage respectfully with their stories.

▶ **In silent prayer**
The Church of St. George in Luková, Czech Republic, was abandoned in 1968 after its roof collapsed, and locals claimed it was haunted. Since 2012, artist Jakub Hadrava's plaster ghost art has brought visitors back to the building.

Most haunted

Philadelphia's Eastern State Penitentiary is said to be one of the most haunted buildings in the United States. It first opened its doors in 1829, not closing until 1971. The prison was based on a radical new approach to incarceration that centered on inducing penitence through isolation. For many years, prisoners were unable to speak to each other and forced to wear bags over their heads for anonymity. Any communication was strictly forbidden and prisoners were subjected to torturous punishments for minor infractions. It is perhaps unsurprising, then, that tales of hauntings at the prison have existed for decades.

Inmates, guards, and visitors have reported paranormal activity, including shadowy figures in cellblock 6, voices and cries in cellblock 12, and a mysterious male figure in the guard tower. One of the prison's most notorious residents, the gangster Al Capone, was haunted there in 1929. At night, he was heard screaming and begging "Jimmy" to leave him alone. The penitentiary has been the subject of many investigations on television and online, including *Ghost Adventures*, *Most Haunted*, and *Buzzfeed Unsolved*. Today, daily museum tours focus more on the prison's history and debates around criminal justice than on hauntings. Nonetheless, there are public ghost tours and many visitors record strange experiences. There is also a yearly haunted house event that turns the prison into a scare attraction featuring live actors and terrifying scenes.

> "Take a look around.
> If ghosts exist anywhere,
> they must be here."

AMERICAN ACTOR STEVE BUSCEMI IN "THE VOICES
OF EASTERN STATE" AUDIO TOUR

EYES AND EARS EVERYWHERE

modern animist beliefs

Animism is defined by two core beliefs: first, the
idea that all nonhuman things, such as animals,
plants, and objects, are imbued with an *anima* (soul)
or inhabited by spirits; and secondly, that all things
exist as intentional beings, capable of will, purpose,
and agency. This dual acknowledgment informs
animism's respect for the environment, whether
natural or constructed. It also offers different ways
of apprehending the world that affect individual
well-being (the personal) and relationships with
other living and nonliving things (the communal).

Animist beliefs continue to be an integral part of
everyday life in Indigenous Southeast Asian cultures.
In spite of centuries of repression in the region, they
have continued to survive alongside the official
major religions, such as Islam and Christianity,
either by going underground; remaining marginal as
Indigenous practices; or, more commonly, becoming
assimilated into these major religions.

In Malaysia, the various Indigenous peoples (or
Orang Asli) include the Kadazans, the Ibans, the
Mah Meris, and the Senois, among others. Their

> ## "[Animists] recognize that the world is full of persons, only some of whom are human."
>
> **GRAHAM HARVEY**, IN *ANIMISM: RESPECTING THE LIVING WORLD* (2006)

animistic beliefs are especially evident in their hunting and gathering, agricultural, and husbandry practices. For example, earth that is considered sacred or unclean is avoided, and offerings are made to local deities and ancestral spirits, in order to acquire food, breed animals, or harvest the land.

In East Malaysia, the Kadazan-Dusun people believe that local spirits known as the *mogigion* ("guardians of the land") will become enraged if nature is violated or disturbed. For this reason, construction work often only proceeds once shrines have been built and offerings made to appease them.

The Divine Oneness

Balinese cosmology is influenced both by animism and the ancient conviction that the island belongs to the supreme god Sang Hyang Widhi Wasa ("The Divine Order"), who has entrusted it to humanity for safekeeping. The good (male) spirits are thought to dwell in the mountains, while the evil (female) spirits are consigned to the sea. This is the domain of Nyi Roro Kidul, the serpent queen who is part-mermaid. Both must be shown equal respect, because this duality is believed to bring cosmic balance to the universe.

Spirit houses

In Thailand, Cambodia, Laos, and Myanmar, land on which a business or home sits is often accompanied by a "spirit house," which is a miniature shrine constructed to shelter resident spirits and keep them from interfering with, or even harming, the living. The spirit house is regularly replenished with offerings such as food, drinks, flower garlands, and burning incense. It is usually placed in an auspicious spot, established with the help of a shaman and, if well-appeased, its spirits can potentially bring good fortune as well.

▲ **King of spirits**
The legend of Barong, a panther-like deity, reinforces the binary logic that underpins Balinese animist beliefs: as the leader of benevolent spirits, his eternal arch-nemesis is Rangda, the demon queen.

Spirit theater

The puppets, carvings, and gongs of Indonesian puppet theater are at times thought to house ancestral spirits, and animist spirit folklore has inspired many theatrical tales. The character of Semar, while outwardly a jester, is thought by some to be the ancestral spirit of Java, who is applied to for healing or protection. His costume is often black and white, which figuratively represents sacred binaries (such as light/dark, life/death, good/evil) and, despite Semar's status as a clown, he is widely considered to be a symbol of divine wisdom.

This shadow puppet of the clown Semar is recognizable by its protruding belly, black body, white face, and lump on its forehead.

THE SPIRITS RETURN
reviving traditional African beliefs

▲ Woman power
This carved *gẹlẹdẹ* mask is worn during a festival to celebrate the spiritual power of "mothers." This includes Iya Nla, the primordial mother, but also celebrates female ancestors and elderly women within Yoruba-Nago communities in Benin, Nigeria, and Togo.

It is difficult to separate Africa's spiritual and supernatural beliefs because they are understood today from the continent's colonial history. European colonizers suppressed Indigenous spiritual beliefs as "primitive" pagan practices, and imposed Christianity as the dominant religion. Centuries earlier, Islamic conquerors in the north, east, and west of the continent acted in a similar way. Christianity and Islam became embedded, and African practices were marginalized.

By the 20th century, African belief systems had largely been erased. Over the years, various nationalist movements have tried to redress this but failed to remove the stigma colonialism had attached to "superstitious" practices. Efforts to restore faith in traditional African beliefs have continued to flounder due to ongoing hostility from Christians and Muslims, abuses of power within communities and their own tendency toward secrecy, along with the spread of secularism and globalization. Despite these issues, there is new interest within communities and the African diaspora to restore traditional spiritual practices to a place of relative importance among imported religions.

Reclaiming spirits

African deities, nature spirits, and ancestor spirits manifest as ambivalent, benevolent, and malevolent. Yet accounts by missionaries and African converts to Christianity and Islam almost always labeled them wholly malevolent. In southern Africa, missionaries cast the ancestral spirits of the Tswana religion, the *badimo*, as evil. Similarly, Yoruba-born preacher and Christian convert Samuel Ajayi Crowther linked the Yoruba *òrìṣà* (deity) Èṣù (see pp.44–45) with Satan when he translated the Bible into the Yoruba language in the 1840s.

Today, adherents of traditional beliefs fight to dispel such misconceptions. Through cultural activism and social media, the #ÈṣùIsNotSatan movement seeks to celebrate who Èṣù really is—the mischievous *òrìṣà* of crossroads, duality, beginnings, travelers, fertility, and death.

Goddess power

African beliefs focus on the community and its relationship to the natural world, to which women are central. These beliefs can align with progressive ideas, as seen by the Mijikenda people's campaign in Kenya to protect sacred sites within ancestral forest groves from environmental damage.

Various rituals and festivals have been reinstated to emphasize the foundational role of women in African beliefs. In 1996, members of the Zulu community revived an annual festival in honor of Nomkhubulwane, the goddess of rain, nature, and fertility. Subsequent controversy over whether or not the traditional rite of virgin-testing protects the health, rights, and dignity of the girls who participate has opened up conversations about how African communities can meaningfully engage with traditional beliefs in modern times.

▶ Ancestral guards
Carved sculptures of ancestors stand guard in a *kaya* on the southeastern coast of Kenya. *Kayas* are sacred ancestral villages within forests that the Mijikenda people revere and protect as sites of ritual power. The figures protect *kayas* from tree felling, livestock grazing, and farming.

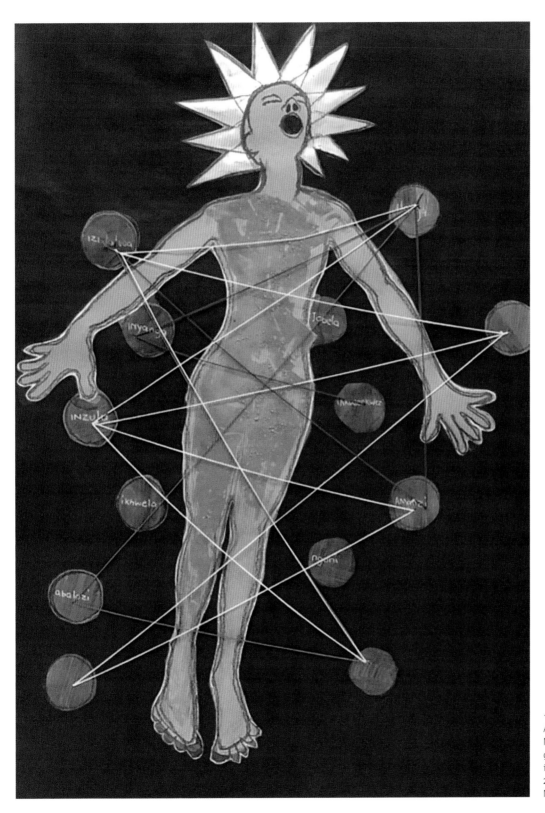

◄ **Mother Earth**
A virgin girl supplicates
Nomkhubulwane, the Zulu
goddess of rain and fertility,
in a mixed media work from
2021 by South African artist
Mandisi Mncela.

BLOODY MARY, BLOODY MARY
urban legends

Stories passed from person to person, told as if they are current and true, are called urban legends. These secondhand stories often narrate a series of odd events, culminating in a plot twist that invokes a strong emotion, such as surprise, fear, or disgust. Mysteries that can only be explained through the supernatural also feature. Examples of urban legends exist all around the world, and not only in cities, despite the "urban" label. They can be told in and about any location, from isolated country roads to busy shopping centers, with their settings in real and familiar places increasing their plausibility for the listener.

◀ **Death's highway**
Depicted in this 2014 film, Highway Sheila haunts a road in Chatsworth, South Africa. The high number of accidents that occur on "Death's Highway" is often blamed on the ghost of a woman said to have died there.

her father refused to let her marry the man she loved. In Quezon City, the Philippines, the story involves a taxi driver picking up a woman in white late at night. When the driver looks behind him, he sees her face is bruised and bloody, and flees the taxi in terror.

Another common tale is that of the Vanishing Hitchhiker—a mysterious hitchhiker (male or female) who suddenly disappears. In Chicago's southwest suburbs, a woman in a white ball gown, known as "Resurrection Mary," asks drivers for a ride home. By the time the car reaches a local cemetery, Mary has vanished without a trace.

Ghostly archetypes

Many urban legends center on a recurring ghost character that appears in different places and cultures. The White or Gray Lady is the ghost of a woman dressed all in white or gray, who died tragically, her story involving love, sex, betrayal, or murder. She is a global phenomenon, with many towns having their own White Lady. Yet her story changes in each location to fit local history or landmarks. In Coventry, UK, the White Lady haunts Whitley Abbey, from where she is said to have jumped to her death after

Summoning spooks

Urban legends also involve ritual games that summon a ghost. "Bloody Mary," for example, is the bloodied ghost of a woman said to appear in a mirror if her name is chanted three or thirteen times. In Japan, it is a girl named Hanako-san who appears in school bathrooms if you knock on the door three times and call her name. Depending on where the game is played, Hanako-san may appear as a girl in red, a three-headed lizard, or a bloodied hand that pulls the summoner into the stall. These games are particularly popular with children.

▼ **Frightening specter**
The imaginary "bogeyman" is often used in stories to frighten children into good behavior. In this 1799 work, Spanish artist Goya depicts the bogeyman *el Coco* as a shrouded figure terrifying two children. The piece was a critique of poor educational practices of the period.

"They're the stories that we use to explain ourselves to ourselves."

NEIL GAIMAN, FANTASY AND GRAPHIC NOVEL AUTHOR ON URBAN LEGENDS

◄ **Woman in white**
The archetypal "White Lady" is depicted in this 1900 painting by Austrian artist Gabriel von Max. A pale, ghostly figure, she carries a bunch of skeleton keys at her waist. The painting hangs in a medieval castle in the Czech Republic that is reputed to house many ghosts.

THE SPIRITS AMONG US
ghosts in popular culture

In modern popular culture, ghosts are more alive than ever. From video games to social-media memes, spirits manifest in a wide variety of genres and guises and they continue to exert a strong hold over the popular imagination. Some ghosts appear in popular culture purely for entertainment, jump scares, or even for comedic value—like the flatulent spirit Slimer from the *Ghostbusters* film franchise. Other ghosts, it could be argued, are manifestations of cultural anxieties about death, and help people to deal with death and grief.

A good read

Ghosts have always been at the center of a good story and many writers—including Stephen King (*The Shining*, 1977; *Bag of Bones*, 1998) and James Herbert (*Haunted*, 1988)—have enjoyed international success from writing in the modern supernatural horror genre. However, ghost characters are used in fiction for more than their ability to chill and thrill. In Ali Smith's *Hotel World* (2001), the ghost of a teenage chambermaid is used to explore the stages of grief. The main character of Shehan

▼ **Dancing specters**
In this scene from the English National Ballet's 2006 production of *The Canterville Ghost*—based on Oscar Wilde's 1887 short story—guests dance at Sir Simon's phantom ball.

Karunatilaka's *The Seven Moons of Maali Almeida*, winner of the 2022 Booker Prize, is a ghost seeking to publicly expose the atrocities of the Sri Lankan Civil War. And Raina Telgemeier's graphic novel *Ghosts* (2016), which follows a young girl's attempts to befriend her town's ghosts while suffering from cystic fibrosis, invites a young audience to think about how we can come to terms with death.

Stars of "reality TV"

Ghosts transitioned easily from the page to the screen (see pp.266–269), and one particularly popular genre is the paranormal reality television show, which peaked in the first decades of the 21st century. Examples include *Most Haunted* (UK), *Ghost Adventures* (US), and *Scariest Places on Earth* (US), which feature teams of ghost hunters, psychics, and demonologists actively seeking out paranormal experiences. Each episode focuses on a specific "haunted" location, the investigators documenting historic ghost sightings and then using infrared cameras and recording devices to capture what they see and hear as they brave an overnight stay. Similar shows also made it to YouTube, a popular example being Shane Madej and Ryan Bergara's *Buzzfeed Unsolved* (and the follow-up, *Ghost Files*). These shows are dramatized; British regulator Ofcom stated in 2005 that *Most Haunted* is "for entertainment purposes" rather than "legitimate investigations." However, they can also offer serious insights into how people might respond to paranormal experiences.

Gaming ghouls

Ghosts also live on in video games, often in the role of the adversary. In *Pac-Man*, players are pursued through a maze by four colorful ghosts, while in *Luigi's Mansion*, a subseries of the best-selling *Super Mario* franchise, the player explores a haunted mansion, capturing ghosts in the "Poltergust 3000" vacuum cleaner and, finally, battles the series' villain, the ghost King Boo.

In games of the survival horror genre, the ghosts are often more sinister and violent, such as the antagonists in *The Fatal Frame* series and *Phasmophobia*. However, they are not always the bad guys and, in the *Zelda* series, ghosts often play mentor figures. In "Beyond: Two Souls," the main character is tethered to a ghost who helps her throughout the game.

▲ **How haunted?**
A steadicam operator films Yvette Fielding, a host on the hugely successful TV show *Most Haunted*, as she investigates signs of the paranormal.

◀ *These Ghosts of Mine*
This art installation by fashion designer and artist Antonio Marras is made from 80 nightgowns, embroidered by students of the Naples Academy of Fine Arts. The lanterns light up at night and float like the friendly ghosts of the city.

▲ Ghostly paintings
Known as the "ghost people," these murals appeared across Savamala, a district of Belgrade, Serbia, in the early 2010s—a time when local people were being pushed out of the area by a controversial redevelopment.

The creepy web

In the past, ghost stories were told around a fire, in hushed voices. Now, they spread virally online, on discussion websites and content-sharing platforms, such as Reddit, TikTok, Instagram, Tumblr, and Pinterest. The internet has played a huge role in the world's increasing fascination with the paranormal and, as content can quickly be disseminated to every corner of the globe, folk tales and ghost stories are being shared on an unprecedented scale. Over time, a subculture known as "creepycore" has developed. The name refers to the widespread creation and sharing of art, photos, and videos that draw on the aesthetics of horror and the occult.

The supernatural has even manifested in social media jargon, with the term "ghosting" referring to somebody who has abruptly stopped responding on an online platform or dating app, vanishing like a ghost. The use of social media in contemporary Pagan communities, meanwhile, has become so extensive that it is known as "WitchTok."

Online, people can share their beliefs in magic and the supernatural with vast, global audiences. Personal experiences with the paranormal can go viral through written accounts or recorded footage—in much the same way as earlier photographs of the Cottingley Fairies (see pp.62–63), the Loch Ness Monster, and Bigfoot were published and spread in the 19th and 20th centuries. However, with the internet, such stories and images can be copied and pasted from message board to message board, moving from platform to platform, and presented as truth but with the original creator unknown or forgotten. This content is called "creepypasta," adapted from the term "copypasta" (referring to a block of text that is copied and pasted), and many stories take on a life of their own.

The legend of Slender Man

There are countless creepypasta stories online. The most notorious is "Slender Man" (or Slenderman), about a terrifying faceless figure, unnaturally tall and thin, who wears a suit and stalks children. This legend originated from a single online post on the "Something Awful" forum, which hosted a Photoshop contest of paranormal images in 2009. Eric Knudsen (under the username Victor Surge) contributed two photographs of children, with an unnerving figure lurking in the background, and an unsettling, unattributed caption (see below).

The images captured people's imaginations and fears, and many contributed their own art and stories. The myth grew and the faceless, elongated figure of Slender Man became a bogeyman for the modern age. By 2014, the legend was so well known that when two young girls in Wisconsin stabbed another child in the woods, they claimed they had not acted out of free will—the Slender Man had told them to do it.

> "Its persistent silence and outstretched arms horrified and comforted us ..."

ERIC KNUDSEN, IN A CAPTION DESCRIBING THE SLENDER MAN

IN CONTEXT

Whisper

Social media is a new frontier for those with an interest in ghosts and the undead—as proven by the popularity of Whisper, a zombie-like character who has become a viral sensation. With ashen skin, pointed fangs, long ebony locks, and a cryptic language of growls and clicks, Whisper emerged in 2022 through Spookers Haunted Attraction's TikTok and Instagram. Fans affectionately dub Whisper "adorable," embracing this eerie persona born to comply with TikTok's guidelines, while sparking a devoted online community.

TikTok/Instagram content creator @spookersnz posts videos of Whisper, featuring fun and silly activities designed to entertain audiences worldwide.

▲ **Faceless figure**
This is one of many artistic recreations of the creepypasta legend Slender Man. In 2018, the *Slender Man* film was released, further cementing his image—the faceless figure with elongated arms—in the public imagination.

GHOST STORIES, GLOSSARY, AND INDEX

GHOST STORIES FROM AROUND THE WORLD

The Americas

The Amherst Poltergeist

NOVA SCOTIA, CANADA, 19TH CENTURY

In 1878, 19-year-old Esther Cox began to experience terrifying phenomena. Small fires started at the Amherst cottage where she lived, items disappeared without explanation, and disembodied voices emanated from the darkness. Esther's eyes became bloodshot, her limbs swelled up, and threatening messages appeared on the cottage walls. Esther and her family moved away but the attacks continued, including a pocketknife that stabbed her in the back. Walter Hubble, a supernatural investigator, believed that the spirit of Bob MacNeal, a local youth who had attacked Esther the year before, was responsible, aided by a demon. The attacks finally subsided about a year later, still without explanation.

The Land of the Dead

CALIFORNIA, US, FOLKTALE

A ghost story of the Serrano people tells how a renowned hunter returned home to find his wife dead. Staring at her funeral pyre, he saw a wisp of dust form above the ashes, whirl in the wind, and set off down the road. In the gloom, he thought he saw his wife's shape, so he followed. When they reached a large rock, the apparition spoke, explaining that this was the boundary between the land of the living and the dead, which he could cross if he climbed onto her back. The hunter went with his wife to meet her ancestors, who were hostile at first, since they had to cook special food for a living person. When they went hunting and instructed him to shoot, all he saw were two beetles, which he crushed. These were the land of the dead's deer, and his wife's family praised him. Finally, he could no longer stay without dying himself, but he was allowed to take his wife back to the world of the living for three days. After that she returned and they were parted forever.

The Night Marchers

HAWAI'I, US, FOLKTALE

In certain sacred spots on Hawai'i—burial sites or old temples—it is said that an unwary bystander might come across the *huaka'i pō* (night marchers), traveling in groups, bearing torches, and moving to the rhythmic pounding of drums. Armed with knives, axes, and clubs studded with sharks' teeth, they chant as they march and protect these sacred places from intruders. Sometimes, they have gods or goddesses in their midst, or the *ali'i* (ruling spirits) there to welcome new recruits to the rank of spirit warriors.

The Headless Ghost

MISSISSIPPI, US, EARLY 19TH CENTURY

Two fishermen from Mississippi decided to spend the night on Deer Island, out in Biloxi Bay. While sitting around their campfire making coffee, they heard a noise in the palmetto bushes. They blamed wild pigs but, upon going to check, they were startled when a headless skeleton came hurtling out of the bush and pursued them to their boat. The petrified fishermen sailed back in haste to the mainland. The next day they returned, but found no trace of the ghost, said to be that of a pirate who stayed behind on the island to guard a hoard of plundered gold. His captain had beheaded him, ensuring his skeletal ghost would remain at his post forever.

The Evil Hour

CHIAPAS, MEXICO, FOLKTALE

Travelers on desolate roads in southern Mexico, especially those approaching crossroads, must be wary, lest they encounter La Mala Hora ("The Evil Hour"). Also called La Malogra, this demon can appear as a beautiful woman dressed in black, but most often manifests itself as a dense, pitch-black cloud that smothers lanterns, envelops travelers, and leads them off the road to perish in swamps or plunge off cliffs. It is said that anyone who looks directly at La Mala Hora will be rendered insane, but one Mayan legend tells how a needle blessed by a priest can trap the demon, allowing the priest to banish it.

▲ **Beware the night marchers**—according to legend, anyone bold enough to look straight at the *huaka'i pō* is doomed to die.

The Headless Gringa

GALAPAGOS ISLANDS, ECUADOR, MID-20TH CENTURY

In the 1940s, a serviceman stationed at the US airbase on Baltra Island, in the Galapagos, suspected his girlfriend of cheating on him and murdered her in a fit of rage by pushing her off a cliff. As she hit the beach, it is said that her head became detached from her body. Ever since, a female ghost has appeared to lonely servicemen on the base. In the guise of a beautiful woman, the ghost lures them to a remote spot and then transforms into a hideous headless apparition, smelling of rotting flesh and the sap of the sacred Palo Santo tree. One Ecuadorian soldier who fell victim was found days later, bound, raving, and foaming at the mouth. Sometimes, La Cabeza Gringa ("The Headless Gringa") is even said to climb into bed with soldiers in their barracks and attempt to suffocate them.

Europe

A Ghostly Plan
ENGLAND, 10TH CENTURY
According to the Anglo-Saxon chronicles of Ælfric, the spirit of Saint Swithun (Bishop of Winchester 852–863) became disturbed about his remains being buried outside church grounds and neglected. He appeared to a local blacksmith in a dream, ordering him to find a priest to petition the bishop to move his bones inside the church. The blacksmith, however, was afraid that no one would believe him and did nothing, until Saint Swithun appeared to him twice more. Even then the priest failed to persuade the bishop, and only when the spirit of Swithun began performing miracles and healing large numbers of diseased people did the bishop relent. In 971, Swithun's remains were reinterred and enshrined inside the Old Minster at Winchester.

The Black Sow
WALES, FOLKTALE
As the bonfires died down on Halloween, marking the beginning of winter, people all over Wales feared the emergence of the Hwch Ddu Gwta from the ashes. An enormous black sow with no tail and huge red eyes, this beast would hunt anyone who did not hurry home, and it would drag their souls down to the Underworld. According to legend, the Hwch Ddu Gwta favored lying in wait around stiles and bridges, especially for children, whose parents warned them to avoid such places in the early winter darkness.

The Blue Room
NORTHERN IRELAND, 19TH CENTURY
Springhill House, north of Cookstown, is one of Northern Ireland's most haunted houses. Olivia Lenox-Conyngham's husband, an army officer, shot himself there after being unfairly court-martialed. Since then, house guests have reported seeing Olivia's ghost, repeating her desperate dash to the door of "the blue room" in a vain attempt to prevent her husband's suicide. Phantom whisperings have also been heard in the room, coming from the wall behind the bed and, decades after the officer's death, a hidden powder closet door was discovered behind the wallpaper; on the floor lay a pouch full of bullets. Olivia's ghost has also been seen keeping watch over sleeping children in the house and emanating a comforting presence.

Plague Island
VENICE, ITALY, 16TH CENTURY
The small island of Poveglia in the Venetian lagoon hides a terrible secret. In the 1570s, when plague struck the city, those suffering from the disease were taken to the island and abandoned there to endure a

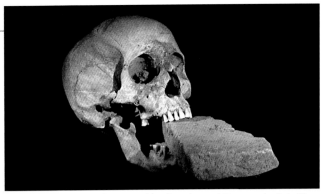

▲ **Like suspected vampires**, many Venetian plague victims were buried with rocks in their mouths, to stop them from eating their way out of the grave.

40-day quarantine. Most died and about 160,000 corpses were buried in huge pits. Many were later found to have large stones wedged in their jaws—the 16th-century way of dealing with vampires. Today, most Venetians refuse to set foot on the island, convinced it is haunted by hundreds of spirits.

The Revenant Baker
BRITTANY, FRANCE, 15TH CENTURY
Not long after the death of a baker in Brittany, his ghost returned to help his family knead the dough. Terrified, they fled, but the ghostly baker became angry and hurled rocks at the villagers. Noting that the apparition's legs were muddy, they dug up the corpse and found it was similarly mud-spattered. The villagers weighed the body down with stones to stop it rising, but the ghost became angrier than ever. At last, they exhumed the corpse again and broke its legs. Only then did the revenant baker stay in his grave.

The Woman in White
GERMANY, 16TH CENTURY
Anna Sydow was the mistress of Joachim II, Elector of Brandenburg. His son, Johann Georg, promised to take care of her, but when Joachim died in 1571, she was imprisoned in Spandau Citadel until her death in 1575. Years later, Johann Georg was visited by the specter of a woman dressed in white, who stood at the foot of his bed. Eight days later, he was dead, but the ghost continued to haunt his family. Finally, in 1709, when a woman's skeleton was found inside the fortress, she was given a proper burial in the hope of ending the hauntings. But some still say they occasionally catch sight of the spectral woman in white.

A Persistent Ghost
SNAEFELLSNES, ICELAND, 13TH–14TH CENTURIES
In the Icelandic *Eyrbyggja Saga*, when Thorolf Half-Foot died and his ghost proved restless, his son, the chieftain Arnkel, had the corpse carried out through a hole knocked in the homestead wall— a ruse to prevent the spirit finding its way back in. Yet the oxen who carried Thorolf to his grave fell dead, and the ghost started terrorizing local farmers. Arnkel moved his father's remains to a hillside and built a wall around the grave to contain the ghost, but when Arnkel was later murdered, Thorolf's spirit broke out, seeking revenge. The farmers dug up and burned the body, but a pregnant cow inhaled the ashes and her calf grew into a ferocious bull, which gored one of Arnkel's killers to death. Avenged at last, Thorolf's ghost was quieter after that.

▲ **Mysterious faces** appeared in the floor of a house in Bélmez, each one different from the last.

Ghost Faces of Bélmez

SPAIN, 20TH CENTURY

The small house at Calle Real 5 in the Andalusian village of Bélmez was unremarkable until 1971, when the form of a ghostly face appeared in the concrete floor of the kitchen. Disturbed, the owners destroyed it with a pickax, but a week later, another face appeared, and then another. Crowds flocked to see the phenomenon, but no one could explain it, and the phantom faces kept materializing on the floor for the next 30 years. Some said they were the spirits of people murdered during the Spanish Civil War who were demanding vengeance, but the faces stayed silent, so no one could be sure.

The Black Ghost

LITHUANIA, 16TH CENTURY

At the harbor in Klaipėda, a port city on Lithuania's Baltic coast, there is an unusual statue. Cast in bronze, a dark, hooded figure, seemingly climbing out of the water, commemorates a ghost that appeared in 1595 to Hans von Heidi, a Klaipėda Castle guard who was patrolling the area at night. Swathed in a black cloak, its face invisible, the specter asked the petrified guard if the city's food and timber stocks were high. The guard replied that they were sufficient, but the ghost advised him that they would soon run out, then vanished. Hans von Heidi reported this encounter to the city authorities, who decided to heed the spirit's advice and stockpiled extra supplies. Famine soon struck the surrounding area, but Klaipėda's citizens did not starve, thanks to the warning from the mysterious Juodasis Vaiduoklis, or "Black Ghost."

Satan's Limousine

RUSSIA, 20TH CENTURY

In the 1960s and 1970s, people in Russia and other parts of Eastern Europe dreaded the appearance of a black Volga car, sometimes with white curtains hiding the driver's identity. The car slowly circled the streets of cities and, if it stopped, its occupant would pull in the nearest passerby, often a child, who would never be seen again. Some said the driver was the Devil, dragging the souls of innocents to Hell. Whoever it was, everyone agreed that the car was best avoided.

Africa

Pool of the Elders

MALAWI, 20TH CENTURY

Dziwe la Nkhalamba, or the "Pool of the Elders," at the base of the Mulanje Mountain, is home to a group of spirits, whom local people advise must be respected or they may turn vengeful. One day, a group of students decided to take a cooling swim there, and one of them climbed to the top of the waterfall to photograph his friends bathing. As he did so, he slipped and fell. One of his friends, a strong swimmer, dived in to pull him out, but felt an incredibly strong force pulling in the other direction and had to let go. The photographer's body was found days later, believed to have been drowned by the spirits.

Hazard Light

SOUTH AFRICA, 20TH CENTURY

Some years ago, it is said, a man killed his wife in a riverbed outside Beaufort West in the arid Karoo region of South Africa. Ever since, people have reported seeing bright lights darting up and down the old river course. Anyone seeing these lights is advised to look away, because a driver who once drove toward them to investigate ended up raving incoherently and was sent to an asylum.

The Cemetery Mule

MOROCCO, FOLKTALE

A woman in the Souss region of Morocco failed to respect the *iddah*, the prescribed period of mourning after being widowed. As a result, she was cursed to become a mule and to haunt the cemetery, bound in iron chains. During daylight, she would sleep underground with the dead and, after sunset, she would dig herself out, dragging her chains behind her, to hunt down unwary men. It is said that the sound of her screams and chains can be heard echoing around the cemetery, and men especially keep their distance, as an encounter with the Cemetery Mule is invariably fatal.

Oceania

Spirit on a Bridge

AUSTRALIA, 20TH CENTURY

Richmond Bridge, north of Hobart in Tasmania, is said to be haunted by the ghost of its overseer, George Grover. During the bridge's construction in the 1830s, Grover was exceptionally cruel and often whipped the convicts forced to build it. When he walked home drunk one evening and paused to sit on the bridge, out of nowhere someone pitched him over and he fell to his death. Now, his ghost is said to pace the spot, inspiring dread in anyone who hears his footsteps, and people are warned never to look back at the spirit or risk Grover following them home.

Castle of Lies

NEW ZEALAND, 20TH CENTURY

Larnach Castle near Dunedin, built in the 1870s by the banker William Larnach, was a luxurious home beset by tragedies. Larnach's

▲ **Larnach Castle**, with its eerily chilly rooms and doors that slam shut, is now a tourist attraction.

favorite daughter, Kate, died at a young age, as did his first two wives. To add to his woes, he was accused of financial misconduct. He shot himself in 1898. The ghosts of Larnach, his wives, and Kate are said to haunt their old home. In 1994, during a performance of *Castle of Lies*, a play put on to tell their stories, a storm began, blowing wind into the ballroom auditorium and scattering ash clouds over the audience. Hail hammered on the tin roof and, at the play's climax, where Larnach shoots himself, a bolt of lightning illuminated the room. The audience thought it was a special effect, but some think it was Larnach's ghost, angered by the spectacle.

Asia

The Cursed Hotel
VIETNAM, 1960S

In 1960, a rich Vietnamese businessman built a hotel at 727 Tran Dung Hao Street in Saigon. His original plan had 13 floors and, even when the architect told him that this might bring bad luck, he ignored the warning. However, accidents kept happening during the construction of the 13th floor: builders were electrocuted, and some fell to their deaths from the scaffolding. Undeterred, the businessman called in an exorcist who, legend has it, had four dead virgins buried in the hotel's foundations. This quietened the angry spirits, but the building soon acquired more, after it served as a hostel for US troops during the Vietnam War. Local residents said they often saw ghostly military processions and heard the screams of soldiers who had died.

Forbidden City Phantoms
CHINA, 20TH CENTURY

Beijing's Forbidden City, home to the imperial family for nearly five centuries, has a rich hoard of ghost stories. A well in the palace complex is said to house the ghosts of several imperial concubines. An iron grid largely keeps them in their place but, every few years, they are said to drag a passerby to their doom. In 1995, palace guards chased a woman with long black hair, whom they suspected of being a thief. She outran them with ease and, when she turned around, revealed the terrible truth: she had no face and was a ghost. Petrified, the guards ran back to tell their colleagues they had seen yet another of the Forbidden City's specters.

The Sankhachurni
BENGAL, INDIA, FOLKTALE

A woman was fetching water one day when she accidentally brushed against a *sankhachurni*, the spirit of an unmarried woman, who lived in a nearby tree. The furious ghost seized the woman and thrust her inside the tree trunk. Then the *sankhachurni* took the woman's clothes and made her way to the village to take her victim's place. At first, the family thought the woman was finishing her domestic chores in half the time but then they noticed that, instead of going to fetch objects, she extended her arm several yards to grab them. When cooking, she did not use fuel but thrust her foot in the fire to light it. Suspecting they had a ghost among them, the family called an exorcist, who held burning turmeric to her nose.

Spirits apparently cannot abide the smell and so, screaming, the *sankhachurni* submitted to the exorcist's demands and agreed to release the woman from the tree.

The Spider Woman
JAPAN, FOLKTALE

In Japanese tradition, a golden orb spider that lives for 400 years transforms into a *jorōgumo*. This half-human, half-spider monster appears as a beautiful woman, who seduces and ensnares men with her charms, then embalms them in spider silk before devouring them. In one story, a young warrior meets a *jorōgumo* but, realizing just in time the danger he is in, he slashes at her with his sword. The wounded spider woman flees to the attic, followed by the warrior. There, he discovers the dead body of a huge spider, surrounded by the rotting corpses of its recent human victims.

▲ **A type of shape-shifting *yokai*** (see pp.182–185), the *jorōgumo*, or spider woman, uses its potent venom to weaken its victims, slowly and painfully.

GLOSSARY

Afterlife A place or realm where a person's spirit or soul goes after death; or what the spirit experiences after death—often some kind of journey that culminates in a final judgment.

Amulet An object, which may be found or created, thought to have protective or healing powers when carried or worn on the body. See *Talisman*.

Ancestor veneration A family group or community's worship of their dead, or other ritual practices and offerings to appease the spirits of their dead.

Angels In Christianity, beings who serve as messengers and intermediaries between humans and God; in the early modern period, some grimoires contained rituals for summoning angels as benevolent spirits (in contrast to the summoning of demons).

Animism The belief that anything natural, such as plants, animals, rocks, water, or weather, has a spirit and can influence human events.

Apparition A ghost or similar supernatural phenomenon that appears, seemingly from nowhere. See *Ghost*.

Astral plane The plane of the universe that the human consciousness, or astral body, can travel through. It is a spiritual plane, existing alongside the physical plane of material objects that human consciousness normally interacts with. The astral plane is often believed to be inhabited by the souls of the dead and those who are not yet born.

Astral projection A person's attempt to detach their soul or consciousness, known as the astral body, from their physical form, to allow it to travel through the astral plane.

Bhuta A restless South/Southeast Asian spirit that has failed to pass through to the otherworld after death, or to be reborn.

Book of the Dead A book (roll of papyrus) found in ancient Egyptian tombs that contains spells to guide the deceased in the afterlife. No two copies are the same.

Burial mound A hill or pile of earth built on top of a burial site or grave; a practice seen in multiple cultures around the world since the Neolithic period.

Catacombs A series of underground passages made by humans, usually for the burial of the dead.

Changeling A creature left behind as a replacement by supernatural beings, such as fairies, after they have stolen a human child.

Conjuring Invoking spirits or practicing illusionist magic.

Cosmos A society or religion's worldview: their conception of the universe, its realms, its deities, its beginning and end.

Cult of the dead Religions or practices in which the dead are celebrated (venerated).

Curse A solemn utterance that is intended to invoke a supernatural power to inflict harm or punishment.

Deity A god or goddess (in a polytheistic religion such as Hinduism); the creator and supreme being (in a monotheistic religion such as Christianity or Islam).

Demon Wicked spirit with access to occult powers. A demon might be summoned to do a magical practitioner's bidding.

Demoniac Medieval term for a person possessed by a demon.

Demonology The study of demons and branch of magic related to them; also a manual produced in the early modern period classifying and describing demons.

Devil, the Most powerful of all demons in the Abrahamic religions (Judaism, Christianity, and Islam). He is variously known as Satan, Lucifer, or Iblis (in Islam). The Devil is believed to have dominion over other demons and evil spirits.

***Dia de los Muertos* (Day of the Dead)** Mexican festival of the dead in which ancestors are celebrated with offerings placed on altars. The Day of the Dead is thought to originate in a mixture of Catholic practices and Indigenous Mesoamerican religious practices.

Disembodiment Separation from the body: could describe a spirit leaving the physical body, or an unattached (living) body part, such as a disembodied hand.

Ectoplasm A substance that is believed to surround ghosts and other creatures connected with spiritual activities. Spiritualist mediums often faked the production of ectoplasm.

Effigy A representation of a specific person in the form of sculpture or some other three-dimensional medium.

Enochian magic A type of ceremonial magic, developed by John Dee and Edward Kelley, that aims to invoke and control various spirits, including angels.

Esotericism Western tradition of mystical, specialized (esoteric) knowledge held only by the privileged few. Rosicrucianism and Kabbalah are examples of esotericism.

Evocation The calling or summoning of a spirit, demon, or other supernatural entity to a location. Often used interchangeably with the term "invocation." See *Invocation*.

Exorcism The process of forcing a spirit to leave a person or place by using prayers or magic. Exorcism rituals are used to drive out demons or spirits. See *Possession*.

Fairy A magical being, often depicted as small and winged, associated with hills, forests, and rivers. Many cultures have their own version of fairies. Even when fairies are thought to be capable of benevolence, they are believed to be dangerous, because they live by their own set of rules and are liable to punish humans for any transgressions, such as stepping into a fairy ring (a circle of mushrooms or flowers).

Familiar Also called an imp, a companion said to be given to a witch by the Devil to carry out her bidding. Sightings of, or attacks by, familiar spirits were used as evidence in the European witch trials. They were believed to be demonic spirits who fed from a witch's own body (via a witch mark, or teat), but many of the sightings of such familiars seem to simply describe animals such as cats and frogs. See *Witch*.

Fetish An object that is worshipped in some societies because it is believed to have a spirit or special magical powers.

Folk magic The magical practices of the common people, rather than learned elites.

Funerary rites A prescribed set of practices carried out after a person dies. Performing these rites could be important for a number of reasons: to help a soul reach the afterlife; to protect the dead from evil spirits; to venerate the dead to appease their spirit and win its favor; or to prevent the dead from manifesting as a ghost.

Ghost Also known as a specter, phantom, or apparition, the spirit of a dead person (or animal); often bodiless, with varying abilities to be seen or heard by the living, or to manipulate objects. Ghosts are often the spirits of those unable to reach the afterlife due to unfinished business, punishment for their deeds in life, or other reasons, and are tied to a person, object, or place.

Ghost pit In the ancient world, a hole dug into the ground as part of ceremonies for raising the dead. Forbidden by Jewish law, ghost pits were used by ancient (pagan) societies such as the Hittites.

Ghost tourism Visiting places specifically because they are thought to be haunted, or with the goal of seeing or sensing a ghost.

Ghoul Originally from Arabic mythology, a shape-shifting spirit that lingers in graveyards and eats human flesh.

Goblin A type of folkloric creature associated with mischief, often depicted as small and ugly. Some, such as hobgoblins, are associated with the home, and are benevolent creatures; others, especially those believed to dwell in rivers and caves, are more malicious.

Gothic A genre of art and literature that flourished from the 1790s onward, blending supernatural elements with romantic tropes. Typical Gothic tropes include damsels in distress, vengeful ghosts, and grand settings such as castles and abbeys.

Grave goods Objects deliberately buried alongside the dead, often in the belief that the deceased can use them in the afterlife.

Grimoire A handbook of magic, which might include spells for summoning spirits or demons, as well as other incantations. The term is most often used to describe texts dating from the medieval or early modern period.

Gui Ghosts in the Chinese tradition; usually translated as "ghost," the term can include all supernatural beings.

Haunting The appearance of a ghost, usually in such a way that causes harm or disturbance to the living.

Hell A realm of the afterlife designated for the punishment of wicked souls.

Heresy Beliefs that contradict the doctrine of the Catholic Church.

Hungry ghost In Buddhism and traditional Chinese religion, a spirit damned to an eternity of insatiable hunger, due to either their actions in life or their families' failure to perform necessary funeral rites.

Incantation (The performance of) words that are believed to have a magical effect when spoken or sung.

Incubus A type of male demon that preys on sleeping women. See *Succubus*.

Invocation Technically, drawing a spirit into one's body; however, the term is often used interchangeably with "evocation." See *Evocation*.

Jinn In Arabic mythology, invisible beings that are thought to be able to grant wishes to humans. In the Islamic faith, jinn are believed to be capable of evil, just as humans are, due to them having free will. The Arabic "jinn" became the English term "genie."

Kabbalah The ancient Jewish practice of mystical interpretation of the Tanakh (Hebrew Bible), first by word of mouth and then by secret codes. Kabbalah includes beliefs in the possibility of being possessed by evil spirits such as *dybbuks* and *ibburs*.

Laying a ghost A Christian method of eliminating ghosts, using scripture to heal restless spirits. This included "reading down," where the reading of Latin scripture would cause the ghost to become smaller until it could be trapped in a bottle or box.

Liminal A description of in-between places—a liminal space is transient, a threshold between one place and another.

Magic circle A demarcated circle, usually on the ground, within which a magical practitioner stands while summoning. Inscribed with runes or other magical symbols, the circle is believed to protect the practitioner from the spirits (often demons) they summon. See *Demon*.

Medium A person who claims to act as an intermediary between the living and the spirits of the dead.

Mermaid A mythological creature with the body and head of a human and a fishlike tail, often depicted as a beautiful woman.

Mesmerism (animal magnetism) Franz Mesmer's theory that all beings are connected by an invisible force, which can be used for healing or inducing trances.

Mounting In the Vodou religion, the possession of a human by a spirit; the term reflects a belief that the human body is akin to a horse the spirit is riding.

Mysticism The belief that life has a hidden meaning or that each person can unite with a deity or absolute truth by deep contemplation of spiritual knowledge beyond the capacity of the human intellect; also used in a more general sense to mean belief in religion, spirituality, or the occult.

Necromancy The magic of the dead, originally a way of acquiring knowledge from them. In the late medieval era it came to mean the conjuring of demons to harness their magical powers.

Necropolis "City of the dead"; term for a large site with many graves, usually located away from the settlements of the living.

Neopaganism A collective term for a number of modern practices that attempt to revive what practitioners believe to be ancient religious traditions. See *Paganism*.

Neoshamanism "New" forms of shamanism, or methods of seeking visions or healing from spirits. Neoshamanism comprises a range of shamanic beliefs and practices. See *Shamanism*.

Netherworld The realm of the dead, another word for the Underworld. See *Underworld*.

New Age A movement beginning in the 1970s that encompasses a range of spiritual beliefs and practices presenting an alternative to capitalism and looking forward to a future lived in harmony with the natural world.

Obsession The external attack on a person by an aggressive spirit, or when a demon takes over a person's senses through dreams or apparitions. See *Possession*.

Occult Hidden mystical, supernatural, or magical powers, practices, or phenomena.

Omen An event regarded as a portent (sign) of good or evil.

Otherworld Another realm of existence; often an afterlife, as it is in the Hindu faith. In Celtic mythology, the otherworld is the domain of spirits, gods, and other supernatural beings.

Ouija A popular talking board patented in the US in 1890. See *Talking board*.

Paganism Polytheistic religious beliefs and practices with origins in the ancient world. The term "pagan" has sometimes been used as a pejorative or to describe any belief system outside the major world religions.

Paranormal Something that cannot be explained by our existing knowledge of science and the natural world.

Parapsychology A field of scientific study dedicated to research into psychic phenomena. Parapsychology is a controversial field, with detractors calling it a pseudoscience because it cannot be tested by the scientific method.

Planchette A small, flat board (often made of wood) on castors, which is employed in seances. A planchette may be used with a talking board to spell out letters or symbols, or combined with a writing tool for psychography. See *Psychography*.

Poltergeist A "noisy ghost," a type of spirit that can manipulate objects.

Poppet In folk magic, a doll made to represent a person, for casting spells on that person to hurt or aid them. Poppets are thought to work by sympathetic magic, the spiritual connection between a person (or thing) and objects that resemble them.

Possession When a person's consciousness is invaded by a spirit or demon, who may then control their movements, speech, and actions. The human body serves as the spirit's host, or vessel. Not all possession is evil—in some cultures, spirit possession is an honor that people actively seek to achieve. See *Mounting*.

Psychography (automatic writing) A method of spirit communication by which a spirit is believed to guide the hand of the practitioner to write out messages, for example via a planchette with a pencil attached to it.

Purgatory In the Catholic faith, a place between Heaven and Hell where sinners must atone for their sins. Souls in Purgatory must undergo purification to enter Heaven.

Relic A token from a deceased holy person, often one of their body parts or something they owned or touched, preserved over time for the purpose of venerating them.

Revenant A corpse that comes back from the dead, from the French word *revenir* ("to return"). See *Zombie*.

Ritual A set of fixed actions, and sometimes words, performed regularly, especially as part of a magical or religious ceremony.

Rosicrucianism A 17th-century secret brotherhood that claimed to have discovered ancient esoteric wisdom and religious principles.

Samhain Also called Samhuinn (Scots) or Sauin (Manx); the ancient Celtic festival of the dead, celebrated halfway between the fall equinox and winter solstice with bonfires and animal sacrifices. Its traditions influenced Halloween. Samhain is celebrated today in Gaelic and Neopagan communities.

Samsara The Hindu and Buddhist process in which a soul goes through cycles of rebirth, with each reincarnation influenced by its actions in its previous life.

Seal of Solomon A symbol said to have been given to the biblical King Solomon by God in the form of a seal, and to have allowed him to control and banish demons.

Seance A demonstration during which a medium channels spirits, acting as an intermediary between those spirits and the people present.

Shamanism The spiritual practices of people in the steppe lands of Central Asia and Siberia, dating back around 40,000 years; the term is sometimes used more generally (and controversially) to refer to wider spiritual and magical tribal traditions, especially those communicating with a spirit world. Prehistoric peoples can be said to have "shamanic" practices.

Shape-shifter A person or thing with the apparent ability to change from one form into another. See *Were-creature*.

Sky burial The practice of leaving the bodies of the dead unburied in high circular structures. This encouraged birds to feast on them, picking the bodies clean before they could be attacked by evil spirits. See *Zoroastrianism*.

Soul A person's innermost essence; may be used synonymously with "spirit."

Spirit A nonphysical entity, sometimes called a soul or spark. Many cultures believe that the spirit is the psychic form of a person, which can live on after their body dies. Some people believe that animals and the natural world have their own spirits—this belief is key to animistic and shamanic religions. "Spirit" can also be used to describe a ghost or supernatural force.

Spiritism (*Espiritismo*) A 19th-century movement inspired by the writings of Allen Kardec, particularly popular in Brazil; the belief that people's spirits survive after death and can be contacted through mediums. Spiritists also believe in reincarnation. See *Spiritualism*.

Spiritualism A movement dating from the 19th century, based on the belief that people who have died can communicate with the living, typically through a medium; also the religious belief that all reality is spiritual, rather than material.

Spirit rapping Knocking sounds said to be made by spirits to communicate with the living. A famous example of spirit rapping is that reported by the Fox family, key figures in the early Spiritualist movement.

Spirit world/realm The realm believed by some to be inhabited by spirits, both good and evil, of people who have died.

Succubus A female demon that preys on sleeping men. See *Incubus*.

Summoning Calling something forth from one place into another; often the calling of a spirit to aid a magical practitioner.

Supernatural Unable to be explained by science or nature; attributed to forces such as gods, spirits, or magic.

Syncretism The combining of different religions, cultures, or ideas.

Talisman A crafted object into which positive powers have been transferred by a magical ritual. See *Amulet*.

Talking board Also called a spirit board or witch board, a spirit communication device with symbols or letters drawn on it for a practitioner to receive messages from spirits. See *Ouija*.

Theosophy A philosophy based on the idea that a knowledge of God may be achieved through spiritual ecstasy, direct intuition, and intense study of the occult.

Theurgy A system of rituals to seek help from a god or benign spirits, particularly angels, to work magic or miracles.

Totem In Indigenous American beliefs, a symbol—often an animal—representing a social unit, such as a family group or clan; also a general term for an object that is revered for religious and symbolic reasons.

Treasure-hunting Also called treasure-digging; the practice of summoning and entrapping spirits who are believed to guard valuable items, in order to acquire riches.

Underworld The realm of the dead, imagined as being under the earth.

Urban legend A story passed on by word of mouth, often about supernatural occurrences, in a particular region or place.

Vampire A type of undead mythological creature believed to drink the blood of the living. In the early modern period, vampire scares (linked to outbreaks of tuberculosis) in Eastern Europe and the United States saw people digging up the graves of the dead to identify potential vampires.

Veil A conceptualization of the barrier between the living and the dead, said to be at its thinnest at Halloween or Samhain. Often misattributed to the ancient Celts, the concept of the veil is probably a 19th-century invention resulting from a revival of interest in Celtic culture and religion.

Were-creature Also called therianthropes; supernatural creatures, such as werewolves, which shift between a human form and an animal one. See *Shape-shifter*.

Wild Hunt A horde of ghosts and other terrifying spirits that ride on horseback across the skies, often during midwinter. The hunt is led by a mythical leader.

Witch Someone believed to have or harness malign magical powers. In the early modern period, witches (often women) were believed to have made pacts with the devil, and to have familiar spirits. See *Familiar*.

Yūrei Japanese ghosts, unable to pass from the world of the living to the afterlife. The term literally means "dark soul."

Zombie A reanimated corpse. Zombies originate in the Haitian *zonbi*, a mindless corpse bound to do the bidding of its maker. See *Revenant*.

Zoroastrianism A monotheistic, pre-Islamic religion of ancient Iran, founded by Zoroaster in the 6th century BCE. It was dualistic—characterized by a struggle between the forces of good and evil.

INDEX

Page numbers in **bold** indicate
main entries

C

ACKNOWLEDGMENTS

DK would like to thank the following: Christine Stroyan, Anoushka Alexander-Rose, Fozia Bora, Madeline Potter, and Cross Cultural Consultants for editorial assistance; Adam Brackenbury for high-res color work; Phil Gamble for design assistance; Diana Vowles for proofreading; Helen Peters for indexing; Assistant Picture Research Administrator Manpreet Kaur

(br). 146 Bridgeman Images. 147 Alamy Stock Photo: Charles Walker Collection (ca). Wellcome Collection: (br). 148 Alamy Stock Photo: Charles Walker Collection (tl); Prisma Archivo (br). 149 Alamy Stock Photo: Chronicle. 150 Wellcome Collection. 151 Library of Congress, Washington, D.C.: https://www.loc.gov/item/59059328 (t). Wellcome Collection: (b). 152 Photo Scala, Florence: Photo Josse. 153 Alamy Stock Photo: The Picture Art Collection (t). Bridgeman Images: Giancarlo Costa (b). 154 Amgueddfa Cymru – National Museum Wales: (bl). Photo Scala, Florence: bpk, Bildagentur fuer Kunst, Kultur und Geschichte, Berlin (r); The Metropolitan Museum of Art / Art Resource (fbl). Science Museum Group: (bc). 155 Alamy Stock Photo: AmityPhotos (bl); Olga Yastremska (tl). Dreamstime.com: Penywise (ftl). Getty Images: Universal Images Group / Godong (tr). Photo Scala, Florence: RMN-Grand Palais / Georges Poncet / RMN-GP (tc). Shutterstock.com: Alwayswin (fbr). US Ghost Adventures: The Historic Lizzie Borden House (bc). 156 University of Manchester: Library. 157 Alamy Stock Photo: Pictorial Press Ltd (t). Bridgeman Images: The Stapleton Collection (b). 158 University of Iceland: (tc). University of California Libraries: (bc). 159 Alamy Stock Photo: World History Archive (tc). Wellcome Collection: (bc). 160 Alamy Stock Photo: BTEU / RKMLGE (br). © The Trustees of the British Museum. All rights reserved: (tl). 161 Alamy Stock Photo: Charles Walker Collection. 162-163 Alamy Stock Photo: Universal Art Archive. 164 Alamy Stock Photo: Universal Art Archive. 165 Alamy Stock Photo: The History Collection (b). Bridgeman Images: © Freer Sackler Gallery / Freer Gallery of Art, Smithsonian Institution (t). 166 Alamy Stock Photo: Evgenii Zolotov (br). Bridgeman Images: British Library archive (l). 167 © Trustees of the Chester Beatty Library, Dublin. 168 Getty Images: Sepia Times (bl). Nationaal Museum van Wereldculturen: (tr). 169 Getty Images: Sepia Times. 170-171 Alamy Stock Photo: Universal Images Group North America LLC / DeAgostini. 172 Alamy Stock Photo: Vintage Archives (tr). Minneapolis Institute of Art: The Christina N. and Swan J. Turnblad Memorial Fund / PD (tl). 173 Photo Scala, Florence: RMN-Grand Palais. 174-175 Photo Scala, Florence: bpk, Bildagentur fuer Kunst, Kultur und Geschichte, Berlin (b). 175 Getty Images: Gerard Sioen (t). 176 Bridgeman Images. 177 Alamy Stock Photo: Chronicle (tl). Rijksmuseum Amsterdam: (cr). 178-179 Bridgeman Images. 180 Bridgeman Images: Photo © Heini Schneebeli (c). Brooklyn Museum: Gift of the Carroll Family Collection, 2019.45.2 (cla). Getty Images: SSPL (br). Science Museum Group: (bl). Shutterstock.com: westernhippie (tl). 180-181 Macquarie University Ancient Cultures Research Centre. 181 Getty Images: Oliver Mohr (c). Los Angeles County Museum of Art: Gift of Mr. and Mrs. Werner G. Scharff (M.91.232.5) / PD (crb). McCord Stewart Museum: (tc). Shutterstock.com: Michael Bann (tr). 182-183 Bridgeman Images: Christie's Images (b). 183 Alamy Stock Photo: Science History Images (t). 184 Bridgeman Images: Minneapolis Institute of Art / Bequest of Louis W. Hill, Jr. (b). 184-185 The Metropolitan Museum of Art: (c). 185 The Metropolitan Museum of Art: (tr). 186 Bridgeman Images: Fototeca Gilardi (b). Zentralbibliothek Zurich: (tl). 187 Getty Images: DeAgostini. 188-189 Dover Publications, Inc. New York. 190 Alamy Stock Photo: Chronicle (bc). Bridgeman Images: © Estate of Gerald Bloncourt. All Rights Reserved 2024 (br). Yale University Library: Heath, Henry, active 1824-1850, attributed name. (bl). 191 Alamy Stock Photo: North Wind Picture Archives (bl). Bridgeman Images: British Library archive (bc). Shutterstock.com: Buffalo Bill Center Of The West (br). 192 Yale University Library: Heath, Henry, active 1824-1850, attributed name. 193 Boston Public Library: Defoe.27.59 (tr). The New York Public Library: Carl H. Pforzheimer (bl). 194 Beinecke Rare Book And Manuscript Library / Yale University Library. 195 Bridgeman Images. © Tate, London 2022: (tr). 196 Albert & Shirley Small Special Collections Library: Sadleir-Black Collection of Gothic Fiction / Special Collections Library, University of Virginia via Project Gothic. Bridgeman Images: British Library archive (t). 197 Alamy Stock Photo: AF Fotografie. 198-199 Getty Images: Pictures from History. 198 Alamy Stock Photo: Brian Perry (l). 199 Bridgeman Images: Christie's Images (r). 200 Alamy Stock Photo: Charles Walker Collection. 201 Alamy Stock Photo: Chronicle (tr). Wellcome Collection: (br). 202-203 Getty Images: Fine Art Photographic. 204 Bridgeman Images: © Estate of Gerald Bloncourt. All Rights Reserved 2024. 205 Alamy Stock Photo: Everett Collection Inc. 206 Alamy Stock Photo: Stig Alenis (l). State Library of Pennsylvania: (br). 207 Rubin Private Collection. 208 Alamy Stock Photo: BBM (t). 209 Alamy Stock Photo: The Granger Collection (tl, br). 210 Alamy Stock Photo: Lebrecht Music & Arts (t). Mary Evans Picture Library: Arthur Rackham (bl). 211 Mary Evans Picture Library: © Estate of Alfred Bestall / ILN. 212-213 Image Courtesy National Gallery Of Art, Washington. 214 Alamy Stock Photo: Chronicle. 215 Alamy Stock Photo: Lordprice Collection (b). Parabon NanoLabs, Inc.: (cra). 216 Alamy Stock Photo: CPA Media Pte Ltd (t). Bridgeman Images: © Archives Charmet (b). 217 Bridgeman Images: © Fine Art Images. 218-219 Alamy Stock Photo: ART Collection. 220-221 Alamy Stock Photo: Universal Art Archive (b). 221 AF Fotografie: (tr). Getty Images: ullstein bild Dtl. (cr). 222 Alamy Stock Photo: North Wind Picture Archives (t). 223 Alamy Stock Photo: Granger - Historical Picture Archive (tr). Senate House Library, University of London: (tr). 224 Wellcome Collection: (tr). Xavier University of Louisiana: (bl). 225 Victorian Spiritualists' Union Inc. 226-227 Potter & Potter Auctions: (c). The Museum of Talking Boards Collection, museumoftalkingboards.com: (bc). 226 Alamy Stock Photo: maximimages.com (c). Reproduced by kind permission of the Syndics of Cambridge University Library: (bl). Sworders Fine Art (GES and Sons Limited): (clb). The Museum of Talking Boards Collection, museumoftalkingboards.com: (cra). 227 Dreamstime.com: Taksina (tr). The Museum of Talking Boards Collection, museumoftalkingboards.com: (tl, r, cl). 228 Getty Images: ullstein bild (t). University of California Libraries: (bc). 229 Bridgeman Images: © Patrice Cartier. All rights reserved 2024. 230 Alamy Stock Photo: Interfoto (b). 231 Alamy Stock Photo: Chronicle (r). Bridgeman Images: Universal History Archive / UIG (l). 232 Bridgeman Images: British Library archive (l). 233 Alamy Stock Photo: Chronicle (b). Getty Images: Whitemay (tr). 234-235 Alamy Stock Photo: Masheter Movie Archive. 236 Alamy Stock Photo: Chronicle (r). The Museum of Talking Boards Collection, museumoftalkingboards.com: (cl). 237 Duke University: David M. Rubenstein Rare Book & Manuscript Library. 238 Library of Congress, Washington, D.C.: (tr). Science Museum Group: (l). 238-239 Library of Congress, Washington, D.C.: (bc). 239 Alamy Stock Photo: Gainew Gallery (cr). Getty Images: London Stereoscopic Company (cl); SSPL (tl, tc, tr); Sepia Times (fcl, c). Library of Congress, Washington, D.C.: (ftl). The Metropolitan Museum of Art: Gift of Weston J. Naef, in memory of Kathleen W. Naef and Weston J. Naef Sr., 1982 (br). 240 Alamy Stock Photo: Pictures Now (br). Shutterstock.com: Buffalo Bill Center of The West (tl). 241 TopFoto: (b). 242 Science Photo Library: Sheila Terry. 243 Alamy Stock Photo: Historic Collection (cra); Penrodas Collection (bc). 244 Rhine Dice Turning Test, University Archives Photograph Collection Box 69, Duke University Archives, David M. Rubenstein Rare Book & Manuscript Library, Duke University.: (tl). The Metropolitan Museum of Art: Gilman Collection, Gift of The Howard Gilman Foundation, 2005 (br). 245 Image provided courtesy of the Rhine Research Center: Previously published by Science Digest, November 1965 (tr). 246-247 Bridgeman Images: Look and Learn. 248-249 Dover Publications, Inc. New York. 250 Alamy Stock Photo: Allstar Picture Library Ltd (bc); Gary Doak (b). Getty Images: Stanislav Tiplyashin (bl). 251 Alamy Stock Photo: Christina Simons (bl); Konrad Zelazowski (br). Dreamstime.com: Keith Gentry (bc). 252 Alamy Stock Photo: History and Art Collection (l). 252-253 Alamy Stock Photo: NB / DeptComm. 253 Getty Images: Corbis Historical (b). 254 Alamy Stock Photo: Charles Walker Collection (b). 255 Mary Evans Picture Library: (b, t). 256 Mary Evans Picture Library: Harry Price Library. 257 Alamy Stock Photo: Associated Press (b); Ira Berger (t). 258 Alamy Stock Photo: Nigel James (cr). Dreamstime.com: Martin Bergsma (tl). Science Museum Group: (tc, tr); National Science and Media Museum (bl). 258-259 Dreamstime.com: Oleksandr Kostiuchenko (bc). 259 Digital Dowsing LLC: (tc). Dreamstime.com: Bigtunaonline (tr). GhostStop: (bc, cla, ca). Shutterstock.com: ViralMind (tl). 260-261 ANGUSalive. 262 Alamy Stock Photo: Charles Walker Collection (br). Bridgeman Images: © A. Dagli Orti / © NPL - DeA Picture Library (tl). 263 Alamy Stock Photo: steeve-x-art. 264 Alamy Stock Photo: Tim Ring (l). Getty Images: Evening Standard (b). 265 Getty Images: Stanislav Tiplyashin. 266 Alamy Stock Photo: BFA. 267 Alamy Stock Photo: Allstar Picture Library Ltd (b); PictureLux / The Hollywood Archive (t). 268 Alamy Stock Photo: Everett Collection Inc. 269 Alamy Stock Photo: BFA (tr); Moviestore Collection Ltd (b). 270-271 Getty Images: Karl-Josef Hildenbrand. 272 Alamy Stock Photo: BFA (c); Media Associates (l); Science History Images (tc); Media Associates (tr); BFA (cr); BFA (bc); BFA (tr). 273 Alamy Stock Photo: BFA (tl); BFA (c); BFA (tc); BFA (tr); BFA (cr); Media Associates / Big Blue Film (fbl); Cinematic (bl); (bc); BFA (br). 274 Alamy Stock Photo: Gary Doak. 275 Ecole Polytechnique Fdrale de Lausanne (EPFL): (bl). Getty Images: Matt Anderson Photography (t). 276-277 Christina Lonsdale: radianthuman.com. 278 Getty Images: Historical Picture Archive. 279 Alamy Stock Photo: BFA / Warner Bros (tc); Lilly Pudding (t). 280 Dumbarton Oaks Research Library and Collections, Washington, D.C.: (tl). Wikimedia: Marie-Lan Nguyen (br). 281 akg-images. 282 York Ghost Merchants: (bl). 282-283 Alamy Stock Photo: Chronicle (tc). 283 Dreamstime.com: Jerry Coli (br). 284 Alamy Stock Photo: Christina Simons (tr). South West Voice Photography: (bl). 285 Alamy Stock Photo: Arcaid Images. 286-287 Getty Images: Dale Fornoff. 288 Getty Images / iStock: lanolan. 289 Dreamstime.com: Keith Gentry (tr). Getty Images: Pictures From History / Universal Images Group (bc). 290 Bridgeman Images: © Davis Museum at Wellesley College / Gift of John Friedman and Jane Furse (Class of 1979) (tl). © Safaricom PLC: Allan Gichigi (br). 291 Thomarts Gallery: © Mandisi Mncela. 292 Alamy Stock Photo: Media Associates / Garuda Motion Pictures (tr); Visual Arts Resource (bl). 293 Alamy Stock Photo: VPC Photo. 294 ArenaPAL: Mark Ellidge Archive. 295 Ian French: (tr). Getty Images: Mario Laporta / KONTROLAB / LightRocket (br). 296 Alamy Stock Photo: Konrad Zelazowski. 297 Getty Images / iStock: John Webb (tc). Spookers Haunted Attraction: @spookersnz (bc). 298-299 Dover Publications, Inc. New York. 300 Kimberly Leahey. 301 Nat Geo Image Collection: (tr). 302 Alamy Stock Photo: Stephen Fleming (br); Alberto Paredes (tl). 303 Alamy Stock Photo: Chronicle of World History. 320 Alamy Stock Photo: Chronicle.

All other images © Dorling Kindersley

"I can call spirits from the vasty deep."

GLENDOWER IN SHAKESPEARE'S *HENRY IV PART 1*, 1596–1597